LA BOHÈME

The Metropolitan Opera Classics Library

THE METROPOLITAN OPERA CLASSICS LIBRARY

GIACOMO PUCCINI

LA BOHÈME

LIBRETTO BY

GIUSEPPE GIACOSA AND LUIGI ILLICA

STORY ADAPTATION BY

V. S. PRITCHETT

INTRODUCTION BY

WILLIAM MANN

GENERAL EDITOR
ROBERT SUSSMAN STEWART

LITTLE, BROWN AND COMPANY   BOSTON   TORONTO

FIRST EDITION

LIBRARY OF CONGRESS CATALOG PUBLICATION DATA

Main entry under title:

La Bohème.

(The Metropolitan Opera classics library)
Discography: p.
Bibliography: p.
Contents: Introduction, Giacomo Puccini, 1858–1924 /
by William Mann — Puccini's La Bohème / by William
Mann — La vie de Bohème by / V. S. Pritchett — [etc.]
    1. Puccini, Giacomo, 1858–1924. Bohème. 2. Operas
— Librettos. I. Mann, William S. II. Puccini, Giacomo,
1858–1924. Bohème. Libretto. English & Italian.
1983. III. Pritchett, V.S. (Victor Sawdon), 1900–
Vie de Bohème. 1983. IV. Series.
ML410.P89B63   1983   782.1'092'4   83-956
ISBN 0-316-56838-4
ISBN 0-316-56839-2 (pbk.)
ISBN 0-316-56840-6 (deluxe)

MV
Published simultaneously in Canada
by Little, Brown & Company (Canada) Limited

PRINTED IN THE UNITED STATES OF AMERICA

FOREWORD

The Metropolitan Opera Classics Library, which honors the Metropolitan's centennial, was born out of the often expressed idea that opera is, at one and the same time, music *and* drama. Those familiar with the managing of opera houses know from hard-won experience that few, if any, operas ever earn a permanent place in the repertory if they do not bring "good stories" to their music. Indeed, the majority of our most beloved operas have been inspired by the narratives of either ancient myth or legend, or of novels, or of classical comedies and great tragedies.

Yet the historical fact that opera is, essentially, European in its tradition has meant that, for much of the English-speaking world, the use in opera of these literary treasures in languages other than our own narrows rather than expands their immediacy and their hold over us. We are all aware of having to "read up" on the story of an opera before attending a performance — or, drearier still, of having to sit through three or four acts without ever really knowing who is saying what to whom. Far too often the drama is lost completely, and the whole opera itself becomes clouded over, dusty like a museum piece, truly "foreign."

It is with this in mind that The Metropolitan Opera Classics Library has asked some of the most renowned writers of our time to retell the stories of operas in their own way, to bring the characters and the action to life. This is, of course, in no way to take away from, or diminish, the central role of music in opera; but rather to enrich or enhance it, so that, ultimately, the marriage of music and drama will be fulfilled, and opera will become more clear and more available — to more people.

Making opera more available to more people is not a new task for us here at the Metropolitan Opera. Over forty years ago, we added millions of listeners to our regular audiences when we introduced the Texaco Saturday radio broadcasts. Half a decade ago, even more millions were able to join us when we inaugurated our "Live From the Met" telecasts. Now, as we move into our second century, we hope to find still others — in schools, in libraries, and in the thousands of cities and towns and villages across America wherever books are read and loved. For surely the more opera is understood as literature, the more opera will be appreciated, both in performance and for its undoubtedly glorious music.

ANTHONY A. BLISS
GENERAL MANAGER
METROPOLITAN OPERA

ACKNOWLEDGMENTS

I am grateful to many members of the staff of the Metropolitan Opera for their continued contribution to *The Metropolitan Opera Classics Library*. In particular, and above all, I must thank Michael Bronson, Director of the Media Department, who, from the start of the work on this second volume, has given generously of his time and of his considerable skill.

I would also like to thank Clemente D'Alessio in the Media Department for his support and Sue Breger for her enthusiasm and for her attention to details too numerous to list here.

Robert Tuggle, Director of the Metropolitan Opera Archives, has again offered sound, scholarly advice and has provided invaluable assistance with the task of gathering research material and historical illustrations. Others who have been helpful in the selection of illustrations and photographs are Nina Keller in the Press and Public Relations Department; James Heffernan, the Metropolitan's Official Photographer; Winnie Klotz, Assistant to the Official Photographer; and Clarie Freimann, Presentations Coordinator of the Education Department at the Metropolitan Opera Guild.

Special thanks must go to Mrs. Dorle Soria for the material she has graciously made available from her private Puccini collection. I am also indebted to Gerald Fitzgerald, Associate Editor of *Opera News*, for his editorial astuteness and for his work on the color photograph selection. Miss Seena Sussman, who served as an editorial assistant, was helpful with photograph selection and with the preparation of the manuscript.

David M. Reuben, Director of the Met's Press and Public Relations Department, has again supported this project in innumerable ways. He has also read the entire manuscript. In addition, Jack Beeson, composer and MacDowell Professor of Music at Columbia University, has read the entire manuscript and made useful suggestions.

My thanks to Deborah Jurkowitz, assistant editor at Little, Brown and Company, for overseeing the various stages in the production of this volume. I must also acknowledge Barry Lippman of Little, Brown and Company — still a faithful and helpful editor.

— R.S.S.

Contents

Oh, beautiful age of deceits and utopias,
one believes, hopes, and all seems beautiful.

(MARCELLO, ACT II)

Introduction

Giacomo Puccini: 1858–1924

Tuscany, the breeding ground of Chianti wine and home of the Italian language in its purest form, abounds in beautiful and antique towns, rich in history and culture. Here are Florence, Siena, Pisa, Arezzo, Livorno (Leghorn to English-speakers of former generations), and here is Lucca, where the composer of *La Bohème* was born. At one time the capital of Tuscany, Lucca was famous for its textiles, and for the splendor of its palaces and churches. The modern visitor will find the center of the old fortified town almost unspoiled, a fascinating maze of narrow alleys and luxuriant boulevards. Lucca prided itself on its church music tradition, maintained in the music school which dates back to the tenth century. During the eighteenth century, secular music flourished too in the work of Francesco Geminiani, Luigi Gasparini, Francesco Barsanti, and the Boccherinis, father and more famous son. In that century, too, the Puccini family lodged a bid to become Lucca's longest-lasting musical dynasty. In 1739 the first Giacomo Puccini, who had studied under Padre Martini in Bologna, was made organist and choirmaster of St. Martin's Cathedral in Lucca, and director of the court orchestra there. Four generations of Puccinis followed him in this post; all were reputable composers as well as executants, all had trained in Bologna. The second Giacomo inherited his operatic genius from three generations of forebears, his father Michele, his grandfather Domenico, and his great-grandfather Antonio, all successful opera composers, and masters of instrumental and church music as well. With five generations of musicians, the Puccinis outstrip Lucca's earlier musical family of Guami, three generations of whom directed musical life in Lucca between 1579 and 1649: the Guamis win on sheer numbers, since ten of them were active musicians during those years.

By the time that Michele Puccini fathered a son, as the fifth of his seven children, it was assumed in Lucca that the position of organist and choirmaster in the cathedral would again pass to a Puccini, in the fullness of years. Michele, mindful of the family's musical prestige, had his eldest son baptized Giacomo Antonio Domenico Michele Secondo Maria, thus commemorating the names of his musical predecessors in chronological order, intimating that the baby was the second to bear those illustrious names, and invoking the protection of the Blessed Virgin. Michele Primo, alas, died betimes, aged fifty-one, when his elder son was only five years old; the town council appointed the dead man's brother-in-law to his post, with the proviso that it must be yielded to baby Giacomo as soon as he was able to perform the required duties.

The boy Giacomo at first showed scant aptitude for music, or for other academic subjects: he preferred outdoor pursuits, chiefly the hunting of wildfowl (and that remained Puccini's abiding pastime in adult life, together with women and motorized transport). His mother suspected that her brother, the temporary cathedral organist, might not be the ideal music master (it was not in his best interests to make the lad an expert musician who would promptly take away his principal employment). She put Giacomo's musical education in the hands of another local teacher, who prepared him in his future duties so that at ten he was ready to be a choirboy, and at fourteen to play the organ for church services in and around Lucca, thus contributing to the family funds. By seventeen he was composing music himself, and studying operatic scores with his teacher. Rather over a year later, learning that Verdi's latest opera, *Aida*, was to be performed in neighboring Pisa, he and two friends determined to see it, and walked the forty miles there and back.

That performance changed Puccini's life: he realized that his musical career must range beyond the churches of Lucca to the opera houses of Italy. As he later phrased it: "Almighty God touched me with his little finger and said: 'Write for the theater — mind well, only for the theatre.'" To learn his craft, he would have to study music at a grander conservatory than the one in Lucca, and it must be the Royal Conservatory in Milan, for which the entrance examination was exacting. In 1880 he won his diploma from the Lucca conservatory with the composition and performance of his *Messa di Gloria* (locally admired at the time, and nowadays still occasionally performed), and passed into the Milan

Conservatory with top marks, where his composition teachers were Amilcare Ponchielli (composer of *La Gioconda* with its "Dance of the Hours") and Antonio Bazzini (best known today for the violin encore piece "La Ronde des lutins," though in the Puccini context it is interesting to learn that his opera *Turanda,* based on Gozzi's play, was given at La Scala in 1867). After three years of study, as much operagoing as he could afford, penury, and unremitting hunger, Puccini graduated with a *Capriccio sinfonico* for orchestra, successfully performed at the Conservatory by a student orchestra under Franco Faccio, Italy's leading conductor before Toscanini. Puccini later withdrew the score, having plundered parts of it for *Edgar* and *La Bohème.*

Some weeks earlier in 1883, the music-publishing firm of San-zogno had announced a competition for a one-act opera. Ponchielli advised his pupil to enter, and found him a librettist in Ferdinando Fontana, who supplied a text based on the legend known to balletomanes as *Giselle.* Puccini hurriedly set it to music in the three months or so left to him before the competition's deadline. *Le Villi* won no prize, perhaps because Puccini's musical handwriting, then and to the end of his days, was so untidy — it had already lost him one prize in his Lucca conservatory years, and remained a perennial thorn in the flesh of his copyists. The poet Fontana, undaunted, arranged for Puccini to play and sing excerpts from *Le Villi* at a musical gathering in the house of a rich and influential Milanese amateur. The guests included Verdi's last librettist, the composer Arrigo Boito, and Italy's leading music publisher, Giulio Ricordi. They and others were so impressed by Puccini's music that they collected the funds for a stage production of *Le Villi* in the Teatro dal Verme in Milan on 31 May 1884. It was warmly received, with some numbers encored, and Ricordi published it, after persuading the composer to recast it in two acts. In this form *Le Villi* was much performed, abroad as well as throughout Italy, and Ricordi commissioned another opera from Puccini, who again turned to Fontana.

It was, after all, Fontana who had got *Le Villi* on to the operatic stage. But if that subject had been poor material for Puccini's talents, Fontana's next libretto, *Edgar,* provided no more potent inspiration: with its medieval tale of a young man torn in love between a pure maiden and a wild gypsy, the scenario is an ill-conceived mixture of *Tannhäuser* and *Carmen* (without either minstrels or smugglers). *Edgar* failed at its La Scala premiere on 21 April 1889, and though Puccini subsequently revised it several times, it now has little more than curiosity value.

It was not entirely the fault of the libretto that Puccini took four years to complete *Edgar*. In 1884, the year of its commission, his beloved mother died, and shortly afterward he eloped to Milan with the wife of a school friend, Elvira Geminiani (was her husband, one wonders, a descendant of the famous violinist and composer mentioned earlier?), whom Puccini had been coaching in piano-playing and singing. Elvira could not obtain a divorce in Catholic Italy, and they were unable to legitimize their son Antonio, born in 1886, until Geminiani died, by which time the boy was eighteen. The liaison of Puccini and Elvira caused an almighty scandal in Lucca: when he visited his family there, he had to leave her behind with their son. Theirs was, even after 1904, not a happy marriage. Puccini refused to involve Elvira in the day-to-day working life of a composer; while he was maturing, as an artist and, increasingly, an international celebrity, she remained in outlook a provincial, small-town woman, narrow-minded, aggressive, haughty and domineering, a jealous prey to gossip about her husband's romantic escapades, a hard-hearted shrew, whose once handsome physical appearance quickly lost its appeal as her expression grew ever more sour, pained, tight-lipped and disapproving. For all this, Puccini was largely to blame: when he was not composing music — which he never discussed with her, or allowed her to listen to — he was with his male cronies, either shooting wildfowl or drinking, playing cards and joking, reciting his own scatological verses. He slept little and that during the hours of daylight. A handsome man and smart dresser, he took pleasure in his numerous female conquests, frequent and the more easy because he preferred socially insignificant, weak-willed girls who looked up to the masterful ways and aloofness that won him, from his publisher, the nickname of "Doge." In later life he lamented that nobody loved him; but Puccini seems to have been psychologically unable to form a loving relationship with anyone. He did not invite intimacy with business associates, nor with fellow sportsmen or cardplayers. The relationships were essentially casual, maintained only in their own context, never absorbed into life at home. His family affections were real but reserved, even to his wife. He poured out his emotions in the workshop, and there no other living soul was invited, any more than into the bedroom when he was mastering a real-life Musetta or Mimi who would yield him her music for his mental library of inspiration. Outside the bedroom and the study he cultivated always his image as Doge. He was bored by formal parties, and made dangerous enemies by his scorn for the corruption, dignified as diplomacy, which ruled public life in Italy. He regarded women, like wildfowl on the lake nearby, as objects to be hunted and afterward cast aside. An exception seems to have been the English society hostess Sybil Seligman, a highly cultured and intelligent woman with whom, after a short-lived and passionate love affair, he was able to maintain a genuine, abiding, affectionate friendship until his death.

Puccini's erotic preference for frail, appealing girls is reflected in the heroines of his most admired operas, Manon Lescaut, Mimi, Butterfly, even Tosca and Minnie, certainly Magda in the less popular *Rondine,* and Liù, who is contrasted, in his last opera, with the icy-hearted, Elvira-like, widow-spider Turandot. It is difficult to entirely despise the condescending, cruel philanderer while yet loving his sweetly suffering heroines.

The first of these, Manon Lescaut, captured his attention as early as 1884 perhaps, certainly while *Edgar* was still on the stocks. Puccini knew Prévost's novel, and loved it. The success of Massenet's opera *Manon* (Paris, 1884) fired Puccini to make his own version, an Italian view of the story which, he believed, he appreciated more fully than Massenet. So far from avoiding a subject that had already been treated by another composer, Puccini seems to have enjoyed the challenge involved in winning ownership of something to which another had laid claim — for him it was like an act of musical adultery: the object of the chase, whether woman or opera, became the more desirable, the more exciting, when somebody else had already claimed ownership — stolen fruit, they say, tastes sweeter. So Puccini lusted the more to possess Manon Lescaut, because she was publicly acknowledged to be Massenet's property, and obstacles of the same nature were to draw him to *La Bohème* and *Tosca.* He was also motivated, to be sure, by the knowledge that the subject had already proved itself in the theater: this was an assurance that he always required (from the straight theater if not the opera house) before choosing material for an opera, a lesson learned from the experience of his first two efforts. Puccini's *Manon Lescaut* had, naturally, to be as different as possible from Massenet's in choice of words, incidents, and general dramatic treatment.

From now on Puccini was to treat his librettists with a calculated exigence that drove them to despair: he had learned, from experience of Fontana's bungling, what would make an effect in the theater, and what would fail or cause difficulty. The libretto of *Manon Lescaut* was not prepared to Puccini's satisfaction until five authors had attempted it, with further contributions from the composer and his publisher Giulio Ricordi. The final version was achieved by the partnership of Luigi Illica and Giuseppe Giacosa, who remained Puccini's regular collaborators: but rather than name all of those who had contributed to it, Ricordi published *Manon Lescaut* without mention of any librettist. Puccini composed the music partly in Milan (unconducive to good work, he said), partly in Lucca (where he resented the absence of Elvira and Tonio), chiefly in the Italian countryside where he worked best. He rented accommodation in various places before settling on a home in Torre del Lago, a small town midway between Lucca, Pisa, and Viareggio, on Lake Massaciuccoli where he could fish, shoot, and boat. He bought a property there by the lake, had a new villa built, and (though Elvira would have preferred town life) left it unwillingly in 1921 when the noise and smell of a neighboring peat factory drove him away to Viareggio. The villa is now a museum and the resting place of his body: the town proudly calls itself Torre del Lago Puccini.

To one of his sisters Puccini had written that he was at work on another opera for La Scala. After the failure there of *Edgar*, Ricordi was against a Milan premiere for *Manon Lescaut*, even more since its thunder was sure to be stolen by Verdi's *Falstaff*, which was due for production at about the same time. *Manon Lescaut* was therefore baptized in Turin, at the Teatro Regio, on 1 February 1893. It was rapturously received and favorably noticed by national as well as local critics. Productions throughout Italy and abroad quickly followed, with like success. Puccini's international reputation was made, and for the first time he was earning good money and could pay his accumulated debts — hitherto he had been embarrassingly dependent on advances from Ricordi.

Puccini had already decided that his next opera would be *La Lupa* (The Wolf), from the same collection of tales about Sicilian life by Giovanni Verga which had given Mascagni has greatly successful *Cavalleria rusticana.* He abandoned *La Lupa* — partly through distaste for the characters, and partly because it had not yet won laurels for Verga in the theater — though not before setting some of Verga's libretto to music which he later prudently transferred to *La Bohème,* the subject which supplanted *La Lupa.* Henri Murger's *Scènes de la vie de bohème* (1848) was based on the author's own experiences as an impoverished student in Paris. The book struck appropriate chords in Puccini's memories of his own student days in Milan. He knew that Murger had turned these tenuously linked short stories into a successful play, and he soon discovered that a former collaborator in the *Manon Lescaut* libretto, Ruggiero Leoncavallo (by now the successful composer of *Pagliacci*), was at work on a *Bohème* opera: Puccini thus had two pressing reasons for deciding on *La Bohème.* Illica made him a draft libretto and brought in Giacosa to write the verses: Puccini bombarded them both with objections, criticism and demands for rewriting that inclined first one, then the other, to give up. Ricordi swore them all to secrecy: Leoncavallo must not discover that his *Bohème* had a rival — though he did find out, and was openly scornful of Puccini's inferior libretto.

Toscanini conducted the première of Puccini's *Bohème,* at Turin on 1 February 1896. It was amiably received, though some critics found it flippant in manner, a disappointment after *Manon Lescaut.* Leoncavallo's *Bohème,* first produced in Venice on 5 May 1897, was received more politely, and modern revivals have shown it to be an attractive, expert treatment of the source material. In the longer run there was no doubt which of these two *Bohèmes* the public preferred.

Puccini's *La Bohème* may, so soon after Verdi's *Falstaff,* have appeared copycat: an opera composer of known melodramatic potential suddenly decides to don clown's greasepaint, and then display, behind it, a simple bourgeois sentimentality — neither aspect becoming to the heroic mentality of romantic serious tragedy. Verdi could afford the luxury of mirth-making, with serious operas by the dozen under his belt, and important ones too, from *Nabucco* to *Otello.* Puccini had only one real success to his name, *Manon Lescaut,* and was expected to continue likewise. *Tosca* would have pleased the cognoscenti much more. *La Bohème* was, for some critics, too easy a success, dangerous for a composer with but one triumph to his credit. The conductor, the young and brilliant and masterful Toscanini, supposed that the operagoers of Turin were still overwhelmed by the marvels of Wagner's *Götterdämmerung* which they had just experienced for the first time. The notion implies a bewilderingly blinkered view of opera, but is not incredible: the human race, when not quite sure of itself, uses solemnity as a mask, almost by natural instinct, and erects invented canons of propriety, intending them to be welcomed as wholesome, though really to cover ignorant confusion. The operagoers of Turin decided not to accept the declared failure of *La Bohème*. It was evidently not grand opera, but it had irresistible charm, great melodiousness, and immediate appeal to basic human emotions. When you emerge from your first *Bohème,* it is not the frivolity that clings to your memory, but the sweet and star-crossed love of Mimi and Rodolfo, the end of the first act, and of the third act and of the fourth act — if it is not thrust down our throats in Act II, we are aware of it all the time, in their persons, and through their voices.

If you are aria-minded, there are solos aplenty in *Bohème:* when gramophone records began to be marketed, soon after the premiere, excerpts from *Bohème* were soon part of the desirable repertory. Before long, every soprano wanted to be heard in "Mi chiamano Mimì," or else "Quando me'n' vo," every tenor in "Che gelida manina"; military bands in the park were expected to play potpourris from *Bohème,* dance floors to sway beneath its rhythms. The names of its first cast are not part of every operagoer's history book, unless that of Antonio Pini-Corsi, who sang Schaunard. But while the opera was still, so to say, in its infancy, the principal roles were acknowledged as excellent vehicles for such great singers as Melba, Farrar, Bori, Caruso, McCormack, Scotti, De Luca, and Ruffo, all of whom recorded extracts. *La Bohème* became an essential challenge to every great opera singer, conductor, and, in the present visual-haunted time, stage director. It is the custom-built opera for young lovers, music that insists on another hand to hold. A *Bohème* that does not make you weep at "O soave fanciulla" and "Mimì è tanta malata," and in the closing bars of the last act, is a disgrace to Puccini's memory.

His next opera, *Tosca* (premiere in Rome, 14 January 1900), had been in Puccini's mind since 1889, two years after Sardou's tragedy, written for Sarah Bernhardt, was first performed in Paris. His ex-librettist Fontana had suggested it to Puccini, who evinced lively interest and asked Ricordi to negotiate with the author for operatic rights. Meanwhile *Manon Lescaut* claimed all his attention. When it was complete and his thoughts reverted to *Tosca,* he learned that Ricordi had bought it for Alberto Franchetti, Puccini's exact contemporary and fellow student at Lucca Conservatory. Illica was making a libretto of *Tosca* for Franchetti: Sardou had approved, and Verdi himself praised Illica's treatment and wished that he were younger and in a physical condition to set it to music. Again Puccini's envy was roused. While at work on *La Bohème* he traveled to Florence with Elvira to see Sardou's play with Bernhardt in the title role, and determined that it must be his to compose. He easily persuaded Ricordi to prefer his claim on *Tosca,* and the publisher contrived to convince Franchetti that the subject was quite unsuitable and should be dropped, whereupon Puccini lost no time in signing for it, his eagerness heightened by an encouraging message from Verdi, who kept a benevolent, if distant, eye on his progress, and by the recent triumph of Giordano's *Andrea Chénier* (libretto by Illica) on a not dissimilar theme.

Sardou's *Tosca* required a minimum of literary adaptation: Illica again brought in Giacosa to write the verse (the latter found the piece ugly and wanting in poetic content), and again Puccini found constant fault with their work. It was not until January 1898 (after prolonged and serious consideration of a libretto by Illica about the last days of Marie Antoinette, an offshoot of the poet's research into the French Revolution for *Chénier*) that Puccini began to compose *Tosca,* his first venture into the fashionable *verismo* style, opera as a slice of seamy, violent life. If *Tosca* seemed remote from the relatively carefree romance of *La Bohème,* Puccini could take courage from Sardou's appeal to his manifest talent which must range beyond the confines of his previous operas. That Puccini found the requisite musical diction for *Tosca* is shown by the speed with which he completed it, notwithstanding constant altercation with his librettists and Ricordi: the first act occupied him for most of 1898; acts two and three were composed between late February and late September 1899.

The premiere of *Tosca* in Rome (chosen because the drama takes place there, each act precisely located in a building familiar to every inhabitant of the city) was a tense affair, with a bomb scare, a nervous audience, and hostile newspaper critics. Puccini already had enemies, some jealous of his success, others of his own making. I have already indicated how openly he despised the bribery and corruption on which Italian public life depended. He did not suffer knaves or fools gladly, however influential. Subsequently performances were well attended and favorably received. Outside Italy, *Tosca* was welcomed as a significant advance in Puccini's development and a worthy challenge for the most eminent opera singers. It has resiliently survived recurrent outbursts of mud-slinging by strict arbiters of taste. Three solo arias in it rank with the most popular of all Puccini's music. It is interesting to recall that he composed the music for Cavaradossi's "E lucevan le stelle" to an improvised text of his own, in place of the heroic and idealistic monologue by which Illica set great store and was most unwilling to jettison.

After *Tosca*, Puccini entertained a host of possible subjects for his next opera, anxious as he was to return to work. He settled finally on one that had been among the first to attract his attention. While visiting London to prepare for the English premiere of *Tosca,* he was taken to see *Madame Butterfly,* a one-act play by David Belasco, the picaresque American writer, based on a short story by John Luther Long, a lawyer by profession. The tale, of a Japanese geisha who cast aside her country's customs and traditions, even her family, to marry an American naval officer, and who was then deserted by him, derived from a real-life story, told to Long by his sister who had lived in Nagasaki where her husband was a missionary. The play reads mawkishly now, but in 1900 it touched the hearts of playgoers, among them Puccini, for all that he understood virtually no English. The content was perfectly clear to him and he at once went backstage and obtained Belasco's permission to turn it into an opera. It took time for the rights to *Butterfly* to be ratified, and this time Illica and Giacosa had much to do in reshaping Belasco's play as an opera in two or three acts (the present Act III followed Act II, in the premiere production, without an interval or pause in the music) before Puccini could begin composing it — whence his consideration of other operatic subjects. As was his custom, he thoroughly researched the subject matter, to acquaint himself with Japanese customs, traditional music, and native speech inflections. Composition was held up in 1903 by a motor-car accident, and by the diagnosis of diabetes, necessitating careful diet, as well as a recurrent throat complaint (he was a heavy cigarette-smoker) which was eventually, as cancer, to cause his death. Nevertheless Puccini completed the opera by 27 December 1903, and it was ready for its premiere at La Scala on 17 February 1904, just over one month after the long-delayed marriage of Puccini and Elvira. The first performance of *Madama Butterfly*, though carefully rehearsed with a magnificent cast (Storchio, Zenatello, De Luca), was one of the most famous fiascos in operatic history. The work was, from start to finish, subjected to noisy interruption, both bitter and mocking, from a section of the audience who communicated their hostility to such of the rest as were not already committed to its merits. Puccini was a prime object of envy, hatred, and malice in Milan, not only for his success, but for his studied independence in private and public life: he refused to curry favor, to seek advancement by the influence of others, to frequent fashionable society, to toe the Italian Establishment's line. His enemies had tried in vain to ruin the first night of *Tosca;* with *Madama Butterfly* they succeeded. Puccini and his librettists promptly withdrew the opera, made some minimal alterations, restored the alternative three-act form, and brought it out again in Brescia on 28 May with the lively success that it has enjoyed ever since — during the 1950s *Butterfly* was estimated to have received more performances than any other opera in world repertory.

Six years were to elapse before the next Puccini operatic premiere. Puccini traveled much, overseeing local premieres of *Madama Butterfly*, anxious that it should not be misrepresented. Avidly he studied the scores of his most adventurous composer-colleagues, and equally avidly he hunted for new, really original and modern operatic subject matter to which he would be able to respond with equally bold and original music. He had been accused in the past of repeating himself musically: there must be no such charges in future. The initial fiasco of *Butterfly,* artificially engineered though he knew it to have been, had served as an amber light to Puccini's self-critical faculty: he must rigorously exclude secondhand as well as second-best invention.

Puccini was a shrewd judge of operatic material: the subjects that he seriously contemplated for his operas, but did not bring to fruition, were later taken up, almost to the last heroine, by other composers — with at least passing success. Some of them became Giordano's *Siberia,* D'Albert's *Tiefland,* Korngold's *Die tote Stadt,* Zandonai's *Conchita,* Mascagni's *Parisina* and *Lodoletta,* Janáček's *From the House of the Dead,* Alfano's *Cyrano de Bergerac,* and Montemezzi's *Hellera.* It was on a visit to New York in 1907, for the premiere there at the Metropolitan Opera of *Butterfly* (in which the composer did not, surprisingly, appreciate the contributions of Geraldine Farrar and Caruso) as part of a six-week Puccini season, that he went to see a more recent play, *The Girl of the Golden West* (1905) by Belasco, the author of *Madame Butterfly,* and again found the subject for his next opera. Puccini was particularly drawn to its mixture of rough realism and honest sentiment, though he admitted that it was "sometimes in very bad taste." The choice of a librettist for once posed problems. The faithful Giacosa had died in 1906, and Illica was busy with the Marie Antoinette project mentioned earlier — he would, in any case, need a collaborator for the actual poetry of the libretto, Puccini knew. Choice fell on Carlo Zangarini, who had learned English from his American mother but was inclined to overwrite in Italian, and the more self-controlled Guelfo Civinni. After the usual skirmishing with his librettists, Puccini retired to Torre del Lago and prepared to compose *La Fanciulla del West.*

Work was interrupted by a family tragedy. In 1903, when Puccini was convalescing after his motoring accident, his wife engaged a local girl aged sixteen to act as a sort of lay nurse, or literally nursemaid, to the invalid. Doria Manfredi proved efficient and likable, and remained on the domestic staff at Torre del Lago. Toward the end of 1908 Elvira Puccini, who had always been painfully aware of her husband's philandering escapades, took it into her head that Puccini was carrying on an affair with Doria, and though she had no evidence for her suspicions, pretended that she had caught the two red-handed. After violently abusing the girl in and out of doors, Elvira dismissed her and continued to shout obscenities about her behavior to all the village, including the girl's family and the priest of the parish. Puccini left home and considered a permanent separation from his demented wife, then returned to face the storm with a clear conscience. In January 1909 Doria attempted suicide and died in hospital a few days later, calling on her family for revenge. They took Elvira Puccini to court for public defamation of character, and the court found against her, the dead girl having been medically examined and pronounced *virgo intacta.* Elvira's prison sentence was eventually quashed, but her local reputation touched rock-bottom, and the scandal resounded throughout Italy and beyond, thanks to Puccini's great fame and the enemies he had made. His own innocence was never contested, except by Elvira who refused to recant; he remained even more popular than before in Torre del Lago, except with his own wife.

The traumatic experience not only prevented Puccini from continuing to work, but temporarily dried up his creative powers when he did find time for composition. In August 1909 he forced himself to pick up the musical threads of *Fanciulla,* and he finished the last act on 6 August 1910. The world premiere went to the Metropolitan Opera in New York, where Toscanini conducted it on 10 December, with a cast splendidly led by Destinn, Caruso, and Amato. Puccini traveled there with his son, and was well pleased with the resounding success. His wife was left at home, tearfully reproving him for his unkindness. She could not imagine herself ever in the wrong.

Again Puccini went in search of new operatic material. In 1912 he lost his staunchest ally and adviser when Giulio Ricordi, his publisher, died, leaving his son Tito in charge of the firm. Puccini and Tito Ricordi quarreled constantly. When Puccini was commissioned in 1913 by the Karlstheater in Vienna to compose a new operetta for performance there, Tito declined to publish it, and Puccini assigned it to the rival firm of Sanzogno. The opera, as it became, was called *La Rondine.* It had its premiere not in Vienna, where by 1917 the First World War was in full spate, but in neutral Monte Carlo. *La Rondine* is blessed with delicious music, light, cheerful and sensuous, with a touch of pathos. It does not deserve its present neglect, just as Puccini did not, at the time, deserve the French newspapers' accusations of treachery for having written it to a Viennese commission, even one dating from peacetime.

Visiting Paris in 1912 when he was still *persona grata* there, Puccini had seen the gruesome one-act tragedy *La Houppelande* ("The Cloak") by Didier Gold, and was captivated by its setting on a barge moored under one of the Parisian bridges which span the river Seine. More than once in the past he had contemplated an operatic triple bill: at one point it was to reflect the three parts of Dante's *Divine Comedy* — Inferno, Purgatorio, Paradiso. Something of the kind underlaid the construction of the French Grand Guignol shows: a thriller, a tear-jerker, and a comedy. Puccini now set about compiling such a triple bill, which he called a "triptych," in Italian *Trittico*. The first panel was clearly "The Cloak," *Il Tabarro;* Giuseppe Adami, a playwright and music critic, also a protégé of Giulio Ricordi, made the Italian libretto, and was soon accepted by Puccini as a staunch friend. The other two panels were to have been contributed by Gabriele D'Annunzio, Italy's most eminent poet, one with whom Puccini had long been discussing possible operas, and the French comic dramatist Tristan Bernard; neither was forthcoming, so Puccini deputed the choice to Adami, who found the tear-jerker in one of his own plays, set in a convent — this became *Suor Angelica*. The comic conclusion was appropriately found in Dante, after all: the tale of *Gianni Schicchi,* elaborated from a few lines in the *Inferno*. Its theatrical credentials were not established, but Puccini completed all three operas by April 1918. The wartime conscription in Italy made it difficult to ensure a first-rate cast for the *Trittico* at the Rome Opera, as had been Puccini's intention. He accepted the offer of the Metropolitan Opera to give the premiere, which took place there on 14 December 1918, so soon after the Armistice that Puccini was unable to travel to New York, a sorrow in triplicate since it was the first time in his life that he had missed any of his operas' baptisms. In Europe as well as America, *Schicchi* was liked best. It took several decades for *Il Tabarro* to be fully appreciated, and *Suor Angelica* lags behind only because the convent setting is found unpalatable by many operagoers, through the character of Angelica's formidable aunt, the Princess, is one of his most startling achievements, surely an Elvira simulacrum.

The end of the First World War found Puccini unhappy to be living in politically restless, militant Italy, and melancholy in the contemplation of his own sixties, the onset of old age. By way of compensation his marriage now entered a new, more serene and frankly affectionate phase. Long ago he had forgiven Elvira, generous man. Now she forgave her blameless victim. He was still waiting impatiently for a new libretto. A new friendship with Renato Simoni, a scholar and playwright who was an authority on Gozzi, brought up the idea of a Gozzi play as operatic source material. Puccini himself may have suggested *Turandot,* of which he knew an operatic version by his former professor Bazzini, as well as incidental music (possibly also the subsequent opera) by Busoni. Adami joined Simoni in making the libretto, Puccini busied himself with research into Chinese music. It was while composing *Turandot* that Puccini was compelled to exchange Torre del Lago for a villa in Viareggio. In 1923 the composer was again troubled by throat pains. Several specialists found nothing untoward to diagnose, until Puccini visited another in Florence who located a cancerous growth in his throat. In November 1924 he underwent X-ray treatment, for relief of the cancer, at a clinic in Brussels. His heart gave way under the intense strain of the treatment and on 29 November 1924 he died. He was buried at first in the Toscanini family tomb — a generous gesture by the conductor whom Puccini had, more than once, wrongly vilified. Two years later his remains were transferred to a newly built mausoleum by the lake at Torre del Lago. *Turandot* was complete, at the time of Puccini's death, as far as the penultimate scene of the last act, the funeral cortège of Liù. Puccini, ironically, had found trouble in finding the music for the last scene, in which the implacable princess's heart is gradually turned to feelings of warmth and love. The initial sketches existed, in the composer's characteristic scrawl: on their basis Franco Alfano built up a closing scene, having much recourse to earlier music in *Turandot*. His completion was performed at La Scala on 26 April 1926, though in a substantially abbreviated version made at Toscanini's behest (the original full finale was discovered and first performed in 1982). But on the previous evening, at the opera's official premiere, the conductor Toscanini silenced the orchestra after Liù's death-march and, turning to the audience, announced "Here, at this point, Giacomo Puccini broke off his work. This time death was more powerful than art."

Puccini brought out his first important and successful opera, *Manon Lescaut*, eight days before the premiere of Verdi's last opera, *Falstaff*. With Verdi's retirement, Puccini had no difficulty in bestriding the Italian opera of his day. His contemporaries were a respectable group of composers, and each of them produced one memorable opera: *Andrea Chénier* (1896) by Umberto Giordano, Puccini's composition teacher; *La Wally* (1892) by Alfredo Catalani, Puccini's exact contemporary as a student, and an enemy devoured by jealousy until his premature death in 1893; *Pagliacci* (1892) by Ruggiero Leoncavallo, another friend who turned foe; its heavenly twin *Cavalleria rusticana* (1890) by Pietro Mascagni, the most creative of all these others; and *Adriana Lecouvreur* (1902) by Francesco Cilèa. None of these had Puccini's melodic fecundity, nor his unsleeping professionalism as a man of the theater.

By the time that Puccini produced *Manon Lescaut,* two operatic failures had taught him precisely what made for operatic success, and how to ensure it within his own admitted creative limitations. His personal style, in particular his melodic language, was fixed in *Manon Lescaut;* thereafter he had only to keep himself idiomatically up to date (he studied the music of Debussy, Richard Strauss, and the young Stravinsky to beneficial purpose), and discreetly to expand his range, so that each new opera would appear to break fresh ground, and protect him from the old accusation, leveled against *La Bohème,* of repeating himself. Calaf's "Nessun dorma" is manifestly from the same pen as Des Grieux's "Guardate, pazzo son" and Cavaradossi's "E lucevan le stelle"; but if you think fleetingly, and in turn, of the music for *Turandot, Manon Lescaut,* and *Tosca,* each has its own identifying atmosphere, as is also true of *Bohème, Butterfly, Fanciulla,* and each panel of the *Trittico.* Nobody familiar with them is likely to mistake one Puccini opera for any of the others; the composer went to some pains to ensure that there could be no such confusion, using his flair for pastiche and capacity for original musical research (e.g., before writing the prelude to the third act of *Tosca,* he climbed to the battlements of the Castel Sant'Angelo in Rome, and took notes on the sounds heard there at dawn). He worked hard to ensure, before he began writing the music, that the new work would impress audiences throughout, visually as theatrical spectacle, and emotionally as a poignant dramatic experience, even if sung in an altogether unfamiliar language — Puccini could remember negotiating rights to *Butterfly* with its author after a performance in London at which he understood barely a word of the play: so it must be with his operas. And so it was: his envious rivals and social enemies could conspire to ruin the success of a first night, as they did of *Butterfly;* and the critics, watchful for their own reputations and convinced that Puccini could not maintain such a high rate of striking forever, were always poised to pounce on any short-falling. Puccini had formulated his rules for success and he stuck to them. There is no substandard Puccini opera after *Manon Lescaut:* not *Fanciulla,* whose abrasive harmony, blunt musical dialogue, and muscular orchestration took some time to grow familiar; not *Suor*

Anglica, an exquisite vignette of feminine frailty *en masse* (no pun intended) with a horrendous gorgon as villainess, and no contrasting male voices in the cast (for such a composer as Puccini, it was like playing the piano with one arm in a sling); not even *La Rondine,* which fails only if you expect it to be less unpretentious than Puccini made it. *Turandot* gave the composer trouble to put into music, I believe, because he realized too late that the characters were all puppets and the action a sequence of rites or ceremonies, not of realistic unpredictable incidents. Despite this handicap to creativity ("I can only compose when my bloodthirsty puppets move about on stage," he wrote to Adami), and failing health too, Puccini made *Turandot* a striking and alluring work of art, even though it remained incomplete.

With his theatrical flair, shrewd artistic judgment, painstaking craftsmanship, and genius for the creation of melody, Puccini was well able to uphold the Italian operatic tradition, during his lifetime, against the German school led, almost as single-handedly, by Richard Strauss (whose rejection of the vanguard, from *Der Rosenkavalier* onwards, coincided with Puccini's more ardent cultivation of new trends, in *Fanciulla* and its successors). A compatriot and perceptive critic, Ferruccio Bonavia, summed up Puccini thus, in his obituary for the *Musical Times* (January 1925): "He wrote for the great audiences of the theatre — not for the more critical and cultured *cognoscenti.* Those felt with him as he felt for them, for their griefs and for their tragedies chronicled in the columns of the newspaper, not in the annals of history." Puccini, that is to say, set his artistic sights too low: heroics were not for him — in *Fanciulla* and *Schicchi* he even has antiheroes, rather in advance of their time. Nearly sixty years after his death, the "great audiences," and the great singers, conductors, and stage directors, still find Puccini inexhaustible; the cognoscenti, while admitting that he respected his own artistic limitations, may find his modesty laudable and sensible (a professional opera composer cannot nowadays afford a commercial flop), and may also find more to study and ponder with interest than Bonavia's generation perhaps thought possible.

WILLIAM MANN
LONDON, 1982

PUCCINI'S
La Bohème

by
WILLIAM MANN

IT is most usual, when great composers are being discussed, for the highest acclaim to go to their later works, when they were at their most experienced in technique, most mature in wisdom and imagination. Late Verdi operas, from *Aida* onwards, are demonstrably more rich and profound than the most enjoyable before *Rigoletto*, or even before *La forza del destino*. However much you enjoy Wagner's *Der fliegende Holländer*, you will not, I hope, try to persuade anybody that it is as profound an experience as *Tristan und Isolde*. Noble opera as *Fidelio* is agreed to be, I cannot help wishing that Beethoven had left it until the time of the Ninth Symphony and the *Missa Solemnis*, only a few years after his final version, but years of great importance for his style. Berlioz's *Symphonie fantastique* is, admittedly, an early work and a masterpiece; *Béatrice et Bénédict*, written thirty years later, is less brilliant, but more subtle and refined in musical invention, boisterous and passionate in a less obvious manner. Even among composers who died young, Mozart attracts us rather through *Le Nozze di Figaro* and its successors, than through the successful achievements of his boyhood before the mighty *Idomeneo*.

So one may continue, comparing Monteverdi's *Orfeo* with his *L'Incoronazione di Poppea*, Handel's Italian operas with his English oratorios (dramatically much more advanced), playing Schubert's *Erlkönig* and *Gretchen am Spinnrade* off against *Winterreise*. When Puccini is reached, *Turandot* is plainly more advanced, perhaps more sure in touch, than *Madama Butterfly*; *Il Tabarro* and *Gianni Schicchi* distill the essence of Puccini respectively grim and satirical. Are they superior to *Tosca* and *La Bohème*? I don't think so. There are some flaws of design and perspective in *Tosca*, if you look for them. I have yet to acknowledge any in *La Bohème*; indeed, I become more and more convinced that it, and not

one of Puccini's later works, is the most perfectly designed and
executed of them all. It does not essay high tragedy, though it ends
very sadly; it doesn't deal in high affairs of state, and involves no
central dilemma of agonizing choice. There is no heroism in *La
Bohème,* unless the heroism of one's own poverty. Those consid-
erations do not make *Tosca* necessarily superior to *La Bohème,*
which sets its operatic sights exactly as high as is appropriate and
then frames the action in a small but identifiable, highly detailed
world of its own, as broad as the Latin Quarter of Paris, as high
as its rooftops, and as various as the people living there in 1830
under the Empire of Louis Philippe. The principal characters are
unpretentious and young, their joys and sorrows as real as our
own, as invigorating or touching as those of gods or monarchs or
other heroes in earlier operas. That *La Bohème* is superficially a
jolly opera counts in its favor, not to its discredit as the Turin
opera critics if 1896 seem to have assumed, especially as the jollity rings so true (if the skylarking of the bohemian lads doesn't
ring true, the stage director hasn't rehearsed his actors properly).
It is a jollity that heightens the romantic appeal of love at first
meeting, Rodolfo and Mimi's scene together at the end of the first
act, and bursts into full gaudy flower with the scene outside Café
Momus. Nor does the jocular banter lessen the melancholy which,
in the big vocal trio and quartet, dominates the third act, and which
also eventually overtakes the fourth. In *La Bohème* the authors
pay homage, in equally balanced proportions, to the penury, pleasure, and pathos of life in bohemian Paris.

    The action, and therefore the diction of text and music, the
choice of words and musical phrases, is swift-moving in *La Bohème,* much more so than is usual in opera, which reckons to pause
and take stock of the situation every ten minutes or so. The tone
of voice in *Bohème* is conversational, almost throughout, but of
old-fashioned simple recitative little trace is to be found, so naturally did Puccini's invention find melodies for situations and moods
and turns of phrase, however apparently humdrum. Melodious invention is prodigally squandered in *La Bohème;* Puccini could afford to throw out an enchanting tune (such as Rodolfo's arioso,
"Dal mio cervel" when introducing Mimi to his cronies at Café
Momus, or Marcello's "Dica: quant'anni ha" to the landlord Benoit), extend it for a moment, and then drop it forever. *La Bohème* is full of vocal ensembles in which the action can move on-

wards, but it has very few set arias or monologues: the famous ones for Rodolfo and Mimì in the first act were added as late as 1894 at an advanced stage of the opera's conception. Mimì has two other solos ("Sono andati" soon becomes a duet), Musetta one, her waltz, Colline his coat song, Rodolfo no other; Schaunard's song about the parrot, just after his first entrance, ought to be a solo, but is firmly gripped by the dynamic, helter-skelter ensemble of his friends. Marcello has no solo as such, but plenty of arioso in ensemble (just after Musetta's waltz, for example). We may notice, in these passages and generally, that the climaxes are quickly achieved and quitted: there is no wallowing over the view from the top of the mountain, so to say, and long-held top notes were strictly discouraged (a pause over the note meant no more than twice its written value, the composer insisted — good guidance for all music, which every student should learn). *La Bohème* is an opera in which something is happening virtually all the time: the notion of a singer standing still and delivering to the gallery is not one to which this opera subscribes, except in the two Act I monologues added later; that is why solos so often become duets. In performance the construction of the four acts may appear easygoing and relaxed, but they are most concisely ordered, words and music articulated with keen precision, internal form linked by brief, pertinent transitions — when they are longer, they feel like scenes in their own right, not bridges at all.

This was as Puccini intended. He was able to bring off a "lyrical action" of this dynamic sort because Luigi Illica and Giuseppe Giacosa gave him a libretto apt for fast-moving music, and a very fine libretto too. It is difficult honestly to admire an opera with a plot that does not make sense, or words that are an embarrassment to comprehension. You can read the libretto of *La Bohème* at the end of this book and it reads easily, as entertainment. Illica raided Murger's novel to advantage, in his search for stageworthy incident, amusing references, and enlightening traits of character. His is the credit for the libretto's dramatic activity. Giacosa, the poet in the partnership, complained bitterly (complaining was his Leitmotiv, as it were, with Puccini) that *La Bohème* was all character and no poetry; eventually he found the poetry implicit in the contexts, and a quantity of it can be savored for its poetic quality, even in passages of everyday conversation, for example during the incineration of Rodolfo's drama manuscript in Act I. In that passage, and in all those involving the bohemian boys, Giacosa was helped by the convoluted, literary, comically artificial vocabulary that Murger assigns to them deliberately — a sort of private language customary in small, closely knit communities of educated people especially, but not exclusively. "Bohemians," wrote Murger, "speak a dialect of their own when they are together, the product of the Studio, the stage, and the editor's office. This vocabulary is the Inferno of rhetoric and the Paradiso of neologism." It is already a sort of poetry, as such useful to another poet in search of heightened speech for lyrical music. It enabled Giacosa to flap his poetic wings when he reached the monologues of Rodolfo and Mimi three-quarters through Act I. Rodolfo's poetic conceit, in "Che gelida manina," about his spiritual millions being plundered by a pair of lovely eyes (Puccini honored it with the most marvelous tune in the whole opera — too good to squander, and so used thematically in later acts) is no more ridiculous, as amorous conversation, than the way Marcello and Colline were discussing a visit to the hairdresser a few minutes earlier.

La Bohème is as much Giacosa's triumph as Puccini's. Their *tour de force* together is Act II, in which several scenes and conversations, each precisely and vividly expressed, take place at the same time; respectable bourgeois families window-shopping, street hawkers and shopkeepers, little urchins, café customers, students, midinettes, classy children and their mothers, Parpignol the toy-seller, Mimi, Musetta with her sugar daddy, and the four bohemians, all are exactly characterized, ripe to be counterpointed in Puccini's conjuring-trick music. Glorious as that conjuring is — a whirlwind of solo voices, chorus, orchestra, tunes, interruptions, and special effects — it obliterates half of the text in performance, and a reading here of the libretto may prove an eye-opener to people who know *La Bohème* quite well. For an example, try Musetta's entrance and Marcello's account of her, while Musetta tries to attract his attention; or after her waltz song, when Rodolfo and Mimi, Schaunard and Colline, Alcindoro and Musetta each to themselves are all talking simultaneously in song — Marcello is too knocked out to utter, but when he finds his tongue and takes up Musetta's tune, that is a dramatic event in the music worth waiting for. The cries of the street hawkers at the beginning of the act may not all be clear in the theater, though they make good reading: Illica, and perhaps Puccini, will have given many of them to

Giacosa, since they are corroborative detail, which was Illica's speciality. Illica, of course, was responsible for shaping Act IV as a part-recapitulatory reflection of Act I, and it was Illica's stage directions for the start of Act III that inspired Puccini's evocative tone poem — with an orchestral curiosity, the notated part for clinking wineglasses off-stage in the tavern, designated by Illica as *cabaré* (the word is really French, *cabaret*). Puccini deserves all the credit we grant him for the greatness of *La Bohème,* and his librettists deserve just as much, as will be appreciated when the libretto has been read carefully, the Italian words matched with the English (if you don't speak Italian fluently — the vocabulary of *Bohème* is quite extensive) for full enjoyment of the music.

What follows is an attempt to exemplify, in greater detail, the above generalizations. It is best read with reference to the printed libretto (with English translation, so that I need not myself translate all my references). In performance one tends to ignore the larger paragraphs or set pieces (aria, quartet, etc.) of each act's construction (I call them "acts" but the score says "pictures," perhaps remembering that Murger's original title for his book was *Scènes de Bohème,* "bohemian scenes," i.e., not a consecutive narration, but cameos or animated tableaux), so cunningly do Illica and Puccini conceal their traces. The annotations below relate to those paragraphs.

ACT I

The curtain rises at once during the opening C major exchanges for wind and strings (borrowed from Puccini's student work *Capriccio sinfonico*) which are marked "ruggedly" (*ruvidamente*) by Puccini. They and the higher answering phrase recur often during the four acts, and are usually taken to represent the four boisterous bohemians; but often they have special relevance to Marcello, as here discovered painting *The Crossing of the Red Sea.* He is the only one of the four without an accredited signature tune, so I refer to it as Marcello's theme. Does it suggest his picture, or merely the bitter cold that makes it difficult for him to hold his brush? The rest of the orchestral introduction is more serene: a lulling figure disturbed by spasmodic gusts, a rising scale, and a cadence with the lulling figure. The whole of this is at once repeated, as

Marcello curses his painting, a fourth higher to arrive in B-flat major for:

Rodolfo. "Nei cieli bigi," which introduces the theme hereafter associated with Rodolfo, a charming, lazy barcarolle, not particularly apt to its text about gray skies and smoking chimneys (Puccini took it over from his abandoned opera *La Lupa,* where it had to do with blue Sicilian skies and smoking Mount Etna!). Here the reference is specifically to smoke from their own, at present inactive, form of heating, a living-room stove. Rodolfo's theme is taken up by Marcello in a second verse that trails away into barely accompanied musical conversation, before reappearing when Rodolfo decides to burn the manuscript of his five-act play (*Le Vengeur* is the title in Murger, and it exists in many drafts, so we do not have to mourn the sacrifice of one of them).

This is the stove scene. The reappearances of Rodolfo's theme are differently scored each time, the last one, for two flutes, tinkling harp and shimmering strings, being particularly lovely, for the first warmth to thaw two cold men, as the drama's first act burns away. The tune is now interrupted and extended by a new melodic section, very loud on horns with violas and cellos, associated with Colline the philosopher (after "Che lieto baglior"), who enters noisily and in a foul temper, unable to pawn his books this Christmas Eve. Colline's theme (it makes one other appearance, when Colline plays mysterious, in the last act, about his evening plans) here sounds grand and tragical, or is it merely his anger and physical clumsiness? Colline at once becomes an interested participant in the premiere (or rather *dernière*) of *Le Vengeur,* whose first act passes all too quickly (a tap on the bass drum marks the last spark). Quickly, the second act! Rodolfo rips the pages apart to strident bitonal chords, and the fire flickers happily again on the orchestra; here the dialogue is as fanciful as the orchestral music. It too dies out, and Rodolfo piles the last three acts on together (Marcello's theme here refers to all those present), but the fire fades even more quickly, with wonderfully delicate orchestral music (three trumpets and harp for the final flicker). The "audience" boos the author with "Abbasso l'autor."

At this point, Schaunard, the musician of the four, enters, preceded by his own swaggering theme, prominent on horns. This is his scene, in two halves, the story of the Englishman and the noisy parrot, and the Christmas Eve carol ("Quando un'olezzo") and in both his solo is interrupted by his friends. The first story brings forward ("E mi presento") a second Schaunard theme, *brillante* on flute and clarinet, and parrot squawks for muted trumpets in harsh duet. This second theme leads, like an echo, into "Quando un'olezzo," which introduces the Christmas Eve theme later associated, more noisily than here, with Café Momus. Schaunard's first theme ends the section, followed at once by the episode with the landlord.

Benoit's knock causes havoc in the room, and hasty consultation before he is let in and treated to soft soap and a wheedling theme, unctuously scored for woodwind and perfectly captivating, to which he responds with a more jerky idea, concerned with rent overdue ("Quest'è l'ultimo trimestre"). Marcello now tries some solo flattery, with another oleaginous theme, sparingly and pointedly scored ("Dica: quant'anni ha"). It develops suggestions of a swagger as Marcello twits Benoit about his prowess as a ladykiller. Benoit falls for the ruse, and the first wheedling theme is resumed ("Ei gongolava") with even lovelier woodwind writing. Benoit expounds his taste in women, with orchestral caricatures of the outsize ("balena") and the skinny ("magra, proprio magra," harsh woodwind). His pompous dictum ("Le donne magre") is happily used to see him off the premises. For, at the mention of Benoit's wife, the young men profess to be gravely shocked, and they break into a would-be *fugato* of solemn outrage ("Quest'uomo ha moglie"), with a more jaunty, unfugal continuation ("Si abbruci dello zucchero" — presumably burnt sugar was a proto-disinfectant), and out Benoit goes, impelled from behind, down the stairs — this is the top floor of a tall Paris dwelling, remember.

Off to Momus. Schaunard resumes his second solo, about Christmastime, now associating the theme with its rightful owner, Café Momus, and it is played *staccato,* more as it will sound in the second act. Marcello tells Colline to get spruced up, calling him a bear (the *Orso* is duly made to growl on drums), and they prepare to go out. Rodolfo (his theme on solo violin, sounding conscientious and idealistic) must stay and write the editorial for his fashion magazine, *The Beaver.* The bohemian (Marcello) theme sees the others down the steep stairs. When they have gone, a clarinet (as it were Rodolfo whistling unconcernedly) recalls the disinfectant theme above — a delightful touch — and he sits down to work. His thoughts are voiced for us, on flute and clarinets, and they are in Puccini's archaizing, Dresden China pastoral tone of voice (we can catch him archaizing somewhere in each of his operas, a personal foible if hardly reprehensible). He means that Rodolfo cannot think of anything topical to write about. "I'm not in the mood," he mutters.

Mimì. A rich hushed string chord breathes expectancy, relieved by a timid knock on the door, and the first female voice to be heard. She is identified by hesitant clarinets (later she will sing the phrase to "Mi chiamano Mimì"), their arch completed by violins — all this is pure magic. Suddenly she feels unwell (an anxious clarinet phrase), catches her breath, coughs, and faints. Rodolfo sprinkles drops of water on her face (held flutes, plucked violins, an exact likeness) and she revives. A hesitant theme seems to start a new section, but it is only transition. Her return to find her key ("Oh! sventata!") does launch a new section.

Duet. This is quite extended, as they look for the key, and its urgent theme will return in the last act, like much else in the first act. For the present it floats lightly on its way, and eases warmly into their first handclasp and the major part of the scene.

Monologues. When Rodolfo sings "Che gelida manina" in the theater, we are listening to the tenor voice. On recordings we can also enjoy the exquisite orchestral coloring of the first, introductory section, the hesitant turn into "Chi son? Sono un poeta," the more confident reprise of Rodolfo's personal theme ("In povertà"), which rises to a new tune, the first really passionate one, due to be brought back and made the most of ("Talor dal mio forziere" — henceforward the *Talor* theme). The orchestra takes up the theme, doubling up on it, sumptuously supported, to the long-awaited top C (only an alternative, and without any pause-mark on it!) and fervent descent to the solo's end.

Mimì's solo, "Mi chiamano Mimì," follows with only a violin cue to the singer — the key is going to change from A-flat major to D major, very far away in terms of musical tonality. It begins with Mimì's theme and clinging high string chords, most appealing; they lead to a second tune ("Mi piaccion quelle cose") that rises to a brief climax, for *amor* and *primavere,* uplifted and essentially innocent. This almost functions as her second theme. After a return to her (first) theme, she rattles on cheerfully about her lonely existence, but returns to the topic of springtime ("ma quando vien lo sgelo") for a glorious burst of passionately sensual melody supported by a luxurious carpet of string harmony, after which the aria can only sink to its close, via a rerun of the "Mi piaccion" tune, more grandly scored. Her breathless apology is almost too formal, like a recitative.

There is an interruption. The other three bohemians call to Rodolfo from the street below. He opens the window to lean out and answer them. A ray of moonlight floods the room and illuminates Mimi too, as Rodolfo reveals to the others that he is not alone. With suitable jocularity his friends walk toward the café. Marcello comments, "He has found poetry" — Giacosa at his best!

Finale. Rodolfo turns from the window to see Mimi floodlit by the moon, and love overcomes him. The *Talor* theme wells back, a semitone higher than before (this is a familiar Puccini effect to increase emotional tension) but pitched lower down on the orchestra for more grandeur. Marcello's mocking call floats poetically up from below again, as a reminder that he guessed correctly. The orchestra sweeps Mimi and Rodolfo to a climactic reprise of the *Talor* melody, and from there the tension drops quickly and remains simmering, through melting chord progressions ("No, per pietà!"), and a blatant but wonderfully inventive link ("Sarebbe così dolce," clarinet, oboe, violins, each registering exactly) until the melody of "Che gelida" returns and they leave the room arm in arm, singing its last phrase offstage — Rodolfo should *not* follow Mimi up to her top C, according to Puccini. The harp (how diversely Puccini uses it in this opera!) quietly draws the curtain.

ACT II

Outside Café Momus the air is crisp with frost and aglow with Christmas Eve excitement. The gently ambling tune to which Schaunard, in the first act, evoked the smell of fritters in the streets ("Quando un'olezza") now bursts from its old cocoon and is blared forth by trumpets in brash accented consecutive triads (a feature of this score already heard on the harp in the scene with Benoit), for which Puccini won grave academic disapproval, as he did for the parallel fifths which open the third act.

The trumpets' theme acquires a rhythmic pattern and runs into a full chorus of street traders, urchins, and shoppers. The traders' cry of "Aranci, datteri!" brings out a relevant thematic bass line.

The curtains are still closed when the chorus begins. They are raised during three sequences of loud full orchestral chords, and a bar of silence allows us to absorb the brilliant, active spectacle on stage. The foregoing is repeated with additional choral and orchestral parts that add weight and detail. The goods offered by the hawkers in this scene make lively reading, comic and evocative (not all may be heard in the theater, but are the *fringuelli* and *passeri* songbirds or food?). After the curtain-chords, the music switches from F to A-flat major, and the street cries are resumed; the voices of café customers calling inside for service are added to the scene — only one table is outside the café on this frosty night, occupied by "honest burghers."

In the middle of this throng the four bohemians are discovered: first Schaunard, buying a horn (of the hunting or coaching variety, perhaps, rather than an orchestral instrument) from a junk shop, and trying to get the price reduced, because the D on it is out of tune (the orchestral horns play D-*flat* against the trumpet's E-flat, so that D natural would be wrong in either case). The traders' theme is blown away. Rodolfo, with Mimi, walks toward a milliner's shop. Colline has bought a capacious overcoat which is being darned for him; he stuffs the pockets with books. A new theme in A-flat major steals in (Colline's "È un poco usato"), to dominate this short subsection about the bohemians. As it grows it turns pitiful to embrace Marcello's slightly tipsy and lovelorn mood ("Chi vuol, donnine allegre"): so many pretty girls, and none for him. He has spotted Rodolfo with Mimi, and the sight reminds him of Musetta, the girl who was his until she left him for a wealthier protector. In desperation he offers his virgin heart to a passing damsel in exchange for a sou — "Prunes from Tours" shouts a hawker, as if in sarcastic comment (if so, Puccini placed it there, as he later similarly does with unconnected remarks). The A-flat melody is lost behind traders' calls, with a new high-pitched variant of the earlier theme, and the bohemians use it too, as they assemble, though they miss Rodolfo and Mimi, coming out of the milliner's with her new pink bonnet, to a gentler next line of this tune, which turns back into the preceding A-flat major theme (Rodolfo's "Ho uno zio milionario," a likely story). It is cut short by a chorus of jocular urchins, chortling to a version of the Momus theme which returns proudly in its trumpet chordal form, as the bohemians bring a table out of the café on to the pavement for supper *al fresco* in more senses than one. The "honest burghers" find them too boisterous, and move away, leaving an empty table for — wait and see whom. Mimi has been watching a group of students who rouse Rodolfo's jealousy, as he admits ("Chi guardi?") to a new version of the *Talor* melody: the authors are preparing us for his behavior in Act III. For the moment he is blissfully happy. The A-flat tune returns briefly as they join their friends at table — from the distance comes the cry "Here are Parpignol's toys!" and perhaps Puccini again connected the unconnected as a comment.

The A-flat tune's section is over (but the tune not yet retired), and it may already be sensed that Puccini's Act II is a musical club sandwich with alternate layers of public and private episodes, based on the Momus and hawkers' themes, with gentler interludes like the foregoing, and like Rodolfo's mini-aria which now follows ("Questa è Mimì") as he introduces the flower-girl to his friends. She is identified by the strings with a welcome snatch ("Mi piaccion quelle cose") from her first act monologue, and Rodolfo adds a short but rapturous lyrical outburst on the conceit that he is a poet and she Poetry. The young men welcome her distantly and in Latin, to gloomy chords for woodwind, harp and drums. Parpignol the toyseller cries again, "from very far away" says the score, but a second later he is outside Café Momus, followed by crowds of eager boys and girls, and a jovial ditty in his praise. At the end of it the bohemians give their order to the waiter, and the mothers of Parpignol's customers descend angrily upon their progeny with a reproachful verse of their own. This verse also has its coda, carefully (sardonically?) placed by Puccini:

BOY: I want the trumpet, the little horse!
RODOLFO: And you, Mimi, what do you want?
MIMI: *Crème brulée.*

The children pay no attention to their mammas, but follow Parpignol as he moves to the next street, still singing his praises. The lilt of their song is sustained, as a conversation between Mimi and Marcello comes into earshot. She shows him her new bonnet, and now a fresh episode begins, with its own melody, launched by a rising scale ("Una cuffietta a pizzi") and sometimes punctuated by Marcello's "Red Sea" theme. Mimi's little arietta, in praise of Rodolfo's expertise at mind-reading, is extended eloquently in Mar-

cello's wistful expression of longing for her naïve, credulous Uto-
pianism; she carries the melody to its peak, capped by a general
toast, hurriedly called to prevent Marcello from hurting Mimi's
feelings with his cynical view of love.

As they drink the toast, Marcello shouts out for poison instead.
He has spotted Musetta in the distance, and a moment later the
others see her too. The orchestra breaks into the first of her two
personal themes: like this act, one of them is public (this one), and
the other more private. Her public motto explodes with vivacity,
and even calls the shopkeepers' wives to their doors to admire her
latest finery (that's Musetta, one day in a state coach, the next in
an omnibus, says Murger). Part of this theme is distorted amus-
ingly to lampoon her elderly, pompous companion Alcindoro, who
is indeed a minister of state, at present given much to complaint
about the unstately dance Musetta's caprices are leading him. She
is given to calling him, with the swooping extremes of her public
motto, as if he were a dog, "Come, Lulù!" and "Sit, Lulù"; "Such
pet names, please, save them for when we're alone," he mumbles
in vain. Musetta has observed Marcello, fetches Lulù to the vacant
table beside him, then to her fury finds that Marcello turns his
eyes away, while Schaunard is watching her discomfiture with open
amusement. "La commedia è stupenda," he keeps repeating, and
it really is a moment of high theatrical fun.

With Musetta's arrival, Puccini's music has drawn breath, and
now plunges into what sounds like a distinct second part of Act
II, though the composer will presently show that the act is still an
unbroken musical entity. The second, more intimate, Musetta
theme materializes on flute when Marcello volunteers information
about this newcomer ("Domandatelo a me"), and his solo is turned
into a duet by Musetta's incessant chatter all the while. This theme
alternates with the Alcindoro variant (she breaks a plate to attract
Marcello's attention, but only draws a crowd of passing students
and shopgirls), then comes to a halt.

At Musetta's open appeal to Marcello ("Tu non mi guardi!"),
the music begins, I believe, its introduction to her waltz song, from
the trilling figure for flute and clarinet. It is quickly interrupted by
a lazy melody for clarinet, a moment of privacy while Rodolfo
puzzles Mimi with his suggestion that she might one day behave
like that. Schaunard and Colline keep up a running commentary
on the stupendous comedy. The moment of lyricism is cut off, and

Musetta returns to her waltz introduction, with a salient phrase for clarinet and three pings on the harp (manna for a stage director, if the timing can be controlled). The roulades, in the first line of "Quando me'n vo," for flute and clarinet are an integral part of the tune, though Musetta does not sing them, and an integral part of the middle section's climax ("felice mi fa"). The scoring for woodwinds throughout is greatly sensitive; they dominate the middle section, which charmingly splits into two melodic strands when the violins take up the tune. The stage directions show that Musetta is sitting down and gazing at Marcello throughout; I do not recall ever seeing this, in hundreds of performances, though it must make a cogent effect. The music was imported by Puccini from an orchestral waltz for the launching of a battleship at Genoa, and that lifted from a piano piece conceived while rocking in a boat on Torre del Lago, which explains the lazy undulation and lilt of Musetta's song, but does not banish the thought that the crew of the battleship, hearing it, must have been uncomfortably reminded of seasickness. Puccini recognized that this waltz of his would perfectly enshrine the philosophy of Musetta. He apprised Giacosa of the prosody required for the song in doggerel, such as he regularly invented for his Torre del Lago cronies, beginning with the immortal line "Cocorico, cocorico poeta" (literally "Cockadoodle-do, cockadoodle-do poet").

Those who only know Musetta's waltz as sung by itself in a solo recital, live or on record, are surprised, when they meet it again in the context of the whole opera, to find Mimi and Alcindoro joining in this supposed monologue. It is also much longer than the recital item suggests, continuing to monopolize the music right until the start of the finale. At first Puccini sets up an intermezzo (Rodolfo's "Marcello un dì l'amò") involving one of the Momus themes connected with street urchins' laughter, and a broad yearning continuation for Musetta ("Ah! Marcello smania"). All the assembled principal characters are involved except Marcello, who has remained silent, greatly perturbed in spirit, ever since Musetta began her song and he begged, like Odysseus confronted by the Sirens, to be tied to his chair. With Schaunard's comment, "Quel bravaccio a momenti cederà," the music turns into our old friend the A-flat melody which supported an earlier episode (Colline's "È un poco usato"). The reprise continues, and seems to herald another verse of Musetta's waltz when she goes into her screaming

routine about a tight shoe. Marcello breaks silence and leads the
expected reprise of the waltz ("Gioventù mia" — Puccini consis-
tently gives Marcello great-hearted lyrical outpourings such as this,
perhaps to console the singer for the absence of a real solo aria),
grandly doubled up by the orchestra and set as a big ensemble
with counterpoints galore. Musetta gets rid of her shoe and Lulù,
trumpets and trombones thunder out "Quando me'n vo," and she
hurls herself into Marcello's arms (I saw Ljuba Welitsch, a sub-
stantial Musetta, actually jump several feet and be caught by Paolo
Silveri, to which every cricketer in the Covent Garden audience
cried out "How's that?"). The melody continues, softly lingering,
while the other bohemians investigate their supper bill, horror-
struck.

The waltz is lost behind the approaching strains of a military
band, sounding the retreat to music of Louis-Philippe's reign (Ricordi found it for that irrepressible archivist Puccini). Here begins
the finale in which Puccini extravagantly combines or contrasts the
military march with numerous themes heard earlier. Some com-
mentators disparage Puccini for his abandoned thematic largesse
at this point, questioning the dramatic relevance. They are obliged
to confess that the effect is a brave one, and a little more familiar-
ity with the libretto would show that there is dramatic justification
for every theme's reappearance. Schaunard has lost his wallet, hence
his theme. Musetta will leave their bill with hers for Lulù to pay
on his return; so her first theme is required. Parpignol's theme is
motivated by his small customers, now clamoring to see the soldiers. The hawkers' theme is there, with them as named spectators.
Musetta has a new, short-lived melody, her hail-and-farewell to
Alcindoro. The military procession, with stage band of trumpets,
fifes, and drums, marches through the singing crowd, which in-
cludes the clientele of Café Momus, its theme naturally bringing
the act to its close as Alcindoro returns to find his bird has flown,
having left an expensive cuckoo behind in the nest.

ACT III

The curtain rises at once: the introductory orchestral music is an
accompaniment for the stage picture and mimed action on stage.
It is as well to read the initial stage directions in detail, since we
are unlikely to see them all represented on stage at once. The per-

emptory full orchestral rat-tat which brings up the curtain mirrors the one, a third lower, which closed Act II (presumably there bringing the curtain down, though exceptionally Puccini forgot to say so in the score). The bare fifths on flutes and harp evoke the dropping snowflakes and the lonely spot to perfection, one would think, particularly with the persistent drone bass below (it remains, at one pitch or another, almost unbroken, until Marcello's entrance). It seems surprising that academic musicians could have complained. Old Verdi knew their meaning and said so openly: the fifths have to be bare and consecutive because it is so cold. Soft strings and wind build up the snowflakes into heaps now and then. The melodious harp solo, with twinkling triangle spots, draws attention to the *cabaré,* or tavern, seen to one side; it is the song of the all-night boozers within. All this is repeated with voices (as happened in Acts I and II), like the double exposition of a concerto movement: the orchestral rat-tat now becomes the shout of the scavengers, streetsweepers. The harp solo is now sung offstage by nine female drinkers who clink glasses to keep time (Puccini writes an orchestral part for the glasses).

Musetta is heard among them, singing a snatch of "Quando me'n vo" — this was at the request of Giulio Ricordi, to warn the audience of her presence in the *cabaré* with, as it happens, Marcello, whose painting of the *Crossing of the Red Sea* now hangs outside as an inn sign. A steamboat had been added to it, and with the new title, *At the Port of Marseilles,* it was sold to the innkeeper in return for board and lodging. Murger is entertaining about this picture, which was revised and retitled many times, and could have found its own way to the Louvre, if given wheels, it had been rejected so many times. After Musetta, nine male drinkers are heard in a song about Eve and Noah. There is a brief reprise of the opening, as the customs officer lets six dairymaids through the city gate (the open fifths now *legato,* even more wan). The milk-sellers arrange to meet later, in a tiny duet of jeweled structural precision, typical of others in this score. It is echoed by flute and clarinet; strings add a *pizzicato* echo of the drinking song, now dissolved into snowflakes.

Mimi, footsore, cold, and ailing, enters with her personal theme, tenuous and helpless on strings, and sends for Marcello in another miniature *cantilena.* There is a structural reference to the snowflake fifths, a jangle of church bells for matins at the Hospice Ste.

Marie Thérèse, and a gust of Marcello's initial theme as he comes out of the tavern. The drone-bass now ceases.

Duets. The first duet, for Mimi and Marcello, begins with her reluctance to see Rodolfo, who is asleep in the bar ("C'è Rodolfo"). The melody, mostly Mimi's, is shared with poignant flutes and clarinet, and is tugged by the heart to a grand climax. Its second verse, in the minor, expands into a further, harrowing tune doubled at the octave below, in typical Puccini fashion, and is again Mimi's solo. With the third verse ("Quando s'è come voi") Marcello makes a duet of it. Verse four trails away on the orchestra into an uncompleted melody about Mimi's exhaustion. Rodolfo's theme perks up on the oboe. Mimi is advised to go home (the text was evidently different at the first performance and Toscanini, who conducted, retained the earlier words for his recording decades later — Mimi is to hide in the trees, thus explaining her subsequent reappearance).

The orchestra muses quietly on the Rodolfo and *Talor* themes, then on those of Marcello (this is why I don't call it a general bohemian quartet theme). The Marcello–Rodolfo duet begins with the poet's theme, quite frank and zestful: he is going to leave Mimi. Why did he not say this last night on arrival? We know that he arrived tired, and perhaps did not want to talk in Musetta's presence, since Mimi has become a firm friend of Musetta's (and will have learned some of her gold-digging ways by Act IV). In the original libretto Marcello does specify to Mimi that Rodolfo did not explain the reason for his sudden appearance in the tavern "an hour before dawn," though Marcello must have guessed. Rodolfo explains in another arioso ("Già un'altra volta") his falling out of love; he is still buoyant, and he speaks insincerely, but Marcello answers him buoyantly too ("Se non ride" — his first line, "Dei pazzi è l'amor," was quite sober). Mimi has stealthily moved closer to hide behind a tree within earshot. Goaded by Marcello's taunts of jealousy, Rodolfo bursts out, ironically and bitterly, in another arioso, that Mimi is an open flirt ("Mimì è una civetta"); the languid Puccini octaves again suggest that he is lying, as Marcello appreciates. The tune is resumed and extended to passion and despair (the uprushing chromatic scales on strings are much found in Puccini, and never fail), but it too peters out, because these short ariosos have found their full realization in the truth.

Trio. Rodolfo now admits it ("Mimì è tanto malata"): Mimi is dying of tuberculosis, and Rodolfo is too penurious to be able to have it cured. The musical theme is dark and solemn (low wood-wind, strings and harp, cello and English horn on top), like tolling funeral bells. The continuation ("Una terribil tosse") brings back Puccini octaves and close harmony with claustrophobic oppressive sweetness (the smell of a chest ward in a hospital); then the funeral bells toll again, and all three are singing. The coughing motif wells gently on the orchestra as a coda, and the sun seems to shine as Rodolfo runs to Mimi, whose sobs and coughs had betrayed her whereabouts. Here is her theme, sung by him with orchestra, but here too, appropriately, is its original continuation, the theme of her fainting fit. What I called Musetta's private theme interrupts; and her loud laughter is heard from inside the *cabaré*. Marcello hurries in to investigate.

Addio. Mimi softly says goodbye to Rodolfo. She will return ("Donde lieta uscì") to her little lonely garret and her embroidered flowers. The solo is almost entirely a varied recapitulation of her solo in Act I, somewhat reordered, though there is a new and glorious climax before she ends with the famous phrase "Addio senza rancor."

Quartet-Finale. Rodolfo pauses on the threshold and is pushed, by oboes and clarinets, into this farewell duet with interruptions, set in sumptuous G flat major, its music lifted by Puccini from a drawing-room song of his called "Sole e amore," the loan well justified by his new orchestral accompaniment, delicately featuring woodwind. The refrain ("Soli l'inverno è cosa da morire" — "being alone in winter is a thing to die of") is especially captivating with its typical end in unharmonized octaves (Puccini took this device to extremes with Johnson's last solo in *La Fanciulla del West*). The second verse gives the melody to strings, and is enhanced with the rapid patter of Musetta and Marcello at cross purposes, and with plentiful accompanimental interest, some of it jocularly echoing the slanging match. At his "Vana, frivola, civetta!" the brass softly interpose Marcello's original theme (an apt trick already played in Act II) and continue so even after he and she have left the stage in opposite directions, at the beginning of the third verse, with shouted farewell insults. The lovers are alone again with "Sole e amore," in ecstatic duet as they stroll away together, singing their last line in octaves offstage, as in the first act. Violins on their bottom strings end the melody gorgeously, and with it the third act.

ACT IV

We are back in the top-floor garret of the first act. Spring must have arrived, because Mimi is no longer there, and Marcello has returned from his lodging in the *cabaré*. He is standing, brush in hand, at his easel, when the curtain rises, which is at once, and Rodolfo is biting a pen at his desk. Much though each would like the other to believe that he is the soul of industry, we in the audience can see through the double pretence. They are gossiping, and each has an item of special interest for the other.

Puccini's Act IV is musically a recapitulation of the first act, and dramatically they both fall into two parts, first the bohemians, and then Mimi. There is, predictably, some new music; Puccini was never at a loss for a new tune, just as he never liked to repeat a passage without altering it in some way, even if only by varying the orchestral texture. So the orchestral introduction to Act IV is abbreviated. Instead of the surging and rumbling announcement of the short bohemian tag (which I hesitantly likened to Marcello's painting of *The Crossing of the Red Sea*, we have the tag just once, fully scored now and very loud, a clatter to bring up the curtain. Then its brilliant, lighthearted, mocking continuation, also fully scored. In Act III both ideas became specifically associated with Marcello, not more generally with the four bohemian fellows, though in this last act they have both connotations. Rodolfo has run into Musetta in the street. She was being driven in a carriage-and-pair with liveried attendants, thoroughly pleased with her newfound standing, and wearing finery luxurious enough to stop her from thinking about falling in love. Puccini brings back both her musical themes, in order, perkily set for woodwind, and a dour, low-pitched chord-progression for Rodolfo's muttered recognition that Marcello's exclamation of pleasure at the news is patently insincere. Back to the beginning again, as was often Puccini's way, now a tone higher (another of his calculated devices), for Marcello's news that he has met Mimi, and she too was finely dressed in a carriage, having gone off with the foppish Viscount of whom Rodolfo was complaining in Act III (Mimi had been showing him her legs). Her theme accordingly returns, its beginning extended while Rodolfo savors the implications of the meeting at which he was not present. Marcello, to twist the knife in the wound, decorates her motto with a frivolous mordent. The strings' dummy accompaniment to Rodolfo's "Evviva!" suggests the horses clopping down the street. Back to work, they agree: but the jaunty music, with trilling flute and clarinet and chiming bells, tells us that their minds are on their sweethearts trotting through Paris in spring sunshine. They throw aside the tools of their trades (a dull thud on low oboe, bassoon, and violas matches the action).

Duet. With a juicy burst of heartache the strings return to Rodolfo's *Talor* theme, the voice of unforgettable romantic young love. It is, strangely enough when we think of faithless Musetta, also that voice for Marcello, for he pulls from his overalls pocket a silk ribbon of hers, and secretly covers it with kisses. Rodolfo begins the duet, whose music is altogether new, with a fervent, arching melody for the tiny hands, snow-white neck, and fragrant hair that cling so closely to his brief youth's memories (Giacosa is at his most potent in lyrics of this kind — we remember "Mi chiamano Mimì" and "Addio, dolce svegliare," and indeed the love duets in *Tosca* and *Madama Butterfly*). Marcello, who takes the second line, thinks of his painting and how, no matter what his subject is supposed to be, he cannot help painting Musetta's dear face. These thoughts take the duet into its middle section ("Se pingere mi piace"); Marcello's rise to a top F-sharp is accompanied by a rapid clarinet *arpeggio* designed to boost the head of emotional steam (I mentioned this earlier, and there are many examples in *La Bohème* and throughout Puccini, often suggesting torture in *Tosca* and *Turandot*). Their voices are joined in unison with independent words at the return to the first phrases, though the voices have to part company soon, and the duet is greatly appealing. Rodolfo has pulled out Mimì's pink bonnet to fawn upon: Murger's Marcel, noticing this, comments to himself "Good, at least he's as bad as I am." Considering the intimate, indeed private, content of this duet (the authors wrote brackets round its extremes to indicate that it is all "aside"), Puccini scores it rather fully, though he omits trombones and percussion, and uses trumpets only in one bar, but there most effectively. The orchestral coda is scored with utmost delicacy, solo violin and cello replacing the singers, and maintaining the unison as the baritone Marcello

cannot. To tear himself from daydreams Rodolfo asks the time.
Marcello equally absently mentions the time for yesterday's dinner. What, and Schaunard (evidently in charge of the bohemian
commissariat) not back yet?

Mealtime. Here, with a great whirlwind around his motto theme,
indeed is Schaunard, with Colline close behind him. Gone, alas,
are the days of Christmas Eve and the makings of a full larder.
For supper they bring four breadrolls and one herring. "Salata!"
adds Schaunard; he means that the herring is salted, not that there
is a side-dish of lettuce and the like. They share the food and con-
sume it, with great comic ceremony and extravagant addresses,
pretending that the bread is a choice between trout, salmon, and
(for Schaunard's special benefit, curiously underlined in the
rhythmic flow) parrot's tongue — a reference to his exploits in Act
I. The carafe of water is served in Colline's top hat, as if it were
champagne. Schaunard has to refuse the nonexistent second help-
ings, on the grounds that he has an appointment at court; his theme
from Act I has reappeared, lightly scored this time and extended
to convey the mystery behind this disclosure — his business, it turns
out, is not with the Emperor but one Guizot, a historical character, indeed a fine historian, but a poor statesman, of Louis Philippe's reign. Schaunard demands the only drinking glass and, in
extravagant language, proposes a toast. The others shout him down
(as Puccini rightly shouted down his librettists who, at this point,
wanted all four friends to toast one another in turn — this cur-
tailed speech of Schaunard's is all that is left) and he offers an
alternative choice of "choreographic action" which they eagerly
accept.

Dance. The initial bohemian theme (not only Marcello's here)
reflects their enthusiasm for this impromptu frolic. Tables and
chairs are set to one side and Puccini gladly indulges in some pastiche old-time dance music, not excluding a Spanish fandango.
Colline suggests quadrilles for which Schaunard, as house musician, has to sing the music (it sounds a little like Musetta's themes),
Marcello adopting falsetto for Rodolfo's female partner. There is
an interruption when Colline takes exception to Schaunard's calling instructions. The orchestra boils with excitement as these two
prepare for a mock duel, with fire-irons for weapons. Rodolfo and
Marcello prefer meanwhile to dance a rigadoon — a spirited musical specimen that scampers all over the place — while battle is in

progress. At the height of the confusion, Musetta bursts through the door. Jollity in B-flat major gives way to shuddering, doom-laden E minor.

Finale. Musetta has brought Mimi here, so weak that she cannot climb to the top of the stairs. Violins surge violently to the top of an E-minor chord and down again as Rodolfo, greatly distressed, runs outside to lead her in. Schaunard and Colline bring out a small bed for her to lie upon. Musetta fetches the carafe of water to refresh her. Mimi is wan and wasted, as we hear from the version of her theme dragged out by English horn and violas with altered, poignant harmony, and only wants to know if Rodolfo will allow her to stay with him — she sings a plaintive, touching variant of her illness theme from Act I — and of course Rodolfo is perfectly delighted. Musetta relates to the rest how she searched everywhere (she still sounds out of breath) for Mimi, who, she heard, had left her Viscount protector and was dying — violins murmur Mimi's "Mi piaccion quelle cose" — but only wanted to die at Rodolfo's side. The musical reminiscence continues, as Mimi sits up and admits to feeling born again, turning into yet another transformation of the *Talor* theme. All the others join in regretting, to solicitous Musetta, that there is no food or drink in the house, though Schaunard can see that Mimi will be dead within the half-hour. Mimi feels cold, and wishes she had a muff, or somewhere to warm her hands. Rodolfo clasps them in his own, to a new, welling phrase. Now Mimi feels well enough ("Buon giorno, Marcello") to greet all her friends here. She has special commendation of Musetta's goodness to give Marcello, and indeed Musetta has just removed her earrings for Marcello to sell, buy medicine, and call a doctor. The music remembers Mimi's new bonnet at Christmas, and the acute joy it gave her (a curious, leaping phrase for clarinet, more gently recalled now): Musetta will go with Marcello, and buy Mimi a muff. Marcello's warmhearted appreciation is characteristic of Puccini's special regard for this good friend.

Colline has brought out the winter overcoat which he bought that Christmas Eve. Now he will pawn it for Mimi's sake (*il sacro monte* is Italian slang for the pawnbroker's shop), honorably as it has served him and his books. He takes farewell of the antique garment ("Vecchia zimarra") in a gaunt, dignified, stoical arioso, whose hobbling accompaniment seems to pre-echo Colline's reluctant walk to the *Monte di Pietà*. The key of his coat song is C-sharp minor, hardly used in *La Bohème* but due to end it in Rodolfo's mourning for Mimi. Nor is this a coincidence: the heavy, resonant chords that end the song are brought back to end the opera too. Quietly Colline suggests that Schaunard too can do Mimi a kindness and leave her alone with Rodolfo. Schaunard's melancholy assent, prefaced by a drooping clarinet phrase, is purely conversational but voiced with as much melodic grace as if it were an aria: this epigrammatic effect is typical of Verdi's *Falstaff*, still an inspiring new work for Puccini at the time of *La Bohème*. They go out quietly, and Schaunard's theme accompanies them on strings, calm and slow and philosophical. How Schaunard has altered since we first met him! Woodwinds answer with Rodolfo's *Talor* theme, ideal love at first timidly stirring, then with more passion though still softly, the fires banked in suspense.

Mimi has opened her eyes, consoled to see herself alone with the man she adores. She begins to tell him of her boundless love and devotion. The music of "Sono andati?" is quite new, intimately expressive, yet with a spacious sadness in its drooping melody and closely contained harmony. It begins as a solo monologue, and rises to a climax, which Rodolfo echoes and it becomes a duet, already a tragic reflection of the love duet which they sang in the first act. After a momentary, hushed allusion to the doomed Mimi of the third act trio, when she mentions the beauty of sunset, she harks back to her first monologue. Rodolfo caps this with the second section. In doing so he reveals her bonnet, which he keeps by his heart, and she reminds him of the duet when they looked for the key. It is even more delicately scored now, with solo clarinet and harp, as they exchange memories. Hers of "Che gelida manina" are cut short by a spasm of pain (a sharp dissonance on two clarinets) and she falls back to her illness motif. Rodolfo cries out, and Schaunard hurries back into the room, shortly followed by Musetta and Marcello, who place Mimi's hands inside the muff which they have bought, pretending it came from Rodolfo. A relevant musical allusion tells them that her tiny hands are frozen no longer. She whispers broken phrases of comfort against soft, sustained, disjointed harmonies, uncannily redolent of the sickroom, and drops off to sleep. A struck cymbal and a loud horn chord in the stillness tell us that Mimi is no more. The others remark nothing, though Musetta lights a candle and mutters a feverish prayer.

Rodolfo expresses optimism. It is Schaunard who tiptoes to Mimi's side and observes that she is dead, as Marcello confirms with a shudder reflected vividly on lower strings. Colline too returns with money, as a shaft of sunlight falls on Mimi's face. "Mi piaccion" on four solo violins at once matches the rays, Nature's requiem, and recalls that other moment when Rodolfo turned from the window to behold Mimi bathed in moonlight. He draws the curtains at that same window, notices the others whispering anxiously and pacing the room. Marcello, his closest friend, has to tell him, "Courage!" He falls upon her corpse, calling distractedly for Mimi. The brass thunders mighty lamentations, and the rest of the orchestra mourn for Rodolfo as well as Mimi, in the melody of 'Sono andati," with all the sadness that Puccini's bass-doubling can confer upon it.

La Vie de Bohème

(HOMAGE TO HENRI MURGER)

by

V. S. PRITCHETT

"WE'RE finished, my poor Rudolphe," Marcel was saying to me. "Dead and buried, the whole crowd of us. You're going bald at the back, I'm gray at the ears. We've turned twenty-seven years old; we'll never be twenty again, youth is over, Paradise is lost, the fun has gone, old age is upon us! I went into a bookshop this morning and everyone was raving about your poems. Worse — the critics are *praising* them! And the Salon has taken two of my pictures and the disgusting government has bought one of them! We've 'arrived' — but where? We are taken up by Society: Princesses next! No more starving in attics. Goodbye the Latin Quarter! Look at you, you've got a carpet on the floor, you're sitting in an armchair! One that really *belongs* to you, not a broken-down thing left behind by the previous tenant who couldn't pay the rent. You've got your clothes out of pawn." He stared at me. I said nothing. He went on. "It's the same with Schaunard — those catchy little songs of his are the rage all over Paris: he's coining money. Next stop the Opéra and Mademoiselle Sidonie screaming them out and her parrot copying them. And Colline: he has found out how to button his collar and has married a rich woman who can't understand his terrible puns or a word he is saying about classical philosophy — thinks Plato is a town in Greece — as he goes handing round fancy cakes at her parties, English-style! He'll be elected to the Institut any time now — you'll see! And talking about marriage — my Musette, bless her faithless heart — is getting married tomorrow, to a postmaster in Clermont-Ferrand or somewhere! I must say she and I had a farewell night together! Wild, heartrending, of course: it was like the bad version of a masterpiece."

"Marcel," I said. "Your irony will kill your heart."

"It's dead already," he said. "But I wrote a little poem about it.

That's the cure, a poem, Rudolphe. Shall I read it to you? It's very touching."

"No, thank you," I said. "Stick to your painting."

Marcel is a dear friend. I know he was only trying to get me out of my misery.

I said: "Let's go and eat at the Café Momus."

"For God's sake, stop torturing yourself," he said.

I looked at him and he changed his tone.

"I *know*, Rudolphe," he said. "I feel the same." And then he changed again. "Momus! They starved us there. One artichoke, one pickled herring, and the wine was vinegar. If you want to brood over the past, let's go to a decent place where at any rate the wine is drinkable. I'm corrupted, Rudolphe. I can't stand anything but the best these days. Look at Balzac — he doesn't stint himself."

"Villon was sentenced to death," I said.

"But he got off on appeal," said Marcel.

"And disappeared," I said.

"All right," said Marcel, "if that is your mood, we'll go to Momus and suffer."

And we did.

It was a shock. The place was as shabby, as bare and crowded as it had always been, but there was not a face either of us knew. I recognized only one of the waiters. No one recognized *us*. Only three years had passed and I could not believe this was the place where we had all talked our heads off. Now for the first time in my life, I felt I was a ghost and had perhaps *never* existed. And then a crowd of students started singing with mocking bravado and its lines came back to me.

> *Ton honneur sera perdu.*
> *Comme les autres*
> *Tu feras, ma pauvre fille*
> *Comme les autres font.*

The song cheered Marcel who hummed it as we sat there, but it was too much for me. I hissed at the students and they looked back at me and one said loudly, "I hear the voice of the bourgeois!"

After this Marcel became serious. He said earnestly, "Rudolphe,

I'm sorry. Stop blaming yourself about Mimi. It was not your fault. You can't go on feeling guilty all your life. It is pure egoism."

We left early. The waiter rushed with the bill — the waiters at Momus never trusted any one. He watched us suspiciously as we argued about who was going to pay — a real Rouennais — and then he seemed to recognize us. He said in an insinuating voice:

"Not for Councillor Alcindoro this evening?"

His dart pierced us. I forget who paid, but as we left we could hear him snapping a contemptuous napkin at us. Marcel said, "We honour the Café Momus with our distinguished custom after a mere three years and the only person who recognizes us is Satan! But he has performed a miracle: he has made Alcindoro immortal."

We both laughed. For myself I laughed myself back to that piquant moment one Christmas Eve. Three years ago — I was twenty-four again. We were all there. We had run off leaving Councillor Alcindoro (who had eaten nothing and had been dragged there by Musette) to pay the bill and indeed he had been sent by Musette to buy her another pair of boots because her feet were sore. This was the night when I first met Mimi and my life suddenly changed. I had laughed Mimi back out of the cemetery.

I have never felt the cold as biting as it was on that Christmas Eve when I was twenty-four. Marcel and I had an attic on the cul-de-sac — how fitting that name — off the Rue du Four, on the sixth floor. The shouts and street cries of the fête were coming up from the street and I was shivering at the window, which had a long crack in it. I had taken over the attic from Schaunard, who had left a table and two or three chairs behind because he owed rent to a real slug called Benoit. I must have bought them, though where I got the money from I can't imagine. The place smelled of many things other people had left behind in those days. The custom must have started centuries back in the time of Villon. There was also the smell of generations of mice and unwashed feet, and it was freezing cold. I had been trying to write one of those hack articles I used to do for a fashion rag called *The Beaver,* but my fingers were so stiff that I couldn't hold a pen and I had put a blanket over my shoulders. I stood at the window looking at the

snow dribbling down onto the roofs opposite and watching the
smoke blowing out of the chimneys. I hated them: there was no
smoke coming out of ours. No wood, no wood in our stove! (And
my uncle who used to give me an allowance which I had spent
before I got it was a stove-maker. His allowance would not have
kept a sparrow.) No wood and — Christmas Eve and everyone
gorging in the streets and cafés below — no food. We were down
to one meal every two days — one sardine, one artichoke, one piece
of bread, a diet that gave us at any rate an appetite for the future.
Under my bed was a manuscript of my tragedy, *Vengeance,* several
versions of it. (Shakespeare was all the go in those days.) It had
been turned down by all the theaters in Paris. And down below in
the street the bourgeois stuffing themselves with sausage and fritters. We could smell them. *Our* lives were mere metaphors or fan-
tasies.

Marcel was in the same state as myself. He had been working
for God knows how long on a terrible picture, *The Israelites
Crossing the Red Sea.* He kept blowing on his hands and he could
hardly hold the brush, and he was keeping warm by stamping his
feet and rushing at the canvas. An enemy keeps one warm! Every
year he sent the picture to the Salon: every year it came back rejected. The thing could have found its way to the place on its own.
He kept changing the title according to the weather. This Christmas Eve and seeing the snow he was putting splodges of white in
it and shouting "Another pharaoh drowned": the new title was
Napoleon Crossing the Beresina.

"I'm sick of you poets," he shouted to me. "You're always
whining about being driven to hack work. There's something wrong
with your stomachs. You're always writing about girls like Psyche.
What you need is a strumpet with a temper, like my Musette."

Musette, of course, had suddenly left him for that senile old
fellow Alcindoro — the Councillor! — and Marcel was in a rage
as he struck at the picture.

"It is Christmas. Girls want to eat," I said.

Presently Colline came in puffing up our five flights of stairs and
he was in a rage too, red and sullen with it, unusual for him. We
thought of him as sweet and old because he was fat and because
he was a bookworm. He was wearing his enormous overcoat,
which was like a pilgrim's cape. It had deep pockets into which he
tipped the books he couldn't stop buying on the Quays. "I feed

the mind," he always said. He had a greedy face with bubbly lips. As usual, one side of his stiff collar was undone and the wing stuck in his ear. When he came to see us he spouted bad puns or classical quotations, but this afternoon the cold had got him too. He marched to the table and unloaded a new lot of books in silence. Then he turned on us.

"Christmas Eve and no fire here," he accused us, pointing to the stove. "And all the pawnbrokers closed. Not even the smell of yesterday's meal. No candles."

Marcel said candles were inedible and when Colline roared that we could at least have lit them, Marcel said we were waiting for the moon to get up. We were treating candles as a Platonic ideal. This distracted Colline, who made some remark about classical philosophy and looked in one of his books peacefully for a quotation. Then he closed it and stared at the stove again.

"Can't you burn that chair?" he said. "The leg is broken."

I said the chair was Marcel's and Marcel said it would soon be the landlord's. "The rent's due today."

Colline looked at Marcel's picture and said vehemently:

"Burn the picture!"

"I can't bear the smell of burning oil paint. It will choke us," said Marcel. "What about your books?"

"Books!" said Colline. "Burn the immortal classics!" Then he put on his sly pathetic look. We were all friends, weren't we? he said. We shared everything? We would sacrifice anything for another, wouldn't we? And then I saw he was looking at my pile of manuscript under the bed.

"Is that your play?" he said in an innocent way. "What's it doing idling its life away?"

I went over to the bed and Marcel called to me:

"For God's sake, no one's asking you to read it to us again."

I suppose I was mad. When we were all together we relieved our feelings by fooling about. I stood up with dignity, took a few pages of the manuscript and said I, at least, was prepared to make a sacrifice to save human life. No one protested. I pushed the pages into the stove. Marcel came with a light, the pages blazed and the stove roared. Colline moved his chair close up to the stove.

"Ah," cried Colline. "The first act. A brilliant beginning. But more! More! Where is the action? It lags. . . ."

I got a fat bundle and stuffed it on the stove. Colline said: "Ah, splendid! Now there's a talent. What a gift that stove has! Scintil-lating. It grows. Is that the second act? Where is Act Three? Why didn't you think of this before? That stove has genius."

We all gathered round. Colline called for Act Four. The Grand Finale. "Look at it — a true emblem of art rising to the stars from the vulgar debris of reality and composition," he said. "Ah, it is going down. Yes, down, down. Curtain!"

"Author! Author!" cried Marcel.

"Boo. Boo!" cried Colline. "Throw the author on."

Marcel fell back into the moralizing state he had been in all day since Musette had left him and came back to his inevitable theme.

"Love is like a stove that burns too fast. We're just firewood. A woman blows on the flame, then blows it out. Hot one moment, drizzle the next."

"But *we* have the fuel," I said.

"Poets," Marcel said, "have no need of fuel." He was mocking me because at this time I was off girls. Dreams and self-love kept me in a blaze, he said, dreams of blue-eyed girls wearing long white gloves, but only because I wanted to write sonnets to them. And he said, "That means nothing to them. They're all ignorant, like my Musette."

"When marriage comes in at the window, love flies out," said Colline; irrelevantly, for the idea of marrying had occurred to none of us. That obscene institution was for the bourgeois! Someone asked, "Where is Schaunard?"

Yes, where was Schaunard? The man we called Marshal Ney. Schaunard's long nose had military genius; it had system. The middle and the end of the month were terrible days for us, but he kept a notebook with dates, names and addresses of the likely "touches" all over Paris. We waited. Then the door was opened: in came two shop boys carrying trays and Marshal Ney himself shouting to the boys,

"On the table and buzz off."

And he started to sing: "Tara. Tara. Tara. Food! Pies, bread, four bottles of the best Bordeaux, cigars. And — firewood! Get the firewood out. Don't touch the food."

"Firewood!" I rushed at it. Colline was at the food. Schaunard stopped him.

"Put it in the cupboard for tomorrow. No one eats at home on Christmas Eve. By Order. We're going to eat Chez Momus!"

And then — for our ears were extremely sensitive to this evocative sound — we heard coins jingling in his pocket, as he pranced about the room.

"I've robbed the Bank of France!" he sang. And he pulled the money out of his pocket and threw a stream of coins all over the floor. We were awed.

"Genuine stuff! Every bit with the head of King Louis Philippe on it, the 'soft pear' himself. Glasses! Pour the wine and I'll tell you the story."

Schaunard's stories always began far from the point, like a spy's. He was not a man for the tale in a nutshell. He would always digress. Did we know Mlle. Sidonie? Did we not! She was famous and large and sang at the Opéra. Did we know that she had a parrot? That was news: we did not. The parrot was the heart of the matter. The wretched parrot had to listen to her rehearsing in her flat and knew by heart all the arias in her repertoire. The bird screeched them day and night. Listen! Mlle. Sidonie had let the room below to a totally mad Englishman who wanted piano lessons, a man rolling in money. He had heard of "my fame as a pianist" and, "as you know" — all musical instruments.

"He offered me hundreds — what am I saying? — thousands if I would play the piano all day and drown the screeching of the parrot."

"Drink up," we said. "Get on with it."

"Now, I happen to know all about parrots," Schaunard said. "The only thing to do in a case like this is to kill them. What is the most civilized way to murder any creature with Christian mercy? Discover its dominant passion! Gratify it! I happen to know that parrots have a lust for parsley. They eat it and in a couple of days they drop dead. I wheedled the parsley out of Mademoiselle Sidonie's maid, stuck it in the cage, the bird dropped dead almost at once. The Englishman paid up instantly and even doubled his money."

Then Schaunard imitated Mlle. Sidonie and the parrot and went over his tale again, adding the parrot's last squawk and the giggles of the maid and how the Englishman kissed him and Schaunard argued with Colline who said Socrates had been given parsley not hemlock and Marcel asked whether there was any parsley in the pies Schaunard had brought. We were warming up. We lit our cigars. Then we were stopped by a knock at the door.

Marcel and I knew who was there. So did Schaunard. The ghost who always ruined our celebrations — Benoit the landlord coming for his rent. We still owed the previous month.

"Pick up the money. Hide it," we whispered. Marcel, the born plotter, picked it up and didn't hide it. He put it on the table.

"It'll show him we're in the money," he said.

There it was, waiting for Benoit's greedy eyes. We were uneasy. Marcel went to the door, but he waved an arm to calm us.

"Ah, the honest Monsieur Benoit!" he said. "A happy Christmas to you, Monsieur Benoit. Delighted to see you, Monsieur Benoit. You come at the right moment. Come in. Look." He pointed to the money on the table. "You've come for the rent. There it is. For once we are solvent. Gaze at it. The rent is yours! First of all, a toast. A glass for the good Monsieur Benoit. A happy Christmas, Monsieur Benoit."

Benoit was a fat spongy little man. He said he wasn't much of a drinker, "not like you youngsters. I am an old man, you know. Well, just a glass."

"You — old! Monsieur Benoit," said Marcel. "Don't talk nonsense. You're a young spark."

Benoit blushed as he drank.

"Happy Christmas, gentlemen."

"What do you mean pretending you are *old,* Monsieur Benoit?" said Schaunard. "You're full of spunk. Drink up."

And the old boy was soon on his second glass. He toasted us. We toasted him.

"Didn't we see you at the Bal Mabille with a blonde the other night, you old rascal?" Marcel said.

Schaunard said "Ah! We know you, Monsieur Benoit. You're like a field gun with the ladies."

"Well," said Benoit, "I don't mind saying that if I am not as young as you I can still do my duty."

He looked at the label on the wine bottle and said, "Excellent." And he held out his glass and Marcel filled it.

"To the Bal Mabille," we cried.

"You know, you young gentlemen," he said, warming up. "I may have been on the backward side when I was young — things weren't so free and easy as they are with you. Times were different but I don't mind admitting I got to be a bit of a devil. I don't mean with any kind of women, like you gentlemen. I don't say I like big women, I mean like . . ."

"Like what?" Marcel said.

"I mean," said Benoit, "not like — whales or the map of the globe, with a red face like a Dutch cheese. . . ."

He swayed as he drew their contours in the air.

"We don't either," we said. "Who does? They're terrible."

"No," said Benoit. "I have my tastes. And I don't like them skinny either. Skinny women complain and nag — like my wife. The wretch is always getting at me."

We sorrowed with him.

"What I like . . ." he began, but his mind was spinning.

"Yes, tell us what you like, Monsieur Benoit," Marcel said.

"Well," he said, "what I like is, you know — well, I *know* what I like," and he grinned and drew a curving shape in the air. "Someone you can put your arms round in bed. Come to that — anywhere!" he added. "I mean when I see one."

"Listen to this disgusting Casanova," said Schaunard, suddenly stern. "What does your poor wife say about that?"

"My wife?" said Monsieur Benoit in confusion.

"Yes, the poor faithful woman whom you married," said Schaunard.

"I am shocked," Marcel said. "Monsieur Benoit confesses he has no regard for morality — I can't believe it."

"Monsieur Benoit, it's shameful. On Christmas Eve too."

"My wife is . . ." Monsieur Benoit said.

"I mean on Christmas Eve surely you ought to be with your wife, not picking up girls in the Bal Mabille."

"I'm . . ." he said, but couldn't go on. He was drunk. Schaunard got up and turned him round so that he didn't know where he was.

"Go home to that good helpless woman," Marcel said and walked Benoit to the door. Benoit was now alarmed.

"Our regards to Madame Benoit," we said. "Make her happy this Christmas."

He looked back at the money for a moment as we got him out of the door.

We stood listening.

"Wait till the old humbug gets down those stairs."

We listened and then we were shouting with laughter.

"Come on," said Schaunard. "Share out the money." And he counted it out to us. "As I was telling you when that fool came in — I gave that parrot parsley and it dropped dead. We ought to have given it to Benoit. Come on, we'll go to Momus and eat. The whole Quarter's out in the streets."

I said, "I'll follow in a minute. I was clearing the glasses off the table. "I've got to finish my proofs for *The Beaver*. The printer's waiting for it at the office. I'm late. It won't take long."

This astonished them.

"Typical writer," said Marcel.

"Make it short this time," said Schaunard. "Cut off the last paragraph. Cut the Beaver's tail off."

They all went off.

"We'll keep a place for you," he called.

Nothing but interruptions in my life. I was glad to be alone for once. The peace, the alertness, the sense of boundlessness in an empty room! I lit a couple of candles. It was warm now, the fire still burned. I looked at the ashes of my play. I did not regret burning it. I was liberated. I suppose I was overexcited by the wine. The wind was thumping at the window. The moon had risen and I sat at my table. But now, as I read what I had written, it meant nothing. I tore up the page and started over again. Marcel calls me a pedant. That is not so. I'm a Perfectionist; a man like Schaunard had only to pick up his fiddle, a trumpet or touch the keys of a piano and the tunes just came to him. Marcel splashed and daubed away at his pictures as if he were a boxer, talking to anyone who happened to be there as he did it. At the same time he's convinced every blob is right. And then, the snow-speckled moon distracted me — like a woman's flitting face. Street cries came up from below, but the room was silent. Presently I heard a scratching at the door. A mouse? It had smelled the food. These old houses are infested with mice. I looked for something to throw. I got up quietly and tiptoed to the door, my foot ready to flatten the creature. The scratching turned into a timid knock. I opened the door suddenly. Not a mouse, but a girl, half crouching in her shawl, stood there holding a key in her hand and an unlit candle.

She gave a small cough and said in a weak, hoarse voice "I live downstairs on the fifth. I'm sorry to disturb you when you have people. My candle's gone out. Could you give me a light?"

She was a very thin shy girl and the hoarse voice made her seem at once of the earth yet ethereal. She had thick brown curls and she swayed: one of those hungry ones you see about the Quarter. "Ma chandelle est morte, je n'ai plus de feu": but strange and how charming, I thought. She tottered as if she were going to faint. I took her by the hand. It was stone cold and small. She was shivering as I led her to the stove. She dropped down in the chair where Colline had sat and her candle fell to the floor, and her key.

I went to the jug and sprinkled water on her face. The fancy came to me that I was watering a flower. There was a little wine left and I held the glass to her lips. We said nothing for a while and slowly her color came back. Then she looked at my table and my pen.

"I thought there were people," she apologized. "I'm sorry. You were working. I am all right now. It was the stairs. I just want a light," she said, and got up.

"Don't go," I said, but she stood up and watched me light her candle.

"I must. You were studying. I am sorry." And like a ghost she went to the door carrying her candle, but when she opened it her candle was blown out by the draft and so were mine. But for the glimmer of the moon we were in darkness.

"Oh," she said. "I've dropped my key."

And she knelt down groping for it on the floor. I shut the door.

"I'll find it," I said and began groping too.

We crawled about like a pair of children on the floor.

"Are you sure you dropped it here, not near the fire?" I said.

"I don't know," she said.

I could smell the scent of her hair and her young breath and when we bumped into each other once I touched her foot and we both said "Sorry" together. Then we were silent and I could hear her heart beating. Now and then the moonlight caught her face and I saw her delicate nose and her fine forehead and she looked angelic for a moment: then we ducked and were crawling again and our hands touched. I let my hand rest firmly on hers. It was a small hand, warmer now and I could feel the bones in it as our fingers mixed; hers were long, smooth at the tips and the nails delicate. The warmth of my hand passed into hers and it was at that moment that I felt I was touching her life and she became alive to me and even strong, not a stranger, not a vision, but a real girl. Who? A model? No, too thin. A sewing girl, as so many were in the Quarter? No, the fingertips of sewing girls are rough with needle pricks. And while I held her hand so briefly, my other hand was feeling about the floor and soon it touched her key. I said nothing, but slipped it into my pocket. I let go of her hand and went on groping. "I've got her, I won't let her go," I thought. That was the moment, I am sure, I fell in love.

"It would be more sensible, don't you think," she said, slyly, "if we had a light," kneeling up.

"Stupid of me," I said. "You're right. Stay there till I light the candles."

I was transformed and proud as I got up and lit the candles.

"Get up," I said. "The floor is dirty."

I helped her get up from her knees and now she changed in my eyes.

"Come and sit by the fire," I said. "Don't worry about it. We'll soon find it."

She came over to the fire, glancing over the floor, and, then, there was amusement in her eyes for a moment and she sat down confidently.

"I've seen you somewhere, I know," I said. "Where was it?"

"On the stairs, I expect," she said. "I've seen you."

"No, not on the stairs. Somewhere in the Quarter." I was determined not to let her go. She did not look timid now.

"What is your name?" I said and to put her at ease I told her about myself. "My name is Rudolphe. I'm sure I've seen you. You caught me finishing a stupid fashion article, but actually I am a poet."

"Fashion!" she said eagerly and rearranged her shawl.

"There's no money in poetry," I said.

"Oh dear," she said like a child putting on airs. "Awful money!"

(Long afterward Marcel mocked me about this. A pretty girl comes to your room, he said, asking for a light, and the first thing you do is to crawl about the floor, steal her key and say you're a poet writing hymns to ideal love. She is Juliet and you are Romeo and you say you may be poor and starving but a poet's riches are in his soul. And then you tell her that sometimes thieves break into your attic. She is frightened when you say "Thieves." And you tell her the thieves are her beautiful eyes.)

Now it is true. I did say that her blue eyes had stolen my heart. They were very still eyes but with the sudden coquettish questioning quiver in the pupils.

Schaunard and Colline had come back and started bawling up the stairs.

"For God's sake hurry up."

I went to the door and shouted, "Nearly finished," and then went back to her.

"You still haven't told me *your* name," I said.

"It's Lucia. Some people call me Mimi, I don't know why, the people where I work. At the dressmaker's. I do piece work. Embroidery. Flowers."

"With delicate fingers like yours — I don't believe you," I said.

"In silk," she said.

"Ah, now I see why they are as smooth as rose petals."

She blushed and said she liked embroidering flowers.

"Only they don't smell — not like real flowers. In the spring, you know? I dream of them — Paris has such horrible smells."

There was always a question in her voice. Shyness.

"You are a poet. I can tell by your voice," I said.

"Am I? No one ever said that. I don't know grammar. I didn't go to school much."

"Better talk it than write it," I said. And I felt suddenly old and grand. "It's a lonely life, being a poet."

"*I'm* not lonely," she said. "There are all the girls where we take our work to the dressmaker's. It's just that they are slow in paying. Some girls have got rich friends — you know? On Sundays I used to go to the country if I had a friend but now, it's funny, I don't. I get tired. So I rest and think. I don't even go to Mass on Sundays — that's a fault, I know — but I think if you pray by yourself it's all right, isn't it? I'm lucky to be on the fifth floor — not so many stairs to climb as you. I hate stairs, don't you?"

Marcel and the others were shouting again.

"Well, thank you. Your friends are calling. I'm sorry I interrupted you." And she put out her hand. I held it.

"Stay with me! You can't go anyway. I've got your key." And I pulled her toward me and kissed her cheek. "I'm falling in love with you. Stay here."

"I saw you take it," she said and held out her hand for it.

"They're not coming back," I said. "Stay. Please stay."

I didn't give her the key. Her fingers pinched my arm. "I don't know. Are you my friend?" she said.

"You are the prettiest wild flower I've ever seen," I said. "And you're hungry too. And so am I. I haven't eaten anything since yesterday. Come along and eat with us. And," I said, "we'll come back here."

Her pretty eyes were very sharp. "I don't know about that," she said. "Are you sure your friends won't mind?"

For an answer I put her shawl round her and she gave in and we went down the steep stairs and into the street. The snow was now falling lightly; it fell in little diamonds in her hair so that she looked like crystal. I took her arm and we hurried. What a crowd there was! I wanted to call out, "Look at the prize I've won," but if anyone had said a word to her I would have said, "Clear off. She's mine."

"Marvelous lights!" she cried at the sight of the lit-up windows, the torches and the flares on the stalls. Our mouths watered at the smell of sausages and smoke coming up from the fritters. The crowd was as warm as a cloak.

We soon caught up with the others. Schaunard took a tin trumpet from a stall and blew it, everyone laughing at him. Colline was haggling over a coat at a secondhand shop. We slowed down at every stall and shop. Then Marcel called to me but I left him because Mimi was looking into a hat shop.

"Rudolphe!" she called. "Bonnets."

"Bonnets. D'you want one? I'll buy you one." I was thinking of the snowflakes melting in her hair. We pushed our way to the counter. I was on fire with excitement. I would have bought the whole of Paris for her if I had had the money. She was soon making the woman in the shop pull down the bonnets and if Mimi tried one on she tried on a dozen.

"How does this look? No, I don't like it," and she threw it away. There was nothing shy about Mimi in a hat shop. She'd have "this one" she'd say, only she'd need a new shawl. And the next was not in the fashion. She was like a bird darting about looking for new feathers. And sharp about it. She was revelling like a child. I was hungry, but she looked as though she would feed on bonnets. And then, the prices! Well, I had my share of Schaunard's money in my pocket. In the end she saw one, very simple, trimmed with roses. I saw her eyes and her whole body change as she put the bonnet on. "Adorable," said the woman in the shop and so did I. "You truly think so?" Mimi asked, her full red lips pouting. The woman said to me — these women are cunning — "With that beautiful skin she needs a coral necklace." And brought one out. Tears of desire were in Mimi's face as she looked at me. I whispered to her that I knew a better place for coral in the Rue de Rivoli. And I said, joking, "I've got a rich uncle. I'm his heir. When he drops off the hooks I'll buy the best necklace you've ever seen and it won't be coral — it will be pearls." And I kissed her.

So we bought the bonnet and as she gripped my arm and walked away, she turned her head this way and that for all to admire. Many people turned round to look at her and indeed there was an awkward moment — how often I have thought of it when I remember that night — when one of those rowdy groups of students stopped dead by the sight of her and cried:

"Look at the darling. Give us a kiss." She was so excited that she went up to them and for a moment I thought she was going off with them. I pulled her away sharply.

"Poor students," she said. "They get up to such tricks."

"Mimi, this is the way. You're not listening to what I'm telling you about my uncle. It is true. Hold my arm."

"You're jealous!" she said, delighted.

"It's because I love you," I said sternly.

"Oh yes!" she said and hung possessively to my arm. "But I don't want your uncle to die. I don't want anyone to die. Don't die, Rudolphe" — like a child giving an order.

And so we got to the Café Momus. Marcel, Schaunard and Colline were there sitting outside on the terrasse, under the awning. "Outside on a cold night like this," I said, thinking of Mimi. "He'll keep you warm," Marcel said to her. We were making such a noise, especially Schaunard, who was still talking about Mlle. Sidonie's parrot. Some quiet elderly people got up and went indignantly inside.

"Artists!" one of them said. "All drunk. No manners." My friends bowed to Mimi, and Marcel, seeing the bonnet, said, "The poet of love, the new Victor Hugo, arrives with the Muse herself, adorned with roses. We know how you finished your article for *The Beaver*!"

"The master has graduated at last," said Colline, "bringing his Diploma with him."

"I want to sit close to you," Mimi whispered to me.

"They need only one chair!" Schaunard called out to the waiter. "Food! Food! Chicken, lobster, everything."

"And no parsley!" said Marcel.

But did we order? No. Parpignol, the toyseller, was going by in the street and the children were swarming around, one or two chased by their mothers. But at last, everyone ordering different things and the waiter going mad, Schaunard said: "Wait! The lady first!" The waiter came to Mimi and she said, "I would like a custard."

"That's not enough," I said.

"A custard!" called Schaunard. "Waiter, not one of your simple custards but the Queen of Custards."

"With honey?" said the waiter.

"Yes, with honey, with everything," said Marcel. And to Mimi: "May your honey never turn to vinegar."

"It's all right," I said to Mimi, "Marcel makes remarks like that. He's thinking of his Musette, his mistress. She's left him."

And almost at once, like an explosion or riot in the street outside we all heard Musette's voice. It was — I am sure it still is — a country girl's voice that suddenly fills any cabaret she is singing in, a voice that makes a man's beard stiffen and starts him rolling his shoulders. It was a voice fresh as a hayfield blowing in the wind, laughing, then sexy and insinuating, at times out of tune. She came swinging toward us in splendid clothes, a stunning blonde as ripe as corn. She turned round to her escort, Councillor Alcindoro, no less, who was on his dignity, and who had a mustache that looked as though it had been dipped in oil and waxed. He was leading a little dog — *her* little dog, of course. She called out: "Stop dragging behind, Lulu" — her name for the Councillor — "Come and meet my friends." She was carrying a billiard cue which she must have taken from some café on the way and was waving the thing about. She made a tour of the terrasse looking for us. Lulu was muttering sharply, "Musette, please! I order you to behave yourself."

Colline said, "What have we here? The chaste Susannah and her Elder."

"Not chaste," said Marcel, for Musette had left him for this fool. Marcel turned his back on her and pretended she was not there.

"She has come here," I whispered to Mimi, "to cause trouble. She always does."

"Oh what a lovely dress! Real silk! The embroidery," Mimi said. "She's beautiful." Mimi's blue eyes were large with awe.

Musette was one of those healthy, bouncing girls, a real baggage, a good-hearted in-and-out-of-bedful.

It was strange, I thought, to see a girl as quiet and exquisite as Mimi was, whose features were, it seemed to me, as delicate as those painted on a Persian vase, admiring a country hoyden like Musette.

"What is her real name?" Mimi said.

"She calls herself Musette," I said, "but her real name is Temptress," I laughed.

"Did she tempt you too?" Mimi said.

"I'm not a fool," I said.

"She keeps *looking* at Marcel," Mimi said, fascinated.

"She's only behaving like this because Marcel is taking no notice of her. And to annoy her old man, of course. She's just playing for attention. She loves a scene. Mimi," I said firmly, "don't look at her. Look at Schaunard. He's mimicking her. He had a girl like that once. He cured her with his walking stick."

Musette came and sat down with us and near enough to Marcel to put out a fine leg and tickle him with the tip of her elegant boot. But Marcel had his back to her, as I said. The old man was furious. He kept saying, "Control yourself, please, Musette! Stop throwing yourself about."

She started singing one of her cabaret songs at the old man:

"All the men give me the eye
When I go by."

Marcel muttered to Schaunard, "Tie me to my chair or I'll kill her. Don't let that bitch near me."

Musette got up and waved the billiard cue at Marcel. It is still
my opinion that Marcel pretended to be a tough man of the world
because he was really timid. He was certainly afraid of being caught
by Musette's claws that evening. The old man, her Lulu, was muttering: "Will you please put that billiard cue down. It's dangerous." She glanced thoughtfully at him. We saw she was thinking
of some way to get rid of him.

"Lulu!" she said. "These boots you bought me are pinching me
to death. Go and buy me a new pair."

Instead of refusing the dotard said, "Yes, my darling. Certainly,
my darling. I'm sorry, my darling," and got up.

"Well, take them off first," she said. He kneeled down and he
removed a boot. She gave him a push with her other foot and he
fell over, but he got up and did as he was told. Musette got up at
once and plomped herself on Marcel's knee and started stroking
his hair and took his fork and helped herself to his food, drank
his wine and then got up and dropped his plate on the floor. It
smashed. There was silence in the café for a moment. Our waiter
came to pick up the pieces: he hated us all.

"Poor Musette," said Mimi.

"Poor! She's rich. She just does what comes into her head," I
said.

"I mean you can see she truly loves Marcel, but she's got a
temper. I have too."

"You! I don't believe you," I said. I had my arm around her.

"Oh yes, I have," she said, shaking her head. "You don't know,
Rudolphe. Great love, like Musette's, ends in great sorrow."

But our talk was cut short by the noise of the military band
sounding the Retreat. We got up and rushed into the street. The
bugles were blowing, the cymbals were clashing and the man with
the big drum was thumping hard.

"Boom, boom, boom," Mimi cried out. "Look at him."

"A man with two bellies," said Colline. "What a man."

"Come on," said Schaunard. "Fall in. Quick march."

Seeing us scrambling into the street the waiter came after us
with the bill. We passed it round from one to the other — it was,
I must say, our custom when we ate at Momus. It ended with
Marcel, who left it on his plate because he and Schaunard had
grabbed Musette and heaved her onto their shoulders, and they

marched off with her. She was waving the billiard cue, and the crowd cheered them. She blew kisses.

"Boom, boom, boom," Mimi cried, as we marched behind. "I love the big drum, don't you?" she cried hanging on to my arm.

She was breathless and we did not walk as fast as the rest and the band was getting far away, though we could see Musette's tossing head. "Who is going to pay the bill?" Mimi said.

"Lulu, of course," I said. "When he gets back with Musette's new boots. He's rich. The waiter will pounce on him. She's made an ass of Lulu."

The last thing I would have thought myself doing when I got out of bed in the morning was that I would be following a band down the street by that night. When I was a child, perhaps; but my flag-waving, band-following days were far off. My character is very different from Marcel's: yet here I was marching along with a girl I hardly knew. And even now, it seemed to me, I was on an entirely new journey that some hidden part of myself had been secretly traveling on all my life. How inspired I had suddenly become. Everything was extraordinary about this hour of self-revelation. It was almost divinely fated. It was extraordinary that Mimi lived below in our house, half-known but now known. Paris itself had changed and was new. I looked down at her: we were making for new country and she was all mystery. The mystery was in the bonnet I had bought for her — and, she was my prisoner. I had her key in my pocket and she knew I had it. What did she mean when she said, "We'll see about that?" when I hinted that she should come back with me? In reality, we were not marching but were soon dawdling and dragging behind and the band and its bugles and drum were almost out of sight and the crowd was beginning to pass us. She became more and more real to me, until at last we stopped dead and glanced without interest at the passing people and then stared at each other. The snow sprinkling us, catching us in snow madness. We were an island and people had to step out of our way. We did not seem to belong to the same world as they. The solemn, almost sullen, intention of desire was in my eyes and in her blue eyes a disguised invitation. We were so paralyzed that when a student turned round and called out, "Ah ha! The lovers!" we were almost grateful to him. If we gazed, it seemed that our skins rather than our eyes were reading deeply into each other.

"Do you want to get out of this?" I said. Her fingers tightened fiercely on my arm.

"Oh yes! I want to," she said. We got on to the pavement.

"Marcel will be back in the attic with Musette," I said. (It was an unwritten law of the Quarter that none of us went to a friend's room if we knew he had a girl there — at any time of the day.)

"You've got my key," she said carelessly.

"Well . . ." I said.

She held my arm even more tightly.

"I want to — terribly!" she said and the snow flying across our faces seemed to heat us. We half ran as best we could in a comic three-legged race, laughing because we had our arms round each other.

When we got to the house and went laughing past the concierge's window I saw that fat woman sitting on the knees of the postman who was lounging with his legs splayed while she was squeezing out wet kisses all over his complacent face.

We went up to Mimi's room and I put the key in the door and she pulled me into the darkness. There was just enough moonlight to see that her room was barer than mine but that the bed was neatly made.

"The candle!" she said.

We both laughed.

"We forgot it at Marcel's," we said together.

And so by moonlight I saw her body for the first time. Our hands were all over each other avidly exploring, as if we were astonishing countries. Once when I looked down at her I saw her hot face turned in profile so that one eye looked at me with that horror which is part of ecstasy, and as if asking a question. I know that question. "Will you love me forever?" In those moments when we lay back and talked she pouted at my praises, she listened pressing against me, as if waiting for the question to be answered and seemed to be telling invisible people in the room to listen. Long after midnight she started chattering about Musette.

"I can't think why you didn't fall for a wonderful girl like that. I love her. She's so strong. I'd love to be like Musette."

"I'm glad you're not," I said.

"Oh, I don't know." She wriggled against me. "She's so free!"

"*You're* not!" I said.

She was inciting me.

It was very late when I woke up the next day. I saw Mimi sitting naked at the table with the bonnet on her head, looking at herself in a small mirror. The room was poor and was cold. I must find another place for us, I thought. I must get her away. I wanted to avoid my friends, to get her away by herself, to hide her. I did not ask but knew she might have had other lovers.

She paraded up and down the room in her bonnet and I pretended to chase her, but she coughed and I told her to put her dress on.

"I hate it," she said. "Look at it."

I said I'd get her a new one. We went back to bed because of the cold.

Everything was changed for me in those idiotic happy weeks. We moved secretly to a better room out of the district. It is easy to lose oneself in Paris only a few streets from your neighbors. People like to stick to their districts and their cafés. I did not tell Marcel or anyone. Our new room, she said, was "chic" and she begged me to buy her a prayer book. She explained to me that she liked to go to Mass "in her heart." I bought her a bracelet that hung on her thin wrist. She went out to see if there was any work going and I stayed in writing and she tiptoed round the room when she came back and saw me still at work.

"How long does it take to write a play? A week?" she asked, "one day?"

I had told her of the play I had burned and she was indignant about this.

"No, longer," I said.

"Two, three? How long?"

"The last one took three years."

"So a poem would be shorter?" she asked.

"I'll be quicker now," I said.

"Oh how I hope you will!" she said. "When will you buy me the dress?"

The new dress gradually became an imaginary person in our lives: we talked of the shops it might be hanging in. That phrase

of hers: "How I hope" enchanted me; it was an echo of her "I
want to terribly" — at first childish and gradually becoming the
wish of a woman longing for the dress she was obliged to en-
broider for another woman. Naturally I had my debts. I got money
in advance from *The Beaver*. I had pawned my jacket. Still, we
managed to eat better than I did with Marcel and the others. We
didn't work all the time. We were so transformed, both of us, that
we felt we were entitled to time off, for a walk in the Luxembourg
or to sit over a coffee in a café, watching people not as happy as
we were. We couldn't afford the boulevards but we went there
because she liked to see what women were wearing and she was
sharp about that. "Not sleeves like that!" she'd say. "Not in green,
but in velvet." I preferred the Luxembourg — her feet did not feel
as tired there — and I told her about the statues of famous artists,
gods and goddesses. I was educating her. "Bah! What a lot you
know," she said sincerely. "Is that true?" Sometimes I had to repeat what I had said because she was not listening. One day I was
telling her about Psyche because she often seemed like Psyche to
me. "Marvelous goddesses!" she said. I pointed out that Psyche
was a nymph. "That one! She's got a gentleman protector?" She
often came out with bits of gossip about "*lorettes*" and the demi-
monde. What she liked most was to go out to the tollgate at the
Port d'Orléans because the air is better and the country begins
there. We'd look for wild flowers. She loved finding flowers more
than anything else: she would kneel down to smell even a daisy.

But because she had two names — Lucia and Mimi — she
seemed, as the months went by, to become two people, one who
was frail, who was *here* with a small hoarse cough and who picked
over her food; and another whose mind and even her eyes and
body with its pearly skin were living in a dream elsewhere; even
knitting her brows, working out how to get to that "elsewhere."
She always woke up and hid what she was thinking when she saw
I had been watching her and would put on a merry laugh, and
became excitable. I watched her because her cough worried me:
she said she only coughed indoors. She did not like to be watched.
Once I made her come back from the window because of the cold
air.

"I'm looking at people," she said. "They're funny." But her
expression was sad. "Do stop about my cough. It was my sister
who was always ill, not me. I told you. When the spring comes

we'll go to Saint-Cloud and sit by the river under a tree. You wrote a poem under a tree, the last time."

As I have said, she had to go out to the dressmakers and sometimes she was later than I expected. She came back full of chatter. She liked to chatter from our window and wave to people in the street.

"Who was that?" I asked once or twice.

"I don't know. They've gone." But her imagination was following them.

"When did you first know you loved me?" I asked.

"I don't know," she said. "When you said you loved me."

"I loved you the first moment I saw you at the door," I said reproaching her.

"Tell me about it again," she said.

It disappointed me that she did not know when she first loved me. I half wondered whether she knew whether she loved me at all. And whether, suppose Schaunard or Marcel or even one of those people passing in the street, one of those students say, had answered the door, she would have dropped into their arms as she had done with me. The thing to do, I thought, is never to let her out of my sight, to keep an eye on her.

"You're a chatterbox — when you go out," I said.

"People talk to me, I don't know why." Her airy theme song "I don't know why!"

"You *do* know why," I said. "You lead them on."

One day she said a student had followed her and talked to her. What did he say? I could imagine the conceited strutting young man.

"Bah," she said. "He talked about his courses. They always do."

"He was trying to make a rendezvous," I said. "Wasn't he?"

For the first time I saw a hard, ugly careless look on her face and her voice had echoes of the dressmakers' workroom.

"Students," she said, giving me a pinch, "are not good at it if that's what's worrying you. They're not old enough."

Oh, I thought, not so innocent, is she? Yet she said this in the most innocent way in the world.

We quarreled about this. I noticed she had been chatting with some dressy women who lived on the corner of the street. That student had stopped to talk to her and these women had laughed at the way she had dealt with the impudent boy.

"I know those women. They're cocottes," I said. "On the look-out for rich men. Their talk is dangerous. I forbid you to talk to them."

They would look her up and down, ask her questions and would soon be telling her that if she took their advice she could better herself. They're nothing but perfumed cats.

And so Mimi and I had another quarrel.

"I'll see who I like. They're very polite." And she described the satin dress one of them was wearing, with a "gorgeous" hat.

"I am just a poor poet," I said.

"And you haven't finished your poem! Three months and all you do is tear up paper," she said.

I had never dreamed of Mimi in a temper. And I who thought of her as wan and needing care! Her voice shook with a harsh, even violent note that vibrated as if it boiled in her throat, and shouted. We both raised our voices. It was all "Monsieur" and "Mademoiselle" to each other as if we had never met, but were miles apart in the room that, in my imagination, was filled with the luxurious shapes of rich pretenders to her body. The neighbors in the room next door knocked on the wall and she turned on them too. They did a lot more knocking when the night came and we were reconciled in tears of love. "Other people want to sleep," the neighbors jeered. We lit the candle and she said, as if nothing had happened, "Rudolphe! Look at your nails. Get me the scissors and the file. You neglect your hands. Look at mine."

Her nails were perfect. Like pearls.

She was an angel again.

It was not our last quarrel. She kept on seeing those women. When she was asleep beside me I used to look at her beautiful forehead and say to myself, What is going on inside that head where the bones are burning? There was a change in our lives: we were happy but jealousy had put its clamp on my mind. And *she* would watch *me* work. Every day she said: "How many lines?"

And when I told her, she sighed.

"Oh my poor dress."

By this time Colline had nosed out where we were living and, of course, the others were soon round with us. Schaunard brought in lobster and insisted on carving it himself. We all noticed he gave himself the biggest part. I had bought Mimi a blue apron in which she looked very pretty. No Musette.

"Gone again," said Marcel cheerfully. "You see!" Mimi nodded to me.

It was good to see Marcel again and to talk frankly. I made a point of going to see him.

"You're both bored. You're not married, thank God, but you've fallen into married habits," he said.

I said this was not so. Mimi and I loved each other passionately. "But she makes me suffer."

"Passion is the mistake," he said. "You're too exalted. It is *you* who make Mimi suffer. She is not strong. This jealousy of yours has changed you. You used to be a Romeo, my boy, but now you're turning into an Othello."

"Look at you and Musette," I said. "What are you?"

"It's different," he said. "Jealousy is come-and-go with us. She's Doll Tearsheet — different play. We amuse ourselves. Anyway Musette is bursting with health. Jealousy doesn't last with us; it's the sauce to the dish, piquant. It's how we love. But with you jealousy's your whole life, it multiplies. You Othellos are tyrants, even sadists: you pick up Desdemonas because you are drawn fatally to the weak and sick."

"Mimi is not sick," I said. "Neither was Desdemona."

"Her love for you is a fever that spends faster and faster every day. Rudolphe, you poets are a gang of egotists. You chew people to nothing with your suspicions."

"But there *is* someone I'm sure. Or might be. Or will be. The way she looks at people, inviting them. Mimi is out and about. How do I know what she is doing?" I said.

"Rudolphe, why should you?" he said. "Take care. You'll drive her away. Stop questioning her."

Marcel is a cynic, I thought. Sensible, a good friend, but a cynic. But what he said *did* change my attitude. I will keep my mouth shut. I will be silent, I decided. I won't ask Mimi any more questions.

And so I was silent with her. But the effect of this was to encase me in my jealousy.

"You are so serious," Mimi said. "You don't talk. I think you have stopped loving me."

At this time she was working on a dress for a very rich woman, in fact one of those cocottes — as I found out — to whom I had forbidden her to speak. This woman was living with a Vicomte,

Mimi said. She thought all rich men were Vicomtes. She had to take the dress to the "Vicomte's" house and the woman complained about the roses in the embroidery. The woman said she wanted the roses to be open and full. The "Vicomte" was always there to calm her down. Obviously a woman like that would make a scene, out of coquetry, to annoy him. The "Vicomte" said, "But you are in bud, my darling," to her. Now, wasn't that a compliment, Mimi said, and truly witty and gallant, because really "She is thirty if she is a day." "The Vicomte gave me a funny look and said, 'I'm sure Mademoiselle agrees with me. She is an artist.' It was very nice of the Vicomte to say this, in front of me," Mimi said because the woman had upset her. "I was nearly crying," Mimi said.

But I could imagine the kind of look the "Vicomte" gave to Mimi.

"Why," I asked, "does this woman make you go to the house? She should go to the manageress of the shop. You should refuse to go to the house — treating you as a servant."

"It's a mansion! You should see it. Servants, everything," Mimi said.

I said, before I could stop myself: "Take care or you'll find *your* Lulu there."

Then I said quietly, "All right. Since you are tired of me, get another lover."

"You're telling me to get someone else," Mimi said.

"I didn't say that," I said.

"You did," she said.

"You've got a rendezvous with the 'Vicomte,' " I said. "Tell the truth."

All my suspicions burst out of the silence I had been living in. A whole list of the places she went to and the houses she came back from, day after day, poured out of me.

"You're just like Musette. You're making a fool of me. But *I'm* not Marcel. I do not love like that."

"You don't love me at all," she said. And she flew into a temper. Her rage, the things she said, turned her into a devil once more.

"All right," she cried. "We'll see. I used to be happy. I hate this room."

"Well, go," I said.

And she rushed out, screaming back at me.

I was out of my mind. I was mad. I know I was mad because everything was so clear to me as if a brilliant light seemed to light up everything in the room. And I felt I was seeing reality for the first time. I was mad because I was so calm and could see in detail what I had to do. Jealousy — I see it now — is one of those poisons that turn one into another person. Even in the mirror I saw another man, a clear-headed judge. I set to work to remove all traces of Mimi. I collected the things she had brought to the room and packed them carefully into a parcel. Then I made a parcel of the few things I had given her: in such situations, a scrupulous sense of justice possesses me. I was not going to have it said that I'd stripped her of everything. I wanted her to know that I was above that kind of pettiness. I hoped when she saw what I had given her she would realize the man she had so easily given up.

A few hours later she came back, timidly for a moment and then defiant. I was preparing for a grand scene. Afterwards I would kill myself. I even thought of a spectacular death before her eyes.

She stared at me. Her face was hard and white. We were both left with nothing to say. We were really too tired to say much.

"Those are yours," I said coldly, pointing to the two parcels. She looked at me with unbelief, then she picked up one of the piles and said in her practical voice, "I'll send a friend for the rest tomorrow." And left.

Not the first time a man has thrown her out, I thought.

There was horror in her face — not that half-smiling horror on a girl's face, not the horror of ecstasy, but of despair.

With cold curiosity I looked at the alcove, drew the curtains and looked at our bed. Then I drew them back and the rings chattered back at me, the first sound in a soundless room. I stared at the pillows. I did not eat that night: jealousy itself is a kind of food, I suppose. I did not lie on the bed. My anger had gone. I sat on the chair beside the bed and stared at the history of our love. My eyes had no tears but were stretched and open, yet I must have slept about an hour for I was woken by the hiss and smell of the guttering candle. The silence after that was terrible.

I half expected her to come back but she did not. I could not work. In the following weeks I went out wandering in a haphazard way from street to street, free but in a wilderness. I sat in cafés and sometimes thought of telling some stranger what had happened, but the moment I opened my mouth I could say nothing. People looked stupid to me. I talked, often out loud, to myself saying "Mimi is no better than Musette" or "You have deceived yourself." I was sometimes in the Luxembourg and sat on a stone bench under the trees and sneered at the statues of gods and goddesses in their ridiculous embraces: everlasting love turned to stone. They mocked my dream. The birds flying from one tree to another jeered at me. What do those birds know, I said — those pompous cooing pigeons; those perpetual, licentious "Vicomtes." Week after week I watched the leaves fall faster and faster. Soon I could feel winter coming nearer. Once when I went back to the room I was startled to see the mark of a girl's shoe heel on the floor of my room. She had been there: the parcel of *her* things had been collected, but the parcel of the things I had given her was untouched. I rushed down to the concierge, who put on a high moral self-congratulating voice.

"The little girl came. She's gone," she said.

It was the sight of that heel mark on the floor she used to polish that made me decide to talk to Marcel one night when I had had no sleep. It was five in the morning, a few flakes of snow were falling when I got to his place. The loose pane on the glass of the concierge's door rattled. The sight inside the concierge's room was squalid. It smelled of the chamber pot. The woman was sprawled like a pig with her nightcap on and her fancy man snoring beside her. She woke up at once: these women live for suspicion too.

"They left weeks ago," she said.

"They're up at the Tollgate, Rue d'Enfer," she said. "The key's in the door if you want to go up," she said. She recognized me — the return of the Prodigal.

There was malice in her voice.

"Artists!" she used to say and her face curdled with contempt.

I went on toward the Rue d'Enfer, on that long slow climb up dead and silent streets. I think I passed only two people. One was a drunken young man who came out of a brothel with a bowl of hard-boiled eggs. Seeing me he dropped one and then another and another on the pavement and called after me "Love is dead." All the windows of the houses were shuttered and stained by their gray secrets and the light snow was blowing across them. I remembered Mimi and how I had gone by omnibus this way when I took her to the country in our earlier happy days. At night now the drains stank. One seems to be trudging through one's past. Somewhere I nearly trod on a beggar who was sleeping on a baker's grating. At any rate there was one happy man!

At the end of the Rue d'Enfer the city ends in open spaces and I heard the bell of the Santa Teresa hospital, a sound that seemed to fill the night with groans and tears. Up here the snow was falling faster. There were now a few wan lights, tired of their vigilance, the lights of the tavern next to the tall iron gates of the Toll. The market people from the country wait to come in at this hour. By the time I got there the gates were opening and the Customs officers were looking at their loads. I made for the tavern for I thought I saw two people walking behind the trees, but perhaps I was confused by the veil of snow and the shadows. In my state I could have believed in ghosts — perhaps I was seeing myself. Customers who had made a night of it were singing and shouting in the tavern and as I got to the door I heard the rollicking, bawling voice of a woman and men calling out to her. It was unmistakable: Musette's voice. The concierge had not lied. She and Marcel must be there. There was Marcel's picture *The Israelites Crossing the Red Sea* hanging as the inn sign, but now a new title was daubed on it in garish letters: *A la Porte de Marseilles*. Marcel had been driven to selling it to an Inn! On either side of the door were two full-length paintings of a Zouave and a Turk. Marcel was down to decorating a cabaret!

"Gone out," said a man at the door when I asked for him, and waved at the trees, "with some woman."

I was so weak that I nearly fell when I sat down on a bench inside the door. The singsong was still going on in an inner room. I must have dropped off to sleep. I don't know for how long, but I was wakened by Marcel himself.

"What are you doing here?" he said. I stared at him and couldn't speak for a time. Then I said the only thing I could say:

"Mimi's left me. I must talk to you."

He looked about him furtively.

"Don't talk. Come right inside and rest. What's been happening to you?" he said.

He said shortly that he and Musette were back together but had been on their beam ends and that he had sold that picture and done the door, and Musette sang every night in return for food and lodging. I was nodding off again.

"I'll be back," he said, and went outside again.

❧

I have forgiven Marcel for what he did that night. I know he was acting as a friend. When you are young you don't realize how cruel you are — not viciously, but without thinking. No harm is meant, but a careless word comes out and sometimes it is fatal, even among people who share everything as we all did. Marcel's weakness is that he sees everything as a comedy: he cannot resist, with the best intentions, setting up as a puppeteer, pulling the strings. But it is dangerous. The wrong word is spoken and he finds himself turning comedy into tragedy without knowing. He is really an actor who intrigues and ad libs at the expense of the rest of the cast.

Some customers were pushing past me, leaving the tavern, and now the dawn had come. What with the noise of the market people I woke up fully. From outside I heard a voice that froze me: it was Mimi's voice. She was talking frantically to Marcel. I couldn't hear what they were saying first of all, but they were arguing. I heard Mimi saying, "Tell me what to do. . . ." And then, "He's mad with jealousy. I can't stand it. Even when I'm asleep he spies on me." And again: "He told me to find another lover."

They came nearer. I stood back against the wall. I did not want to be seen.

"You walked all that way to tell me this," Marcel was saying. "Mimi, we've been over all this before. A cat-and-dog life is no good to anyone. Break. Leave him alone."

She was coughing.

He said, "You're coughing badly. Come in out of the snow. You're cold. All right, if you won't come inside, walk up and down. It will warm you. Don't stand there shivering."

"You're right," she said. "We must break. I want to. But I love him. We don't know how to do it. Please help us to break for good."

Marcel said: "You haven't come to see me. You *knew* Rudolphe was here, didn't you? He's inside now, fast asleep."

"I thought he'd come to you. He always does. Yes, I did hear he had come up here."

Their voices faded as they walked away, but presently they returned and Marcel was saying:

"The trouble with Rudolphe is conceit. He knows nothing about real life. Rudolphe thinks of no one but himself. I've told him a dozen times he is as mad as Othello. . . ."

"Who is Othello?" said Mimi.

"Stay here. Rudolphe is inside. I'll go and get him."

He came into the doorway where I was standing. He knew I had heard. That is what I mean by Marcel's stage tricks. Well, I can play them too.

"I heard every word," I said. "I'm mad, am I? You don't know what life with Mimi is like. She's chasing men all the time, any one, 'Vicomtes,' anyone. I don't know. And she comes back as if nothing had happened. She's just after people with money, like all the girls we know. Musette and her Lulu, for example. We've got no money. It's as simple as that. I suppose you can't blame them."

Marcel said he would never believe that of Mimi.

"I wish Musette was like her. All the same why shouldn't girls do what they like? We do. You take everything so seriously," he said.

"I love her," I said.

"You said it's all over. You're in love with yourself, Rudolphe."

And then, quickly, I said something I wish I hadn't said:

"I am *afraid* of my love," I said. "I've shut my eyes to everything. Because, Marcel, Mimi is ill. Don't you see — she's consumptive. She's dying, Marcel. What can I do for her? My room is cold. She won't eat. I pretend to be asleep because I have seen the fever in her eyes. I listen to that cough eating her lungs away. She laughs when I say anything. Even my love can't save her."

Marcel studied me when I said this. How unjust, I thought, to be made to feel guilty for what lies outside one's power.

"What can I do?" I said.

"Look after her, of course," said Marcel.

And then, on the spur of the moment, I said something for which I will never forgive myself. I was saying what might have been one of Victor Hugo's worst lines, like a ham actor, I felt myself swell up and declaim:

"If it were only a Vicomte, any one you like. But Death himself is my rival!"

"Don't shout it, at any rate," said Marcel glancing furtively outside the door. "There's no need to tell the world. Death is everyone's rival. Mimi is not going to die."

And now Mimi stood in the doorway. How was I to know she was there? Marcel should have stopped me saying that. He had made Mimi hear me sentencing her to death, as if she were a prisoner and I the judge.

I rushed to her with tears of remorse in my eyes.

"Mimi." And I held her in my arms.

But now a common country dance tune had started in the tavern and Musette inside was shouting "Take your hands off!" and laughing. Marcel pushed past me and went inside.

"Musette," he was shouting. "Leave that man alone. I heard you carrying on. I saw it."

Mimi got away from me and stood looking hard and frightened.

"Goodbye, Rudolphe," she said. "I came to see you. I heard you. If I'm going to die I'll die with people who love me. I hope things will be good for you."

"You can't go," I said.

"And the rest of the things you gave me," she said in a dead voice — "the bracelet, the prayer book — just wrap them up. I'll send for them as I said. Oh, and there's the bonnet you bought. It's under the pillow — no, not the bonnet. Perhaps you'd like to keep it. You liked it."

And then she tapped me on the chest.

"And say goodbye," she said, "to jealousy and suspicion next time please! The winter is always bad for me, but I'll be better when the spring comes. I can look after myself. I'm not going to die. And then perhaps in the spring, if you like, you can take me to the country — like you once did to Saint-Cloud and we looked at the river and you wrote a poem. I'll be strong in the spring."

I could see she was horrified by what she had heard me say.

There was screeches coming from the tavern. Marcel had forgotten us. He was in another play of his own making: he came out dragging Musette with him who was saying:

"I wasn't sitting on his knee. He just said, 'Like to dance?' and I said, 'I only dance at night.'"

Her makeup was stained on her face.

"I heard it. I saw it," Marcel shouted at her.

"I'll do what I like," she said and pulled his hair and shook him. And he hit her.

"I've had enough!" Musette cried out. "I'm going. Go home and paint your own front door. It's all you're good for. Viper. Toad."

Mimi and I stood watching them.

"The spring. I mean it, Rudolphe," she said. "And you'll take me to the country." She put her arms round me. "But no suspicions!" she said.

And she ran after Musette. I watched until they were out of sight and Marcel and I were left together.

"Leave them to it," Marcel said. "They can look after themselves. You'll see."

"Where will they go?" I said.

"What does it matter? Girls know how to keep warm. They'll come back," said Marcel.

We drank cognac at the inn.

"You played a trick on me," I said to Marcel.

"You asked for help," he said morosely. "Come back and live with me."

I walked back through the snow to my room. The streets had woken up. The concierge said to me:

"The lady sent for a parcel of some things. I let her have them but I put your cases downstairs until you pay the rent tomorrow."

"Where are my papers?" I said and ran up the stairs.

"Oh you can have those and I haven't touched the rubbish," she called up the stairs. I had a last look at the room. The woman had cleaned it and the maid was stripping the bed.

"I found this," the maid said with an impertinent look. She was holding Mimi's bonnet. I snatched it from her and pushed it under my shirt and left.

"The rent tomorrow, sharp," the concierge called to me from the door. And in the street the people who heard her shrugged their shoulders and laughed at me as I left.

❧

Marcel was wrong. The two girls did not come back. The days went by and the days turned into weeks. Marcel did not talk about

Musette. He had the drastic knack of turning his back on people; as a confident tactic and instead of speaking of her, hummed tunes she had sung and sometimes unknowingly even uttered a few of the words and then broke off. His humming had the effect of bringing Mimi back to me, not as a girl but as an image of the flowers she embroidered and her way of talking about them as real flowers opening in the spring. She had always talked of the future eagerly as if she lived there rather than in the day itself. She was always half dreaming of some fanciful spring and living for it. As I worked I would look at the door of Marcel's room and, in a moment, I would think I could see her coming in timidly — or had it been with design? — asking for her candle to be lit and I would find myself holding my pen in the air. I could remember every moment of our first meeting and then it would pass into the confusion of our time together and now she was a crowd of Mimis in all her moods.

When I went out, especially when I crossed the river on the way to *The Beaver* office with my copy, I sometimes thought I saw her disappearing round a street corner — but she was clearly no longer in the Quarter: it was never she. I was not jealous any longer. In my mind I found myself even pleased to think of her being herself, floating, talking in questions to anyone in that harmless and inviting way of hers.

Instead of Mimi one morning I saw Musette. She was sitting in an elegant carriage with servants in livery behind her and she was handsomely dressed and ecstatic in black velvet which must have cost someone a fortune. Her large earrings glittered. She saw me at once. The carriage slowed down and she waved a gloved hand and called in her strong mocking voice:

"Rudolphe! How's your heart, my dear?"

"How's yours?" I said.

She laughed and said, pleased with her dress:

"Velvet dulls the heartbeats," and she signaled to the man to drive on.

I went back to the attic.

I couldn't resist it: I told Marcel. He was standing in front of his easel.

"Good for her," he said and made one of his violent dashes at his canvas as if he were going to kill it, but before he touched it his hand holding the brush dropped to his side. The next day he

worked furiously and stopped humming. And soon he had his revenge: it was not a revenge but an appeal for truce and pity.

"Rudolphe, I've seen Mimi!" (I'm sure it was a lie.) "She was
riding in the carriage of some Count, got up to kill, like a duch-
ess," he said. "Those two girls have done well, Rudolphe, haven't
they? It's really a compliment to us."

The strange thing is that after this the image of Mimi stopped
coming to the door and I wrote a long poem.

The year rumbled on and once more the wind whistled in the
attic window and slush was on the streets — another Christmas.
We were in our usual Christmas situation: talking of yesterday's
dinner. No food in the place, though we did have a bit of fire in
the stove. We were burning that chair. Schaunard had been out for
days with his list of likely "touches" and for once had failed us.
He was wearing his thin summer jacket and had sold his winter
coat to buy a roll for each of us. Colline was with him in his big
coat and pulled a herring out of a paper bag and said:

"A dish worthy of Caesar."

Schaunard said, "I note it's pickled."

Marcel pulled off Colline's old hat and put it on the table and
stood a bottle of mineral water in it.

"Champagne must be iced," he said.

"Now, my lords, salmon or turbot?" said Schaunard.

"Or a vol-au-vent?" said Marcel picking up his bread and tear-
ing at it.

"I can't touch vol-au-vent today," Schaunard said. "My figure!
I'm dancing in Society tonight."

They began one of their worn-out larks.

We told them to sit down but Schaunard got up and said:

"A dance to get us into form, something Spanish to warm us
up. Choose your partners."

We started a ridiculous dance.

I went up to Marcel and said: "Fair maiden — would you?"

And Marcel said: "Oh sir, I beg you."

"What a scandal!" said Colline.

"You insult me,"said Schaunard. "This is a fandango. Draw your
sword, sir."

We were in this mad state, eating as we danced, crumbs all over
the floor, when the door was opened. Musette was there. In the
black velvet dress.

"Stop it," she said. "I've got Mimi with me. She's struggling up the stairs."

We went to the door. Mimi was sitting on the top stair. She looked haggard and could hardly speak. Marcel and I lifted her up and put her on the bed. She said:

"Rudolphe, will you let me stay with you? I haven't got a room."

Musette whispered to Schaunard that Mimi had been turned out by a "Count" and couldn't get work. "I just found her wandering the streets with nowhere to go, in this weather! She said, 'Take me to Rudolphe. He was right. I am dying.' "

We had eaten those few rolls and there was not a bite left to eat or drink.

I sat beside Mimi on the bed.

"I don't want anything to eat, only to be near you and with you," Mimi said in her hoarse and feeble voice. "I am so cold. If only I had my muff! Oh and there's Schaunard, Marcel and, look, Colline. Oh, Rudolphe, love me."

"I love you," I said.

I told her not to talk.

"I'll whisper," she said. "Don't be frightened if I whisper." And to Marcel, "Musette — how good her heart is, Marcel."

Musette unfastened her earrings and gave them to Marcel and said, "Sell them. Quickly. Get a doctor and medicine. I'll go for a muff."

Colline stood watching us. Slowly he took off his enormous thick coat and said to Schaunard, "Come on. Let's leave them alone. I'll sell it. We've got to get something for her."

I sat beside her and she talked drowsily of how we went shopping that night we met and I bought her the bonnet. I got it out of my cupboard and she tried to sit up and put it on. "You kept it." she said. I told her to rest but she went on talking about that night when she came to this very room.

"I frightened you," she said. "You looked so fierce at first. And then you hid my key! Rudolphe, I'm better already. I love you, Rudolphe. Forgive me. I'll be better in the spring. Am I ugly?"

"No, you're my beautiful Mimi," I said. "I worship you."

I was horrified by the wasting of her body. I was holding a skeleton.

The doctor came and Schaunard and Marcel had bought the medicine. Marcel was heating it on a spirit stove and Musette came back with the muff and Mimi said, as she put her hands in it, "How expensive! I shall be warm. Now I shall sleep." And she closed her eyes.

Musette stood apart from us and suddenly kneeled and started to pray in her real country voice.

"O Gracious Virgin Mary, bless her, I beg of you in your great mercy. Don't let her die . . ." and she stopped and said to me, "Put my cloak over the window, the sun is too strong for her." And she took off her cloak and while I hung it over the window she went on praying.

"Holy Mother, most Holy Mother, make her well. I am unworthy of your forgiveness, but Mimi is like an angel from Heaven."

"She's asleep," said Musette. "Quiet."

I stood near the window away from the bed.

Colline came in without his coat.

"I've sold it," he said to Musette and put the money on the table. I stood gazing across the room at the bed where Schaunard was looking at her. He moved away and whispered to the others and I saw them all, still, gazing at me. I went over to the bed.

"Mimi, Mimi, wake up," I said and I lifted her up.

"She's dead," called Schaunard and he sat down suddenly as if he had been shot.

Musette gave a scream of terror and I fell on to the bed weeping. I looked round half in anger at Schaunard. He had seen her die. Not I.

I do not forgive myself for all that had happened to us. I cannot bear to think of that day. What is the good of the tears in my eyes? Even to write about it, every word of mine, seems like a crime.

LA BOHÈME
AT THE MET

Premiere of the current production,
December 14, 1981

CONDUCTOR, James Levine
PRODUCTION, Franco Zeffirelli
SET DESIGNER, Franco Zeffirelli
COSTUME DESIGNER, Peter J. Hall
LIGHTING DESIGNER, Gil Wechsler

Photographs of the story of the opera by William Harris.
Courtesy of the Education Department, Metropolitan Opera Guild

ACT I

Paris. Christmas Eve. The garret of Marcello and Rodolfo.

It is bitter cold. Rodolfo *(José Carreras)*, a poet, and his friend Marcello *(Richard Stilwell)*, a painter, are trying to work. But they are too hungry and frozen — and too poor to do anything about it.

Two roommates arrive: Colline *(James Morris)*, a young philosopher, and Schaunard *(Allan Monk)*, a musician. Schaunard has had a turn in his luck, and he has brought food and fuel and money. The four bohemians celebrate around their table, make plans to dine out at the Café Momus.

Benoit *(Italo Tajo)*, the landlord, arrives. He demands the overdue rent. The bohemians offer him wine, and when he has drunk too much they ask him about his flirtations. He confesses, and then, in a show of mock indignation, the bohemians throw him out.

Rodolfo stays behind to finish an article. There is a knock on the
door. It is a beautiful young girl, his neighbor Mimi *(Teresa Stratas)*.
She tells Rodolfo that the light of her candle has gone out.
Rodolfo invites her in.

Mimi enters. Suddenly, she feels faint. Rodolfo offers her some wine.

Rodolfo lights Mimi's candle, but it goes out. In the darkness she loses her key. They search for it, and as their hands touch the floor their fingers meet. They are overwhelmed by unexpected love.

Rodolfo hears the voices of his friends calling from the street. He and Mimi look down at them from a small balcony. Then, arm in arm, they make their way to join the others.

ACT II

The Latin Quarter. Christmas Eve.

Rodolfo buys Mimi a bonnet.

OVERLEAF: The streets are crowded with revelers
and children and vendors.

At the Café Momus, Rodolfo introduces Mimi to his friends. They talk and order a sumptuous holiday dinner.

Musetta *(Renata Scotto)*, Marcello's old flame, makes a noisy entrance. She is with Alcindoro *(Italo Tajo)*, her latest, and rich, admirer. Musetta quickly notices Marcello, and to get his attention she bursts into an exuberant song.

Musetta playfully flirts with Marcello. A few moments later, she sends Alcindoro away to fetch her new shoes.

Musetta and Marcello reunite, and as the festivities of Christmas begin, the bohemians march off behind the local band.

ACT III

Outside a tavern near the gates of Paris.
A cold February dawn. There is snow everywhere.

Mimi appears. She asks one of the farm women to do her a favor — to go into the tavern and tell Marcello she is outside.

Mimi tells Marcello how Rodolfo's jealousy has torn them apart.
Marcello tells her that unless lovers can be free and easy
with each other, it is best that they part.

Rodolfo, who has been sleeping in the tavern, unexpectedly comes
outside. Mimi hides from him near a tree. She overhears Rodolfo
confess to Marcello that he loves Mimi more than anything else in the
world, but that he is afraid — afraid that she is dying and
that he cannot adequately take care of her.

Mimi sobs and coughs. Rodolfo hears her. They unite, but Mimi tells
him that they must say goodbye. Rodolfo convinces
her to stay with him until spring.

The lovers are interrupted by the noise of Marcello and Musetta
quarreling. Marcello accuses Musetta of being a frivolous flirt.
Musetta stalks off. Mimi and Rodolfo hold each other. They vow not
to separate until the "season of the flowers."

ACT IV

Several months later. Paris. The garret of Marcello and Rodolfo.

Marcello and Rodolfo try to work, but they are too tormented by the loss of the women they love.

Colline and Schaunard arrive with a scanty meal. They try to distract their friends, to lighten the dark mood with a mock ball, dancing and all.

Musetta arrives unexpectedly. She has come to tell Rodolfo that Mimi is outside, too ill to climb the stairs.

Rodolfo helps Mimi into the garret, prepares a cot for her. Colline offers to sell his coat to buy medicine. Musetta offers to sell her earrings. Marcello leaves to find a doctor. Schaunard goes to fetch fresh water.

Alone, Rodolfo and Mimi renew their vow of love and recall their first meeting. "You are my love and all my life," Mimi tells him.

Musetta and the friends return. Musetta gives Mimi a muff to warm her hands. Mimi grows weaker. Musetta prays for her. Rodolfo draws the curtain to soften the light.

Schaunard discovers that Mimi has died. Rodolfo, turning from the
window, sees her and rushes to the cot. He cries in despair:
"Mimi! Mimi!"

La Bohème

by

GIUSEPPE GIACOSA AND LUIGI ILLICA

ENGLISH TRANSLATION BY WILLIAM WEAVER

Summary

by

William Weaver

ACT I

Rodolfo, a poet, and his friend Marcello, a painter, are trying to work in their Paris garret. It is Christmas Eve, and they are cold and hungry — and without money. Colline, another bohemian, comes in, equally discouraged. But then Schaunard, the fourth and luckiest of the group, enters with money and provisions. The friends decide to celebrate by dining out. After a successful skirmish with their landlord, Benoit, they set out for the Café Momus. Only Rodolfo stays behind to finish an article he must write. When he is alone there is a knock at the door. To his surprise, he finds a beautiful young girl on the landing. It is his neighbor, Mimi, who has knocked to ask for a light. Her candle has gone out. Rodolfo relights it for her, but it goes out again, and in the confusion, she loses her key. In the darkness she and Rodolfo search for it. Their hands touch. Rodolfo and Mimi exchange confidences and, finally, declarations of love. Then they go off to join his friends.

ACT II

Christmas Eve in the Latin Quarter. The group of friends is separated in the bustling of merrymakers and vendors of every kind. Rodolfo and Mimi go into a milliner's, and he buys her a pink bonnet. Later all are reunited at the Café Momus, where they order a sumptuous supper. As they are enjoying themselves, Musetta — Marcello's beautiful but fickle beloved — enters with Alcindoro, an elderly and straitlaced admirer. Seeing Marcello, Musetta contrives to get rid of her escort. She and Marcello are again in each other's arms. The friends all go off, leaving their bill to the hapless Alcindoro.

ACT III

A cold February dawn. Outside a tavern near one of the gates of Paris, Mimi appears and sends for Marcello, who is working in the tavern with Musetta. When he comes out, Mimi tells how Rodolfo's insane jealousy is forcing them apart. Their conversation is cut short when Rodolfo, who was sleeping in the tavern, wakes and comes out. Mimi hides behind a tree. Taxed by Marcello with his fickleness, Rodolfo reveals that he is really concerned for Mimi's health and thinks that another person, less poor than he, could take better care of her. Mimi's presence is discovered, and though she first bids Rodolfo goodbye, in the end they agree to stay together at least until spring comes. As Musetta and Marcello quarrel in the background and finally separate, Rodolfo and Mimi go off reconciled, arm in arm.

Act IV

The garret, months later. Rodolfo and Marcello are again trying to work, but this time each is distracted and tormented by the memory of his lost love. Schaunard and Colline come in, and the four friends clown, making light of their poverty, until Musetta interrupts them, bursting in with the news that Mimi is outside, too ill to climb the last stairs. Rodolfo helps her into the room, where she is settled on the bed. Musetta sacrifices her earrings and Colline his coat to buy medicine and a muff for the dying girl. Marcello goes for a doctor. Left alone, the two lovers renew their vows of love and recall their first meeting. Soon the others return. As Musetta prays, Mimi quietly dies, with Rodolfo calling her name in despair.

CHARACTERS

RODOLFO (a Poet)   *Tenor*
MIMI   *Soprano*
MARCELLO (a Painter)   *Baritone*
COLLINE (a Philosopher)   *Bass*
SCHAUNARD (a Musician)   *Baritone*
MUSETTA   *Soprano*
BENOIT (a Landlord)   *Bass*
ALCINDORO (a Councilor of State)   *Bass*
PARPIGNOL (a Toy Vendor)   *Tenor*
CUSTOMS SERGEANT   *Bass*

Students, Working Girls, Bourgeois, Shopkeepers,
Vendors, Soldiers, Waiters, Gamins, etc.

The time is about 1830.
The place is the Latin Quarter, Paris.

ACT ONE

In the Garret

A broad window from which an expanse of roofs, covered with snow, is seen. At right, a stove. A table, a bed, a wardrobe, four chairs, a painter's easel with a sketched canvas and a stool: scattered books, many bundles of papers, two candlesticks. A door in the center, another at left. Rodolfo is looking pensively out of the window. Marcello is working at his picture: The Crossing of the Red Sea, *with his hands benumbed by the cold. He warms them by breathing on them from time to time, changing his position because of the great chill.*

MARCELLO

Questo Mar Rosso — mi ammollisce e assidera
come se addosso — mi piovesse in stille.
     (he moves away from the easel to look at his picture)
Per vendicarmi, affogo un Faraon.
     (goes back to work — to Rodolfo)
Che fai?

This Red Sea — is soaking and freezing me as if it were raining — upon me in drops.

To avenge myself, I'll drown a Pharaoh.

What are you doing?

RODOLFO

Nei cieli bigi
guardo fumar dai mille
comignoli Parigi,
     (pointing to the stove without fire)
e penso a quel poltrone
d'un vecchio caminetto ingannatore
che vive in ozio come un gran signor!

In the gray skies
I'm watching Paris
smoke from its thousand chimneys,

and I'm thinking of that slacker
of a deceitful old stove
which lives in leisure like a great lord!

MARCELLO

Le sue rendite oneste
da un pezzo non riceve.

For a long time he hasn't received
his just income.

RODOLFO

Quelle sciocche foreste
che fan sotto la neve?

What are those silly forests
doing under the snow?

MARCELLO

Rodolfo, io voglio dirti un mio pensier profondo:
ho un freddo cane.

Rodolfo, I want to tell you a deep thought of mine:
I'm cold as hell.

RODOLFO
(approaching Marcello)

Ed io, Marcel, non ti nascondo
che non credo al sudor della fronte.

And I, Marcello, won't conceal from you
that I don't believe in the sweat of the brow.

73

MARCELLO

Ho ghiacciate
le dita . . . quasi ancor le tenessi immollate
giù in quella gran ghiacciaia che è il cuore di
   Musetta!

I have frozen
fingers . . . as if I still held them plunged
down in that great icebox which is Musetta's
   heart!

(he allows a long sigh to escape him and leaves off painting, setting down palette and brushes)

RODOLFO

L'amore è un caminetto che sciupa
   troppo . . .

Love is a stove that consumes too much . . .

MARCELLO

. . . e in fretta!

. . . and in haste!

RODOLFO

. . . dove l'uomo è fascina . . .

. . . where the man is the kindling-wood . . .

MARCELLO

. . . e la donna è l'alare . . .

. . . and the woman is the andiron . . .

RODOLFO

. . . l'uno brucia in un soffio . . .

. . . the one burns up in a flash . . .

MARCELLO

. . . e l'altro sta a guardare.

. . . and the other stands and watches.

RODOLFO

Ma intanto qui si gela . . .

But meanwhile here we're freezing . . .

MARCELLO

. . . e si muore d'inedia . . . !

. . . and we're dying of starvation . . . !

RODOLFO

Fuoco ci vuole . . .

Fire is needed . . .

MARCELLO

(seizing a chair and preparing to shatter it)

Aspetta . . . sacrifichiam la sedia!   Wait . . . let's sacrifice the chair!

(Rodolfo energetically prevents Marcello's action. Suddenly Rodolfo lets out a shout of joy at an idea that has come to him.)

RODOLFO

Eureka!   Eureka!

(runs to the table and takes a voluminous sheaf of papers from it)

MARCELLO

Trovasti?

You've found it?

RODOLFO

Si Aguzza
l'ingegno. L'idea vampi in fiamma.

Yes. Sharpen
your wit. Let the Idea blaze up in flames.

MARCELLO
(pointing to his picture)

Bruciamo il Mar Rosso?   Do we burn the Red Sea?

RODOLFO

No. Puzza   No. Painted canvas
la tela dipinta. Il mio dramma,   stinks. My drama,
l'ardente mio dramma ci scaldi.   let my burning drama warm us.

MARCELLO
(with comic fear)

Vuoi leggerlo forse? Mi geli.   Do you want perhaps to read it? You freeze
                             me.

RODOLFO

No, in cener la carta si sfaldi   No, let the paper flake away in ash
e l'estro rivoli a' suoi cieli.   and inspiration fly back to its heavens.
(with tragic vehemence)

Al secol gran danno minaccia . . .   Great harm threatens our time . . .
è Roma in periglio!   Rome is in danger!

MARCELLO

Gran cor!   Magnanimous!

RODOLFO
(gives Marcello a part of the sheaf)

A te l'atto primo.   Take the first act.

MARCELLO

Qua.   Here.

RODOLFO

Straccia.   Tear it up.

MARCELLO

Accendi.   Light it.
    (*Rodolfo strikes a tinderbox, lights a candle, and goes to the stove with Marcello. Together they set fire to the part of the sheaf of papers thrown in the hearth, then both take chairs and sit down, warming themselves voluptuously.*)

RODOLFO AND MARCELLO

Che lieto baglior.   What a happy glow.
    (*The door in the background is opened with a racket and Colline enters, frozen, numb, stamping his feet, throwing wrathfully on the table a pack of books tied with a handkerchief.*)

COLLINE

Già dell'Apocalisse appariscono i segni.   The signs of the Apocalypse are already ap-
In giorno di Vigilia non s'accettano pegni —   pearing.
                          On Christmas Eve no pawning is allowed —
(breaks off, surprised)

Una fiammata!   A flame!

RODOLFO
(to Colline)

Zitto, si dà il mio dramma . . .   Hush, my drama is being given . . .

MARCELLO

. . . al fuoco.   . . . to the fire.

COLLINE

Lo trovo scintillante.   I find it sparkling.

RODOLFO

Vivo.   Vivid.
                                                         (The fire dies down.)

COLLINE

Ma dura poco.   But it lasts only a short time.

RODOLFO

La Brevità, gran pregio.   Brevity — a great merit.

COLLINE
(taking the chair from him)

Autore, a me la sedia.   Author, give me the chair.

MARCELLO

Quest'intermezzi fan morir d'inedia.   These intermissions make you die of bore-
                                                                   dom.
Presto.   Quickly.

RODOLFO
(takes another part of the sheaf)

Atto secondo.   Act Two.

MARCELLO
(to Colline)

Non far sussurro.   No whispering.
    (Rodolfo tears up a part of the papers and throws it in the stove: the fire is revived. Colline
draws the chair still closer and warms his hands. Rodolfo is standing near the other two with
the rest of the sheaf of papers.)

COLLINE
(with the manner of a drama critic)

Pensier profondo!   Profound thought!

MARCELLO

Giusto color!   Proper color!

RODOLFO

In quell'azzurro — guizzo languente   In that blue — languishing flicker
sfuma un'ardente — scena d'amor.   an ardent love scene — goes up in smoke.

COLLINE

Scoppietta un foglio.   A page crackles.

MARCELLO

Là c'eran baci!   There were kisses there!

RODOLFO

Tre atti or voglio — d'un colpo udir.   Now I want to hear — three acts at one blow.
(throws the rest of the sheaf in the fire)

COLLINE

Tal degli audaci — l'idea s'integra.   Thus the thought of the bold becomes inte-
grated.

ALL

Bello in allegra — vampa svanir.   It's beautiful to vanish — in a merry flame.
(they applaud enthusiastically: after a moment the flame dies down)

MARCELLO

Oh, Dio . . . già s'abbassa la fiamma.   Oh, God . . . the flame is lowering already.

COLLINE

Che vano, che fragile dramma!   What a vain, what a fragile drama!

MARCELLO

Già scricchiola, increspasi, muor!   It's already creaking, curling up, dying!

COLLINE AND MARCELLO

Abbasso, abbasso l'autor!   Down, down with the author!
(Two delivery boys enter through the center door, one carrying food supplies, bottles of wine, cigars, and the other a bundle of wood. At the sound, the three in front of the stove turn and, with cries of amazement, throw themselves on the provisions carried by the boy and set them on the table. Colline takes the wood and carries it over to the stove. Evening is beginning to fall.)

RODOLFO

Legna!   Wood!

MARCELLO

Sigari!   Cigars!

COLLINE

Bordò!   Bordeaux!

Rodolfo

Legna!   Wood!

MARCELLO

Bordò!   Bordeaux!

ALL THREE

Le dovizie d'una fiera   Destiny destined for us
il destin ci destinò!   the abundance of a fair!

(Schaunard comes in through the center door with an air of triumph, throwing some coins on the ground.)

SCHAUNARD

La Banca di Francia   The Bank of France
per voi si sbilancia.   is going broke for you.

COLLINE
(picking up the coins along with Rodolfo and Marcello)
Raccatta, raccatta!   Gather, gather!

MARCELLO
(incredulous)
Son pezzi di latta!   They're pieces of tin!

SCHAUNARD
(showing him a coin)
Sei sordo? Sei lippo?   Are you deaf? Are you nearsighted?
Quest'uomo chi è?   Who is this man?

RODOLFO
(bowing)
Luigi Filippo!   Louis Philippe!
M'inchino al mio re!   I bow to my king!

ALL
Sta Luigi Filippo ai nostri piè!   Louis Philippe is at our feet!

(Schaunard would like to narrate his good luck, but the others don't listen to him. They arrange everything on the table, and the wood in the stove.)

SCHAUNARD

Or vi dirò: quest'oro, o meglio, argento   Now I'll tell you: this gold, or rather, silver
ha la sua brava istoria.   has its fine story.

MARCELLO

Riscaldiamo il camino!   Let's warm up the stove!

COLLINE

Tanto freddo ha sofferto!   It's suffered such cold!

SCHAUNARD

Un inglese . . . un signor . . . Lord o Milord   An Englishman . . . a gentleman . . . Lord
che sia, voleva un musicista . . .   or Milord
                                                 as may be, wanted a musician . . .

MARCELLO
(throwing Colline's pack of books from the table)
Via!   Away!
Prepariamo la tavola!   Let's prepare the table!

SCHAUNARD

Io? Volo!
Me? I rush over!

RODOLFO

L'esca dov'è?
Where's the tinder?

COLLINE

Là.
There.

MARCELLO

Qua.
Here.

SCHAUNARD

E mi presento.
And I present myself.

M'accetta, gli domando —
He accepts me; I ask him —

COLLINE

Arrosto freddo!
Cold roast!

MARCELLO
(*arranging the victuals*)

Pasticcio dolce!
Sweet pastry!

SCHAUNARD

A quando le lezioni?
"When are the lessons?"

Mi presento, m'accetta, gli domando:
I present myself, he accepts me, I ask him:

a quando le lezioni?
"When are the lessons?"

Risponde: incominciam!
He answers: "Let's begin!

Guardare!, e un pappagallo m'addita
Look!" And he points out a parrot to me

al primo pian, poi soggiunge:
on the second floor, then adds:

Voi suonare finchè quello morire!
"You play till that dies!"

RODOLFO

Fulgida folgori la sala splendida.
Let the splendid hall shine brilliantly.

SCHAUNARD

E fu così:
And so it was:

Suonai tre lunghi dì . . .
I played for three long days . . .

MARCELLO
(*lights the candles and puts them on the table*)

Or le candele!
Now the candles!

COLLINE

Pasticcio dolce!
Sweet pastry!

SCHAUNARD

Allora usai l'incanto
Then I used the spell

di mia presenza bella, di mia presenza
of my handsome appearance, of my hand-

bella . . .
some appearance . . .

Affascinai l'ancella . . .
I charmed the maid . . .

MARCELLO
Mangiar senza tovaglia?   Eat without a tablecloth?

RODOLFO
Un'idea . . . !   An idea!

MARCELLO AND COLLINE
Il *Constituzional!*   The *Constitutional!*

RODOLFO
(unfolding it)
Ottima carta . . .   Excellent paper . . .
Si mangia e si divora un'appendice!   You eat and you devour a supplement!

SCHAUNARD
Gli propinai prezzemolo . . .   I administered parsley to him . . .
Lorito allargò l'ali,   Polly spread his wings,
Lorito allargò l'ali,   Polly spread his wings,
Lorito il becco aprì,   Polly opened his beak,
Un poco di prezzemolo,   a bit of parsley,
da Socrate morì!   he died like Socrates!
   (Seeing that no one is paying any attention to him, he seizes Colline, who is going past him with a dish.)

COLLINE
Chi?   Who?

SCHAUNARD
(shouting, annoyed)
Che il diavolo vi porti tutti quanti!   The devil take you, one and all!
   (then seeing them about to start eating the cold pie)
Ed or che fate?   And now what are you doing?
   (with a solemn gesture he extends his hand over the pie)
No! Queste cibarie   No! These foodstuffs
sono la salmeria   are the reserves
pei dì futuri   for future days,
tenebrosi e oscuri.   tenebrous and dark.
   (and as he speaks, he clears the table)
Pranzare in casa il dì della vigilia   Dine at home on Christmas Eve
mentre il Quartier Latino le sue vie   while the Latin Quarter bedecks
addobba di salsiccie e leccornie?   its streets with sausages and delicacies?
Quando un'olezzo di frittelle   When an aroma of fritters
imbalsama le vecchie strade?   perfumes the old streets?
Là le ragazze cantano contente . . .   There the girls sing happily . . .

RODOLFO, MARCELLO, COLLINE
La vigilia di Natal!   Christmas Eve!

SCHAUNARD
. . . ed han per eco ognuna uno studente! . . . and each has a student as her echo!
Un po' di religione, o miei signori: A bit of religion, O gentlemen:
si beva in casa, ma si pranzi fuor!   we drink at home, but we dine out!

(Rodolfo locks the door, then all go around the table and pour out the wine: they stop, dumbfounded.)

BENOIT
(from outside)

Si può? May I?

MARCELLO

Chi è là? Who's there?

BENOIT

Benoît. Benoit.

MARCELLO

Il padrone di casa! The landlord!

SCHAUNARD

Uscio sul muso. Bolt the door in his face.

COLLINE
(shouts)

Non c'è nessuno. There's nobody home.

SCHAUNARD

È chiuso. It's locked.

BENOIT

Una parola. A word . . .

SCHAUNARD
(after consulting with the others, goes to open)

Sola! Only one!

BENOIT
(enters smiling, sees Marcello, and, showing him a a paper, says:)

Affitto! Rent!

MARCELLO
(with exaggerated care)

Olà! date una sedia. Hola! Give him a chair.

RODOLFO

Presto. Quickly.

BENOIT
(parrying)

Non occorre. Vorrei . . . It's not necessary. I'd like . . .

SCHAUNARD
(insisting, with gentle violence, makes him sit down)

Segga. Be seated.

MARCELLO

Vuol bere?　　　　　　　　　　Do you want to drink?
(pours him some wine)

BENOIT

Grazie.　　　　　　　　　　Thanks.

RODOLFO

Tocchiamo!　　　　　　　　　　Let's touch glasses!

COLLINE

Tocchiamo!　　　　　　　　　　Let's touch glasses!

SCHAUNARD

Beva!　　　　　　　　　　Drink!

RODOLFO

Tocchiam!　　　　　　　　　　Let's touch glasses!
(All drink. Benoit sets down his glass and addresses Marcello, showing him the paper.)

BENOIT

Quest'è l'ultimo trimestre . . .　　　　　　This is the last quarter . . .

MARCELLO
(naïvely)

Ne ho piacere.　　　　　　　　　　I'm glad.

BENOIT

E quindi . . .　　　　　　　　　　And therefore . . .

SCHAUNARD
(interrupting him)

Ancora un sorso.　　　　　　　　　　Another sip.
(fills the glasses)

BENOIT

Grazie.　　　　　　　　　　Thanks.

RODOLFO

Tocchiam!　　　　　　　　　　Let's touch glasses!

COLLINE

Tocchiam!　　　　　　　　　　Let's touch glasses!

THE FOUR
(touching Benoit's glass with theirs)

Alla sua salute!　　　　　　　　　　To your health!

BENOIT
(resuming with Marcello)

A lei ne vengo　　　　　　　　　　I'm coming to you
perchè il trimestre scorso　　　　　　because the last quarter
mi promise . . .　　　　　　　　　　you promised me . . .

MARCELLO

Promisi ed or mantengo.   I promised and now I keep my promise.
(showing Benoit the coins that are on the table)

RODOLFO
(softly, to Marcello)

Che fai?   What are you doing?

SCHAUNARD
(same)

Sei pazzo?   Are you crazy?

MARCELLO
(to Benoit, ignoring the other two)

Ha visto? Or via   Did you see? Now, come,
resti un momento in nostra compagnia.   stay a moment in our company.
Dica: quant'anni ha,   Tell us: how old are you,
caro signor Benoît?   dear Monsieur Benoit?

BENOIT

Gl'anni? Per carità!   My age? For heaven's sake!

RODOLFO

Su e giù la nostra eta?   More or less our age?

BENOIT

Di più, molto di più.   More, much more.
As they make Benoit chatter, they fill his glass as soon as he has emptied it.

COLLINE

Ha detto su e giù.   He said more or less.

MARCELLO
(lowering his voice, and in a sly tone)

L'altra sera al Mabil . . .   The other evening at Mabille . . .
l'han colto in peccato d'amor.   they caught him, in amorous sin.

BENOIT
(uneasy)

Io?!   I?

MARCELLO

Al Mabil . . . l'altra sera l'han colto.   At Mabille . . . the other evening they caught
Neghi.   him.
                                           Deny it.

BENOIT

Un caso.   By chance.

MARCELLO
(flattering him)

Bella donna!   A beautiful woman!

BENOIT
(*half tipsy, with a prompt reaction*)
Ah! molto!　　　　　　　　　　　Ah, very!

SCHAUNARD
(*slaps him on the shoulder*)
Briccone!　　　　　　　　　　Rogue!

RODOLFO
Briccone!　　　　　　　　　　Rogue!

COLLINE
(*slaps him on the other shoulder*)
Seduttore!　　　　　　　　　　Seducer!

SCHAUNARD
Briccone!　　　　　　　　　　Rogue!

RODOLFO
Briccone!　　　　　　　　　　Rogue!

MARCELLO
Una quercia! Un cannone!　　　　　　An oak! A cannon!

RODOLFO
L'uomo ha buon gusto.　　　　　　The man has good taste.

BENOIT
Ah! ah!　　　　　　　　　　Ha! ha!

MARCELLO
Il crin ricciuto e fulvo.　　　　　　His mane, curly and tawny.

SCHAUNARD
Briccon!　　　　　　　　　　Rogue!

MARCELLO
Ei gongolava arzillo, pettoruto.　　　　He swaggered, perky, full-chested.

BENOIT
(*elated*)
Son vecchio, ma robusto.　　　　　　I'm old, but sturdy.

RODOLFO, SCHAUNARD, COLLINE
(*with ironic gravity*)
Ei gongolava arzuto e pettorillo.　　　　He swaggered, perked, full-chestly.

MARCELLO
E a lui cedea la femminil virtù.　　　　And female virtue surrendered to him.

BENOIT
(confiding completely)

Timido in gioventù,	Shy as a young man,
ora me ne ripago!	now I'm getting my own back!
Si sa, è uno svago . . .	You know, it's a pastime . . .
qualche donnetta allegra . . . e un po . . .	some gay little woman . . . and a bit . . .

(indicates accentuated forms)

Non dico una balena	I don't say a whale
o un mappamondo	or a globe
o un viso tondo	or a round face
da luna piena,	like a full moon,
ma magra, proprio magra, no, poi no!	but thin, downright thin, no, no!
Le donne magre sono grattacapi	Thin women mean headaches
e spesso . . . sopracapi . . .	and often . . . horns . . .
e son piene di doglie —	and they're full of complaints —
per esempio mia moglie . . .	for example my wife . . .

(Marcello slams his fist on the table and stands up; the others imitate him. Benoit looks at them, amazed.)

MARCELLO
(terrifyingly)

Quest'uomo ha moglie	This man has a wife,
e sconcie voglie ha nel cor!	and he has obscene desires in his heart!

SCHAUNARD, COLLINE

Orror!	Horrors!

RODOLFO

E ammorba, e appesta	And he corrupts and infects
la nostra onesta magion!	our honest dwelling!

SCHAUNARD, COLLINE

Fuor!	Out!

MARCELLO

Si abbruci dello zucchero!	Let some sugar be burned!

COLLINE

Si discacci il reprobo!	Let the reprobate be driven out!

SCHAUNARD
(majestically)

È la morale offesa . . .	It is offended morality . . .

BENOIT
(aghast, tries in vain to speak)

Io di —	I sa —

MARCELLO

Silenzio!	Silence!

BENOIT

Io di —   I sa —

COLLINE

Silenzio!   Silence!

SCHAUNARD

. . . che vi scaccia!   . . . that drives you away!

BENOIT

Miei signori . . .   Gentlemen . . .

MARCELLO, SCHAUNARD, COLLINE

Silenzio! Via signore!   Silence! Away, sir!

THE FOUR
(*surrounding Benoit and pushing him toward the door*)

Via di qua!   Away from here!
E buona sera a vostra signori . . .   And good evening to Your Lordship.
Ah! ah! ah! ah!   Ha! ha! ha! ha!
(Benoit is driven out.)

MARCELLO
(*shutting the door*)

Ho pagato il trimestre.   I've paid the quarter.

SCHAUNARD

Al Quartiere Latin ci attende Momus.   Momus awaits us in the Latin Quarter.

MARCELLO

Viva chi spende.   Long live he who spends.

SCHAUNARD

Dividiamo il bottin!   Let's share the booty!
(They divide the coins left on the table.)

RODOLFO

Dividiam!   Let's share!

COLLINE

Dividiam!   Let's share!

MARCELLO
(*presenting a broken mirror to Colline*)

Là ci son beltà scese dal cielo.   There, there are beauties descended from
Or che sei ricco, bada alla decenza!   heaven.
Orso, ravviati il pelo.   Now that you're rich, pay heed to decency!
                                       Bear, tidy up your fur.

COLLINE

Farò la conoscenza   I'll make the acquaintance
la prima volta d'un barbitonsore.   of a beard barber for the first time.

Guidatemi al ridicolo	Lead me to the ridiculous
oltraggio d'un rasoio.	outrage of razor.
Andiam!	Let's go!

SCHAUNARD

Andiam!	Let's go!

MARCELLO

Andiam!	Let's go!

SCHAUNARD

Andiam!	Let's go!

COLLINE

Andiam!	Let's go!

RODOLFO

Io resto per terminar	I'm staying to finish
l'articolo di fondo del *Castoro*.	the leading article for *The Beaver*.

MARCELLO

Fa presto.	Hurry up.

RODOLFO

Cinque minuti. Conosco il mestier.	Five minutes. I know the trade.

COLLINE

T'aspetterem dabbasso dal portier.	We'll wait for you below, at the concierge's.

MARCELLO

Se tardi, udrai che coro!	If you delay, what a chorus you'll hear!

RODOLFO
(takes a light and opens the door: Marcello, Schaunard, Colline go out and descend the stairs)

Cinque minuti.	Five minutes.

SCHAUNARD

Taglia corta la coda al tuo Castor!	Cut your Beaver's tail short!

MARCELLO
(outside)

Occhio alla scala.	Keep your eye on the steps.
Tienti alla ringhiera.	Hold on to the railing.

RODOLFO
(still at the door, holding up the light)

Adagio!	Slowly!

COLLINE
(from outside)

È buio pesto!	It's pitch dark!

SCHAUNARD
(*from outside*)

Maledetto portier!   Damned concierge!
(*Sound of somebody tumbling down.*)

COLLINE

Accidenti!   Damn it!

RODOLFO

Colline, sei morto?   Colline, are you dead?

COLLINE
(*from below*)

Non ancor!   Not yet!

MARCELLO
(*from below*)

Vien presto!   Come quickly!
(*Rodolfo shuts the door, sets down the light, clears the table a bit, takes inkwell and paper, then sits down and starts writing, after having put out the other light which was left burning. But, finding no idea, he becomes nervous, tears up the paper and throws away the pen.*)

RODOLFO

Non sono in vena!   I'm not in the mood!
(*There is a timid knock at the door.*)

RODOLFO

Chi è là?   Who's there?

MIMI
(*from outside*)

Scusi.   Excuse me.

RODOLFO

Una donna!   A woman!

MIMI

Di grazia, mi s'è spento il lume.   Please, my light has gone out.

RODOLFO
(*runs to open*)

Ecco.   Here.

MIMI
(*in the doorway, with an extinguished light in her hand and a key*)

Vorrebbe?   Would you?

RODOLFO

S'accomodi un momento.   Come in a moment.

MIMI

Non occorre.   That's not necessary.

RODOLFO
(*insisting*)

La prego, entri.   Please, come in.
(*Mimi enters, she is seized with choking.*)

RODOLFO
(*concerned*)

Si sente male?   Do you feel ill?

MIMI

No . . . nulla.   No . . . nothing.

Rodolfo

Impallidisce!   You're pale!

MIMI
(*seized with coughing*)

Il respir . . . Quelle scale . . .   My breath . . . Those steps . . .
(*She faints, and Rodolfo is just in time to support her and ease her onto a chair, as from Mimi's hands both candlestick and key fall.*)

RODOLFO
(*embarrassed*)

Ed ora come faccio?   And now what shall I do?
(*goes and gets some water and sprinkles Mimi's face with it*)

Così!   Like that!
(*looking at her with great interest*)

Che viso d'ammalata!   What a sick girl's face!
(*Mimi comes to*)

Si sente meglio?   Do you feel better?

MIMI
(*in a faint voice*)

Sì.   Yes.

RODOLFO

Qui c'è tanto freddo. Segga vicino al fuoco.   It's so cold here. Sit near the fire.
(*makes Mimi stand and leads her to sit near the stove*)

Aspetti . . . un po' di vino.   Wait . . . a bit of wine.
(*runs to the table and takes bottle and glass from it*)

MIMI

Grazie.   Thanks.

RODOLFO
(*gives her the glass and pours her something to drink*)

A lei.   For you.

MIMI

Poco, poco.   Just a little.

RODOLFO

Cosi?   Like this?

MIMI

Grazie.   Thanks.
                                               (drinks)

RODOLFO
                                               (admiring her)
(Che bella bambina!)   (What a beautiful child!)

MIMI
                               (rising, looks for her candlestick)
Ora permetta che accenda il lume.   Now allow me to light my light.
Tutto è passato.   It's all over.

RODOLFO

Tanta fretta?   Such haste?

MIMI

Sì.   Yes.
                (Rodolfo lights Mimi's candle and gives it to her without a word.)

MIMI

Grazie. Buona sera.   Thanks. Good evening.

RODOLFO
            (accompanies her to the door, then immediately comes back to work)
Buona sera.   Good evening.

MIMI
                       (goes out, then reappears at the door)
Oh! sventata, sventata!   Oh, foolish, foolish me!
La chiave della stanza   Where have I left
dove l'ho lasciata?   the key to my room?

RODOLFO

Non stia sull'uscio;   Don't stand in the doorway;
il lume vacilla al vento.   the light is flickering in the wind.
                          (Mimi's light goes out.)

MIMI

Oh Dio! Torni ad accenderlo.   Oh, goodness! Light it again.
    (Rodolfo runs with his candle to relight Mimi's, but as he nears the door, his light also
goes out, and the room remains dark.)

RODOLFO

Oh Dio! Anche il mio s'è spento!   Oh, goodness! Mine has gone out, too!

MIMI

Ah! e la chiave ove sarà?   Ah! and where can the key be?
    (groping her way forward, she encounters the table and sets her candlestick on it)

RODOLFO

Buio pesto!   Pitch darkness!
(he is near the door; he closes it)

MIMI

Disgraziata!   Unlucky me!

RODOLFO

Ove sarà?   Where can it be?

MIMI
(confused)

Importuna è la vicina . . .   Your neighbor is a nuisance . . .

RODOLFO

Ma le pare . . .   Why, not at all . . .

MIMI

Importuna è la vicina . . .   Your neighbor is a nuisance . . .

RODOLFO

Cosa dice, ma le pare!   What are you saying? Not at all!

MIMI

Cerchi.   Search.

RODOLFO

Cerco.   I'm searching.
(Mimi searches for the key on the floor, dragging her feet. Rodolfo does the same and, having found the table, he also sets his candlestick on it, then goes back to searching for the key, touching the floor with his hands.)

MIMI

Ove sarà?   Where can it be?

RODOLFO
(finds it and pockets it)

Ah!   Ah!

MIMI

L'ha trovata?   Have you found it?

RODOLFO

No!   No!

MIMI

Mi parve . . .   It seemed to me . . .

RODOLFO

In verità!   Honestly!

MIMI

Cerca?   Are you searching?

RODOLFO

Cerco!   I'm searching!

(Led by Mimi's voice, Rodolfo pretends to search as he comes closer to her. Mimi bends
to the ground and searches, groping. Rodolfo's hand encounters Mimi's and grasps it.)

MIMI
(surprised, straightening up)
Ah!   Ah!

RODOLFO
(holding Mimi's hand)

Che gelida manina,   What an icy little hand,
se la lasci riscaldar.   let it be warmed.
Cercar che giova? — Al buio non so trova.   What's the good of searching? — We can't
                                                    find it in the dark.

Ma Per fortuna — è una notte di luna,   But luckily — it's a moonlit night,
e qui la luna l'abbiamo vicina.   and here we have the moon near.
Aspetti signorina,   Wait, miss,
le dirò con due parole   I'll tell you in two words
chi son, chi son e che faccio, come vivo.   who I am, who I am and what I do, how I
Vuole?   live.
                                                    Would you like that?

(Mimi is silent)

Chi son? Chi son? — Sono un poeta.   Who am I? Who am I? — I'm a poet.
Che cosa faccio? — Scrivo.   What do I do? — I write.
E come vivo? — Vivo.   And how do I live? — I live.
In povertà mia lieta   In my merry poverty
scialo da gran signore   I squander, like a great lord,
rime ed inni d'amore.   rhymes and anthems of love.
Per sogni e per chimere   When it comes to dreams and chimeras
e per castelli in aria   and castles in the air
l'anima ho milionaria.   I have a millionaire's soul.
Talor dal mio forziere   At times from my coffer
ruban tutti i gioielli   two thieves steal all my gems —
due ladri: gli occhi belli.   two beautiful eyes.
V'entrar con voi pur ora,   They entered with you just now,
ed i miei sogni usati   and my familiar dreams
e i bei sogni miei   and my beautiful dreams
tosto si dileguar!   quickly disappeared!
Ma il furto non m'accora   But the theft doesn't grieve me
poichè . . . poichè v'ha preso stanza   because . . . because sweet hope
la dolce speranza!   has taken their place!
Or che mi conoscete   Now that you know me,
parlate voi,   you speak,
deh! parlate. Chi siete?   ah! speak. Who are you!
Vi piaccia dir!   Please tell!

MIMI

Sì.   Yes.
Mi chiamano Mimì,   They call me Mimi,
ma il mio nome è Lucia.   but my name is Lucia.

La storia mia
è breve. A tela o a seta
ricamo in casa e fuori.
Son tranquilla e lieta
ed è mio svago
far gigli e rose.
Mi piaccion quelle cose
che han sì dolce malìa,
che parlano d'amor, di primavere,
che parlano di sogni e di chimere,
quelle cose che han nome poesia . . .
Lei m'intende?

My story
is brief. On canvas or on silk
I embroider at home and outside.
I'm calm and happy
and my pastime
is making lilies and roses.
I like those things
that have such sweet magic,
which speak of love, of springtimes,
which speak of dreams and of chimeras,
those things that are named poetry . . .
Do you understand me?

RODOLFO

Sì.

Yes.

MIMI

Mi chiamano Mimì,
il perchè non so.
Sola, mi fo
il pranzo da me stessa.
Non vado sempre a messa
ma prego assai il Signor.
Vivo sola, soletta,
là in una bianca cameretta:
guardo sui tetti e in cielo,
ma quando vien lo sgelo
il primo sole è mio,
il primo bacio dell'aprile è mio!
Il primo sole è mio!
Germoglia in un vaso una rosa . . .
Foglia a foglia la spio!
Così gentil è il profumo d'un fior!
Ma i fior ch'io faccio, ahimè! . . .
i fior ch'io faccio, ahimè, non hanno odore!
Altro di me non le saprei narrare:
sono la sua vicina
che la vien fuori d'ora a importunare.

They call me Mimi,
I don't know the reason.
Alone, I prepare
dinner by myself.
I don't always go to Mass,
but I pray much to the Lord.
I live alone, all alone,
there in a little white room.
I look out on roofs and into the heavens,
but when the thaw comes
the first sun is mine,
the first kiss of April is mine!
The first sun is mine!
A rose buds in a pot . . .
Leaf by leaf I observe it!
A flower's perfume is so delicate!
But the flowers that I make, alas,
the flowers I make, alas, have no odor!
I wouldn't know what else to tell you about
    me:
I'm your neighbor
who comes at the wrong hour to bother you.

SCHAUNARD
(*from the courtyard*)

Ehi! Rodolfo!

Hey! Rodolfo!

COLLINE

Rodolfo!

Rodolfo!
(*At his friends' cries, Rodolfo loses his patience.*)

MARCELLO

Olà! Non senti?
Lumaca!

Hola! Can't you hear?
Snail!

COLLINE

Poetucolo!   Poetaster!

SCHAUNARD

Accidenti al pigro!   Damn that lazy one!

(More and more impatient, Rodolfo gropes his way to the window and opens it, leaning out a little to answer his friends who are below in the courtyard. The moon's rays enter through the open window, thus lighting the room.)

RODOLFO
(at the window)

Scrivo ancor tre righe a volo.   I'll write another three lines in haste.

MIMI
(coming a little closer to the window)

Chi son?   Who are they?

RODOLFO

Amici.   Friends.

SCHAUNARD

Sentirai le tue.   You'll get an earful.

MARCELLO

Che te ne fai lì solo?   What are you doing up there alone?

RODOLFO

Non son solo. Siamo in due.   I'm not alone. We're two.
Andate da Momus, tenete il posto,   Go to Momus, keep us seats,
ci saremo tosto.   we'll be there soon.

(remains at the window, to make sure that his friends are going away)

MARCELLO, SCHAUNARD, COLLINE

Momus, Momus, Momus,   Momus, Momus, Momus,
zitti e discreti andiamocene via . . .   quiet and discreet, let us go away . . .

(going off)

MARCELLO

Trovò la poesia!   He found poetry!

SCHAUNARD, COLLINE

Momus, Momus, Momus!   Momus, Momus, Momus!

(Mimi is still near the window in such a way that the moon's rays illuminate her. Turning, Rodolfo sees Mimi as if wrapped in a halo of light, and he contemplates her, as if ecstatic.)

RODOLFO

O soave fanciulla!   Oh, sweet maiden!

MARCELLO

Trovò la poesia . . .   He found poetry . . .

RODOLFO

O dolce viso	Oh, gentle face
di mite circonfuso alba lunar,	bathed in a soft lunar dawn,
in te, ravviso	in you I recognize
il sogno ch'io vorrei sempre sognar!	the dream I would like to dream forever

MIMI

Ah! tu sol comandi, Amor!   Ah! Love, only you command!

RODOLFO

Fremon già nell'anima	Extreme sweetnesses
le dolcezze estreme.	already stir in the soul.

MIMI

Oh! come dolce scendono	Oh! how sweetly his compliments
le sue lusinghe al core . . .	descend to my heart . . .
Tu sol comandi, amor!	Only you command, love!

RODOLFO

Fremon dolcezze estreme,	Extreme sweetnesses stir,
nel bacio freme amor!	love stirs in a kiss!

(Rodolfo kisses her.)

MIMI
(freeing herself)

No, per pietà!   No please!

RODOLFO

Sei mia . . . !   You're mine . . . !

MIMI

V'aspettan gli amici . . .   Your friends are waiting for you . . .

RODOLFO

Già mi mandi via?   Are you sending me away already?

MIMI

Vorrei dir . . . ma non oso . . .   I'd like to say . . . but I don't dare . . .

RODOLFO

Di'.   Say it.

MIMI
(with charming slyness)

Se venissi con voi?   If I came with you?

RODOLFO

Che . . . ? Mimì!   What . . . ? Mimi!
(with enticing intention)

Sarebbe così dolce restar qui.	It would be so sweet to stay here.
C'è freddo fuori . . .	It's cold outside . . .

MIMI

Vi starò vicina . . . !   I'll be near you . . . !

RODOLFO

E al ritorno?   And on our return?

MIMI
(mischievous)

Curioso!   Curious!

RODOLFO

Dammi il braccio, mia piccina . . .   Give me your arm, my little one . . .

MIMI
(gives Rodolfo her arm)

Obbedisco, signor!   I obey, sir!

RODOLFO

Che m'ami . . . di' . . .   Say that you love me . . .

MIMI
(with abandon)

Io t'amo!   I love you!
                                             (They go out.)

MIMI, RODOLFO

Amor! Amor! Amor!   Love! Love! Love!

ACT TWO

In the Latin Quarter

Christmas Eve. A crossroads. Where the streets meet a kind of square is formed: shops, vendors of every kind. To one side, the Café Momus. Rodolfo and Mimi stroll in the crowd. Colline is near a rag shop, Schaunard at a junkshop is buying a pipe and a horn. Marcello is pushed here and there at the whim of the throng. The crowd is large and varied: bourgeois, soldiers, maidservants, boys, girls, students, seamstresses, gendarmes, etc. It is evening. The shops are decked with lanterns and glowing lights; a large lamp illuminates the entrance of the Café Momus. The café is very crowded so that some bourgeois are forced to sit at a table out in the open.

THE VENDORS
(at the doors of their shops)

Aranci, datteri!   Oranges, dates!
Caldi i marroni.   Hot chestnuts.
Ninnoli, croci, Torroni!   Trinkets, crosses. Nougat!
Panna montata!   Whipped cream!
Oh! la crostata!   Oh! the pie!
Caramelle!   Sweets!

THE CROWD

Quanta folla! Che chiasso!	What a crowd! What noise!

THE VENDORS

Fiori alle belle!	Flowers for the beauties!
Fringuelli, passeri!	Finches, sparrows!

THE CROWD

Su, corriam! Stringiti a me!	Come, let's run! Hold on tight to me!

THE VENDORS

Latte di cocco!	Coconut milk!
Panna, torroni!	Cream, nougat!

THE CROWD

Quanta folla! Su, partiam!	What a crowd! Come, let's leave!

AT THE CAFÉ

Presto qua!	Quickly, here!
Camerier! Un bicchier! Corri!	Waiter! A glass! Run!
Birra!	Beer!
Da ber!	Something to drink!

THE CROWD

Stringiti a me, ecc.	Hold on tight to me, etc.

THE VENDORS

Fringuelli e passeri, ecc.	Finches and sparrows, etc.

THE MAMMA

Emma, quando ti chiamo!	Emma, when I call you!

AT THE CAFÉ

Dunque? Un caffè!	Well? A coffee!
Da ber, ecc.	Something to drink, etc.

THE VENDORS

Voglio una lancia!	I want a lance!
Aranci, ecc.	Oranges, etc.

SCHAUNARD
(blows into the horn and produces some strange notes from it)

Falso questo re! Falso questo re!	This re is false! This re is false!

(bargains with the junk dealer)

Pipa e corno quant'è?	How much are pipe and horn?

(Rodolfo and Mimi, arm in arm, cross through the crowd, heading for the milliner's shop.)

COLLINE
(at the shop of the rag dealer, who is mending for him the lapel of a long coat that he has just bought)

E un poco usato . . .	It's a bit worn . . .

RODOLFO

Andiam . . .   Let's go . . .

MIMI

Andiam per la cuffietta?   Are we going for the bonnet?

COLLINE

. . . ma è serio e a buon mercato . . .   . . . but it's sober and cheap . . .
(He pays and, with the proper balance, distributes the books he is laden with in the many
pockets of the long coat.)

RODOLFO

Tienti al mio braccio stretta . . .   Hold tight to my arm . . .

MIMI

A te mi stringo . . .   I'm holding tight to you . . .

MIMI, RODOLFO

Andiamo!   Let's go!
(They enter the milliner's.)

MARCELLO

(all alone in the midst of the crowd, with a package under his arm, ogling the girls who are
almost thrown into his arms by the crowd)
Io pur mi sento in vena di gridar: I also feel in the mood to shout:
Chi vuol, donnine allegre, un po 'd'amor?   You merry women, who wants a bit of love?

THE VENDORS

Datteri! Trote!   Dates! Trout!
Prugne di Tours!   Plums from Tours!

MARCELLO

Facciamo insieme . . .   Let's play together . . .
facciamo a vendere e a comprar!   let's play together at selling and buying!

A VENDOR

Prugne di Tours!   Plums from Tours!

MARCELLO

Io dò ad un soldo il vergine mio cuor!   I'll give for a penny my virgin heart!
(The crowd spreads out along the adjacent streets. The shops are full of customers who
come and go. In the café also constant motion of people who enter and go off, some along
one street, some another. After the first moment of confusion is past, the crossroads becomes
a place of constant, very animated comings and goings.)

SCHAUNARD

(comes and saunters in front of the Café Momus, waiting for his friends there; meanwhile,
armed with the huge pipe and the hunting horn, he looks at the crowd curiously)
Fra spintoni e pestate accorrendo affretta Amid shoves and trampling the crowd has-
la folla e si diletta   tens,
nel provar gioie matte . . . insoddis-   running, and enjoys itself
    fatte . . .   in experiencing mad . . . unsatisfied . . .
                                                pleasures . . .

The Women Vendors

| Ninnoli, spillette! | Trinkets, brooches! |
| Datteri e caramelle! | Dates and sweets! |

The Vendors

| Fiori alle belle! | Flowers for the beauties! |

Colline

(comes to the meeting place wrapped in the big coat, which is too long for him and makes folds around him like a Roman toga; triumphantly waving an old book)

| Copia rara, anzi unica, | Rare, indeed unique copy: |
| la grammatica Runica! | the Runic grammar! |

Schaunard

(who comes up at that moment behind Colline, with compassion for him)

| Uomo onesto! | Upright man! |

Marcello

(arrives at the Café Momus and finds Schaunard and Colline there)

| A cena! | To supper! |

Schaunard, Colline

| Rodolfo? | Rodolfo? |

Marcello

| Entrò da una modista. | He went into a milliner's. |

(Marcello, Schaunard, and Colline go into the Café Momus, but they come out almost at once, indignant at that great crowd that is noisily jammed inside. They carry out a table, and a waiter follows them, not at all surprised at their bizarre idea of wanting to sup outdoors. The bourgeois at the nearby table, irritated by the racket that the three friends are making, after a little while stand up and go off. Rodolfo and Mimi come out of the shop.)

Rodolfo

| Vieni, gli amici aspettano. | Come, my friends are waiting. |

Some Vendors

| Panna montata! | Whipped cream! |

Mimi

| Mi sta ben questa cuffietta rosa? | Does this pink bonnet become me? |

Gamins

| Latte di cocco! | Coconut milk! |

The Vendors

| Oh! la crostata! Panna montata! | Oh! the pie! Whipped cream! |

At the Café

| Camerier! Un bicchier! | Waiter! A glass! |

Rodolfo

| Sei brunna e quel color ti dona. | You're dark and that color becomes you. |

AT THE CAFÉ

Presto, olà!	Quickly, hola!
Ratafià!	Ratafia!

MIMI
(looking regretfully towards the milliner's shop)

Bel vezzo di corallo!	Beautiful coral necklace!

RODOLFO

Ho uno zio milionario.	I have a millionaire uncle.
Se fa senno il buon Dio	If the good Lord comes to His senses
voglio comprarti un vezzo assai più bel!	I want to buy you a much more beautiful necklace!

GAMINS

Ah! ah! ah!	Ha! ha! ha!

SERVANT-GIRLS, STUDENTS

Ah! ah!	Ha! ha!

BOURGEOIS

Facciam coda alla gente!	Let's follow the people!
Ragazze, state attente!	Girls, watch out!

THE VENDORS

Oh la crostata!	Oh, the pie!

THE CROWD

Che chiasso! quanta folla!	What noise! What a crowd!

THE VENDORS

Panna montata!	Whipped cream!

BOURGEOIS

Pigliam via Mazzarino!	Let's take Rue Mazarine!
Io soffoco, partiamo!	I'm suffocating, let's leave!
Vedi? Il caffè è vicin!	You see? The café is near!
Andiam là da Momus!	Let's go there, to Momus!

THE VENDORS

Aranci, datteri, ecc.	Oranges, dates, etc.

RODOLFO
(suddenly, seeing Mimi looking, he also turns, suspiciously)

Chi guardi?	Whom are you looking at?

COLLINE

Odio il profano volgo	I hate the vulgar crowd
al par d'Orazio.	as Horace did.

MIMI

Sei geloso?	Are you jealous?

RODOLFO

All'uom felice
sta il sospetto accanto.

Suspicion is always near
the happy man.

SCHAUNARD

Ed io quando mi sazio
vo' abbondanza di spazio . . .

And I, when I sate myself,
want an abundance of space . . .

MIMI

Sei felice?

Are you happy?

MARCELLO
(to the waiter)

Vogliamo una cena prelibata.

We want a choice supper.

RODOLFO

Ah sì, tanto!

Ah, yes, so much!

MARCELLO
(to the waiter)

Lesto!

Quickly!

SCHAUNARD

Per molti!

For many!

RODOLFO

E tu?

And you?

MIMI

Sì, tanto!

Yes, so much!

SERVANT-GIRLS, STUDENTS

Là da Momus!
Andiam! Andiam!

There, at Momus!
Let's go! Let's go!

MARCELLO, SCHAUNARD, COLLINE

Lesto!

Quickly!
(Rodolfo and Mimi join the friends.)

PARPIGNOL
(from the distance, approaching)

Ecco i giocattoli di Parpignoll

Here are Parpignol's toys!

RODOLFO
(arrives, with Mimi)

Due posti.

Two seats.

COLLINE

Finalmente!

At last!

RODOLFO

Eccoci qui.	Here we are.
Questa è Mimì, gaia fioraia.	This is Mimi, a gay flower maker.
Il suo venir completa	Her coming completes
la bella compagnia,	the fine company,
perchè . . . perchè son io il poeta	because . . . because I am the poet,
essa la poesia.	she, poetry.
Dal mio cervel sbocciano i canti,	From my brain blossom songs,
dalle sue dita sbocciano i fior,	from her fingers blossom flowers,
dall'anime esultanti	from exultant souls
sboccia l'amor, sboccia l'amour!	blossoms love, blossoms love!

MARCELLO, SCHAUNARD, COLLINE

Ah! ah! ah! ah!	Ha! ha! ha! ha!

MARCELLO
(ironic)

Dio che concetti rari!	God, what rare conceits!

COLLINE

Digna est intrari.	*Digna est intrari.*

SCHAUNARD

Ingrediat si necessit.	*Ingrediat si necessit.*

COLLINE

Io non dò che un *accessit.*	I give only an *accessit.*

PARPIGNOL

Ecco i giocattoli di Parpignol!	Here are Parpignol's toys!

(Rodolfo seats Mimi. All sit. The waiter returns, presenting the list of dishes.)

COLLINE
(with romantic emphasis to the waiter)

Salame . . .	Salami . . .

(From Rue Dauphine a little cart appears, all frills and flowers, illuminated with paper lanterns. The man pushing it is Parpignol.)

BOYS, GIRLS

Parpignol! Parpignol! Parpignol! Parpignol!	Parpignol! Parpignol! Parpignol! Parpignol!
Ecco Parpignol! Parpignol! Parpignol!	Here's Parpignol! Parpignol! Parpignol!
Col carretto tutto fior!	With his cart all flowers!
Ecco Parpignol!	Here's Parpignol!
Parpignol! Parpignol! Parpignol!	Parpignol! Parpignol! Parpignol!
Voglio la tromba, il cavallin,	I want the trumpet, the little horse,
Il tambur, tamburel,	the drum, the tambourine,
voglio il cannon, voglio il frustin,	I want the cannon, I want the whip,
dei soldati i drappel.	the troop of soldiers.

(The waiter presents the menu to the four friends; it passes around, through the hands of all, looked at with a kind of wonder and profoundly analyzed.)

SCHAUNARD

Cervo arrosto!   Roast stag!

MARCELLO

Un tacchino!   A turkey!

SCHAUNARD

Vin del Reno!   Rhine wine!

COLLINE

Vin da tavola!   Table wine!

SCHAUNARD

Aragosta senza crosta!   Lobster without the shell

MAMMAS
(run up at the cries of the children, try in vain to take them away from Parpignol and scold angrily)

Ah! razza di furfanti indemoniati,   Ah! bunch of devilish rascals,
che ci venite a fare in questo loco?   what are you coming to this place for?
A casa, a letto! Via brutti sguaiati,   Home, to bed! Off, you nasty bawlers,
gli scappellotti vi parranno poco!   Slaps will seem little to you!
A casa, a letto, razza di furfanti,   Home, to bed, you bunch of rascals,
a letto!   to bed!

A BOY

Vo' la tromba, il cavallin!   I want the trumpet, the little horse!
(The children don't want to go away. One of them bursts into tears, his mother grabs him by one ear and he starts shouting that he wants Parpignol's toys. The Mammas, weakening, buy. Parpignol goes off down the Rue de l'Ancienne Comédie, followed by the boys who make a great racket with drums, tambourines, and little trumpets.)

RODOLFO
(softly, to Mimi)

E tu Mimì, che vuoi?   And you, Mimi, what do you want?

MIMI

La crema.   The custard.

SCHAUNARD
(to the waiter)

E gran sfarzo. C'è una dama!   It's great pomp. There's a lady!

BOYS, GIRLS

Viva Parpignol, Parpignol, Parpignol, Parpig-   Long live Parpignol, Parpignol, Parpignol,
nol!   Parpignol!
Il tambur, tamburel,   The drum, tambourine,
dei soldati il drappel!   the troop of soldiers!

MARCELLO
(gallantly, to Mimi)

Signorina Mimì, che dono raro	Miss Mimi, what rare gift
le ha fatto il suo Rodolfo?	has our Rodolfo made you?

MIMI

Una cuffietta	A lace bonnet,
a pizzi, tutta rosa, ricamata;	all pink, embroidered;
coi miei capelli bruni ben si fonde.	it goes well with my dark hair.
Da tanto tempo tal cuffietta è cosa desïatal!	Such a bonnet is a thing I've wanted for such
Ed egli ha letto quel che il core asconde . . .	a time!
Ora colui che legge dentro a un cuore	And he read what the heart hides . . .
sa l'amore . . . ed è . . . lettore.	Now he who reads in a heart
	knows love . . . and he is . . . a reader.

SCHAUNARD

Esperto professore . . .	An expert professor . . .

COLLINE

. . . che ha già diplome e non son armi prime	. . . who already has diplomas and his rhymes
le sue rime.	are not novice weapons.

SCHAUNARD

Tanto che sembra ver ciò ch'egli esprime!	So much so that what he expresses seems true!

MARCELLO
(looking at Mimi)

O bella età d'inganni e d'utopie!	Oh, beautiful age of deceits and utopias, one
si crede, spera, e tutto bello appare.	believes, hopes, and all seems beautiful.

RODOLFO

La più divina delle poesie	The most divine of poems,
è quella, amico, che c'insegna amare!	my friend, is the one that teaches us to love!

MIMI

Amare è dolce ancora più del miele,	To love is still sweeter than honey,
più del miele!	than honey!

MARCELLO

Secondo il palato e miele, o fiele!	According to the palate, it's honey, or gall!

MIMI
(surprised, to Rodolfo)

O Dio! l'ho offeso!	Oh, goodness, I've offended him!

RODOLFO

E in lutto, o mia Mimì.	He's in mourning, my Mimi!

SCHAUNARD, COLLINE
(to change the subject)

Allegri, e un *toast!*	Be happy. And a toast!

MARCELLO

Qua del liquor!	Some liquor here!

MIMI, RODOLFO, MARCELLO

E via i pensier,	Away with thoughts,
alti i bicchier!	glasses high!

ALL

Beviam . . . ! Beviam!	Let's drink . . . ! Let's drink!

MARCELLO
(who has seen Musetta in the distance, interrupts, shouting)

Ch'io beva del tossico!	Let me drink some poison!

(sinks down on the chair)

(At the corner of Rue Mazarine a very beautiful lady appears, with a merry, flirtatious manner, a provocative smile. After her comes a pompous and affected old man. The lady, at the sight of the friends' table, slows down her pace. One would say that she had arrived at the goal of her journey.)

RODOLFO, SCHAUNARD, COLLINE
(at Marcello's exclamation, turn and exclaim)

Oh!	Oh!

MARCELLO

Essa!	She!

RODOLFO, SCHAUNARD, COLLINE

Musetta!	Musetta!

(The friends, their eyes filled with compassion, look at Marcello, who has turned pale. The waiter begins to serve. Schaunard and Colline keep looking discreetly in the direction of Musetta and speak of her. Marcello feigns the maximum indifference. Rodolfo alone has eyes and thoughts only for Mimi.)

THE MAMMAS—SHOPKEEPERS
(as they are retiring suddenly stop near their shops to look at a beautiful lady. Amazed at recognizing her as Musetta, they whisper among themselves, pointing her out to one another)

To'! Lei!	Well! She!
Sì! To'!	Yes! Well!
Lei! Musetta! Tornata!	She! Musetta! Come back!
Siamo in auge!	We're flourishing!
Che toeletta!	What a toilette!

ALCINDORO DE MITONNEAUX
(breathless, overtakes Musetta)

Come un facchino . . . correr di qua . . . di là . . .	Like a porter . . . running here . . . there . . .
No! no! non ci sta . . .	No! no! It isn't done . . .

MUSETTA

Vien, Lulù!	Come, Lulù!

ALCINDORO

Non ne posso più . . .   I can't stand any more . . .

MUSETTA

Vien, Lulù!   Come, Lulù!

ALCINDORO

Non ne posso più!   I can't stand any more!

SCHAUNARD

Quel brutto coso mi par che sudi!   It seems to me that ugly object is sweating!
   (*The beautiful lady, not minding the old man, goes toward the Café Momus and takes a
seat at the table left free.*)

ALCINDORO

Come! qui fuori? qui?   What! Outside here? Here?

MUSETTA

Siedi, Lulù!   Sit, Lulù
      (*Alcindoro sits down, irritated, turning up the collar of his overcoat.*)

ALCINDORO

Tali nomignoli,   Such pet names,
prego, serbateli   please, save them
al tu per tu!   for when we're alone!
         (*A waiter has come over eagerly and is preparing the table.*)

MUSETTA

Non farmi il Barbablù!   Don't act like Bluebeard with me!

COLLINE
(*examining the old man*)

È il vizio contegnoso . . .   He is sedate Vice . . .

MARCELLO
(*with contempt*)

Colla casta Susanna!   . . . with the chaste Susanna!

MIMI
(*to Rodolfo*)

È pur ben vestita!   Still, she's well dressed.

RODOLFO

Gli angeli vanno nudi.   The angels go naked.

MIMI
(*addresses Rodolfo, curious*)

La conosci? Chi è?   You know her? Who is she?

MARCELLO

Domandatelo a me.   Ask me that.
Il suo nome e Musetta;   Her name is Musetta;

cognome: Tentazione!   last name: Temptation!
Per sua vocazione   As her vocation
fa la rosa dei venti;   she plays the compass card;
gira e muta soventi   she turns and changes often
d'amanti e d'amore.   her lovers and her love.
E come la civetta   And like the owl *
è uccello sanguinario;   she's a sanguinary bird;
il suo cibo ordinario   her ordinary food
è il cuore . . . ! Mangia il cuore!   is the heart . . . ! She eats the heart!
Per questo io non ne ho più!   That's why I no longer have any!

MUSETTA
(struck at seeing that the friends are not looking at her)
(Marcello mi vide . . .   (Marcello saw me . . .
e non mi guarda, il vile!   and he isn't looking at me, the coward!
Quel Schaunard che ride!   That Schaunard, who laughs!
Mi fan tutti una bile!   They all make me cross!
Se potessi picchiar!   If I could slap!
Se potessi graffiar!   If I could scratch!
Ma non ho sotto man   But all I have at hand
che questo pellican!   is this pelican!
Aspetta!)   Wait!)
(calls the waiter, who has gone off)
Ehi! Camerier!   Hey! Waiter!

MARCELLO
(to his friends, hiding the emotion that is overcoming him)
Passatemi il ragù!   Pass me the ragout!
(The waiter rushes up. Musetta takes a plate and sniffs it.)

MUSETTA
Ehi! Camerier! Questo piatto   Hey! Waiter! This plate
ha una puzza di rifritto!   stinks of stale fat!
(throws the plate on the ground; the waiter hastens to collect the pieces)

ALCINDORO
(tries to calm her)
No, Musetta . . .   No, Musetta . . .
Zitto, zitto!   Hush, hush!

MUSETTA
(angry, still looking at Marcello)
(Non si volta!)   (He won't turn around!)

ALCINDORO
Zitto, zitto!   Hush, hush!
Zitto! Modi, garbo!   Hush! Manners! Tact!

MUSETTA
(Ah, non si volta!)   (Ah, he won't turn around!)

* TRANSLATOR'S NOTE: the Italian word *civetta* means both "owl" and "coquette."

ALCINDORO

A chi parli?   To whom are you speaking?

COLLINE

Questo pollo è un poema!   This chicken is a poem!

MUSETTA

(Ora lo batto, lo batto!)   (Now I'll hit him, I'll hit him!)

ALCINDORO

Con chi parli?   With whom are you speaking?

MUSETTA
(irked)

Al cameriere! Non seccar!   To the waiter! Don't bother me!

SCHAUNARD

Il vino è prelibato!   The wine is choice!

MUSETTA

Voglio fare il mio piacere . . .   I want to do what I please . . .

ALCINDORO

Parla pian!   Speak softly!

MUSETTA

Vo' far quel che mi pare!   I want to do as I like!

ALCINDORO
(takes the menu from the waiter and prepares to order the supper)

Parla pian, parla pian!   Speak softly, speak softly!

MUSETTA

Non seccar!   Don't bother me!

STUDENTS AND SEAMSTRESSES
(crossing the stage)

Guarda, guarda chi si vede!   Look, look who's to be seen!
Proprio lei, Musetta!   It's she all right, Musetta!
Con quel vecchio che balbetta,   With that old man who stammers,
proprio lei, Musetta! Ah! ah! ah! It's she all right, Musetta! Ha! ha! ha!

MUSETTA

(Che sia geloso di questa mummia?)   (Could he be jealous of this mummy?)

ALCINDORO

La convenienza . . . il grado . . . la virtù!   Decorum . . . rank . . . virtue!

MUSETTA

(Vediam se mi resta   (Let's see if I still have
tanto poter su lui da farlo cedere!)   enough power over him to make him give
                                    way!)

SCHAUNARD
La commedia è stupenda!   The comedy is stupendous!

MUSETTA
(looking at Marcello, in a loud voice)
Tu non mi guardi!   You aren't looking at me!

ALCINDORO
Vedi bene che ordino!   You can see clearly that I'm ordering!

SCHAUNARD
La commedia è stupenda!   The comedy is stupendous!

COLLINE
Stupenda!   Stupendous!

RODOLFO
(to Mimi)
Sappi per tuo governo   You should know, for your guidance,
che non darei perdono in sempiterno!   that I would never forgive!

SCHAUNARD
(to Colline)
Essa all'un parla   She speaks to the one
perchè l'altro intenda.   that the other may understand.

MIMI
(to Rodolfo)
Io t'amo tanto,   I love you so much,
a sono tutta tua . . . !   and I'm all yours . . . !
Chè mi parli di perdono?   Why do you speak to me of forgiveness?

COLLINE
(to Schaunard)
E l'altro invan crudel   And the other, cruel in vain,
finge di non capir, ma sugge miel!   pretends not to understand, but sucks honey!

MUSETTA
Ma il tuo cuore martella.   But your heart is pounding.

ALCINDORO
Parla piano.   Speak softly.

MUSETTA
Ma il tuo cuore martella!   But your heart is pounding!

ALCINDORO
Piano, piano!   Softly, softly!

MUSETTA
(flirtatious, turning meaningfully toward Marcello, who is beginning to writhe)
Quando me'n vo . . .   When I go along . . .

quando me'n vo soletta per la via
la gente sosta e mira,
e la bellezza mia
tutta ricerca in me, ricerca in me
da capo a piè . . .

when I go along, by myself, on the street
people stop and look,
and they seek in me, they seek in me
all my beauty
from head to foot . . .

MARCELLO
(to his friends)
    Tie me to the chair.

Legatemi alla seggiola.

ALCINDORO
    What will those people say?

Quella gente che dirà?

MUSETTA
    . . . and then I savor the subtle

. . . ed assaporo allor la bramosia
sottil che da gl'occhi traspira
e dai palesi vezzi intender sa
alle occulte beltà.
Così l'effluvio del desìo
tutta m'aggira,
felice mi fa . . . felice mi fa!

    longing that breathes from their eyes
and which knows how to appreciate
under the obvious charms the hidden beau-
    ties.
And thus the flow of desire
surrounds me completely,
it makes me happy . . . it makes me happy!

ALCINDORO
    That scurrilous song

Quel canto scurrile
mi muove la bile!
Mi muove la bile!

    rouses my anger!
It rouses my anger!

MUSETTA
    And you know, who remember and suffer,

E tu che sai, che memori e ti struggi,
da me tanto rifuggi?
So ben: le angoscie tue non le vuoi dir,

non le vuoi dir, so ben,
ma ti senti morir!

    do you flee from me so?
I know well: you don't want to tell your suf-
    ferings,
you don't want to tell them, I know well,
but you feel you're dying!

MIMI
    I see well . . . that that poor girl

Io vedo ben . . . che quella poveretta
tutta invaghita ell'è,
tutta invaghita di Marcel,
tutta invaghita ell'è!

    is all infatuated,
she's all infatuated with Marcello,
she's all infatuated!

ALCINDORO
    What will those people say!

Quella gente che dirà!

RODOLFO
(to Mimi)
    Marcello one day loved her,

Marcello un dì l'amò,
la fraschetta l'abbandonò
per poi darsi a miglior vita.

    the coquette abandoned him
to devote herself then to a better life.

	SCHAUNARD
Ah Marcello cederà!	Ah, Marcello will give way!
	COLLINE
Chi sa mai quel che avverrà!	Who knows what will happen!
	SCHAUNARD
Trovan dolce al pari il laccio . . .	They find the noose equally sweet . . .
	COLLINE
Santi numi, in simil briga . . .	Ye gods, in such a fix . . .
	SCHAUNARD
. . . chi lo tende e chi ci dà.	. . . the one who extends it and the one who's trapped.
	COLLINE
. . . mai Colline intopperà!	. . . Colline will never fall!
	MUSETTA
(Ah! Marcello smania, Marcello è vinto!)	(Ah, Marcello's raving, Marcello's defeated!)
	ALCINDORO
Parla pian!	Speak softly!
	MIMI
Quell'infelice mi muove a pietà.	That unhappy man moves me to pity.
	ALCINDORO
Zitta, zitta!	Hush, hush!
	COLLINE
(Essa è bella, io non son cieco . . .	(She's beautiful, I'm not blind . . .
	MIMI
	(to Rodolfo)
T'amo!	I love you!
	RODOLFO
Mimì!	Mimi!
	SCHAUNARD
Quel bravaccio a momenti cederà! Stupenda è la commedia! Marcello cederà!	That swaggerer will give way any minute! The comedy is stupendous! Marcello will give way!
	(to Colline)
Se tal vaga persona ti trattasse a tu per tu, la tua scienza brontolona manderesti a Belzebù!	If such a lovely person were to speak intimately with you, you'd send your grumpy science to Beelzebub!

MUSETTA
(toward Marcello)

So ben: le angoscie tue non le vuoi dir.	I know well: you don't want to tell your sufferings.
Ah! ma ti senti morir.	Ah! but you feel you're dying.

(to Alcindoro)

Io voglio fare il mio piacere!	I want to do as I please!
Voglio far quel che mi par . . .	I want to do what I like . . .
Non seccar! non seccar!	Don't annoy me! Don't annoy me!

MIMI

Quell'infelice mi muove a pietà!	That unhappy man moves me to pity!
l'amor ingeneroso è tristo amor!	Ungenerous love is sad love!
È fiacco amore, ah, ah, mi muove,	It's weak love, ah, ah, he moves me,
mi muove a pietà!	he moves me to pity!

RODOLFO

È fiacco amor quel che le offese	Weak is that love which cannot
vendicar non sa!	avenge its insults!
Non risorge spento amor!	Dead love doesn't rise again!
È fiacco amore quel che le offese	Weak is that love which cannot
vendicar non sa!	avenge its insults!

COLLINE

. . . ma piaccionmi assai più	. . . but I like much more
una pipa e un testo greco,	a pipe and a Greek text,
mi piaccion assai più!	I like them much more!
Essa è bella, non son cieco,	She's beautiful, I'm not blind,
ma piaccionmi assai più	but I like much more
una pipa e un testo greco!)	a pipe and a Greek text!)

ALCINDORO

Modi, garbo! Zitta, zitta!	Manners, tact! Hush, hush!

MUSETTA

Non seccar!	Don't bother me!
(Or convien liberarsi del vecchio!)	(Now it's best to be freed of the old man!)

(pretending to feel a sharp pain)

Ahi!	Ouch!

ALCINDORO

Che c'è?	What is it?

MUSETTA

Qual dolore, qual bruciore!	What pain, what burning!

ALCINDORO

Dove?	Where?

MUSETTA

Al piè!	In my foot!
Sciogli, slaccia — rompi, straccia!	Loosen, unlace — break, tear!
Te ne imploro . . .	I implore you . . .
Laggiù c'è un calzolaio.	There's a cobbler over there.
Corri, presto! Ne voglio un altro paio.	Run, quickly! I want another pair.
Ahi! che fitta! Corri, va, corri!	Ouch! what a pain! Run, go, run!
presto, va, va!	Quickly, go, go!

MARCELLO
(greatly moved)

Gioventù mia, tu non sei morta	My youth, you're not dead,
nè di te morto è il sovvenir!	nor is the memory of you dead!
Se tu battessi alla mia porta	If you knocked at my door,
t'andrebbe il mio core ad aprir . . .	my heart would go to open to you . . .
ad aprir!	to open!

SCHAUNARD, COLLINE

La commedia è stupenda,	The comedy is stupendous!
la commedia è stupenda!	The comedy is stupendous!

MIMI

Io vedo ben, ell'è invaghita di Marcello!	I see well: she is infatuated with Marcello!

RODOLFO

Io vedo ben . . . la commedia è stupenda!	I see well . . . the comedy is stupendous!

ALCINDORO

Imprudente! Quella gente che dirà?	Imprudent girl! What will those people say?
Ma il mio grado! Vuoi ch'io comprometta?	But my rank! You want me to be compromised?
Aspetta!	Wait!

(Desperate, he takes the shoe and rapidly stuffs it into his vest, and majestically buttons up his suit. Then, for fear of greater scandal, he runs hastily toward the cobbler's shop.)

Musetta! Vo.	Musetta! I go.

MUSETTA
(as soon as Alcindoro has left, rises and throws herself into the arms of Marcello, who can resist no longer)

Marcello!	Marcello!

MARCELLO

Sirena!	Siren!

SCHAUNARD

Siamo all'ultima scena!	We're at the last scene!

(A waiter brings the bill.)

RODOLFO, SCHAUNARD, COLLINE

Il conto?!	The bill?!

SCHAUNARD

Così presto?   So soon?

COLLINE

Chi l'ha richiesto?   Who asked for it?

SCHAUNARD

Vediam!   Let's see!

(He has the bill given him; it moves among the friends.)

RODOLFO, COLLINE

Caro!   Expensive!

RODOLFO, SCHAUNARD, COLLINE

Fuori il danaro!   Out with the money!

SCHAUNARD

Colline, Rodolfo e tu Marcel?   Colline, Rodolfo, and you, Marcello?

MARCELLO

Siamo all'asciutto!   We're broke!

SCHAUNARD

Come?   What?

RODOLFO

Ho trenta soldi in tutto!   I have thirty *sous* in all!

MARCELLO, SCHAUNARD, COLLINE

Come? Non ce n'è più?   What? Isn't there any more?

SCHAUNARD

(terrifying)

Ma il mio tesoro ov'è?   Where is my treasure?

(They put their hands in their pockets; they're empty. Nobody can explain the rapid disappearance of Schaunard's money. Surprised, they look at one another. Meanwhile, very far away, the military tattoo is heard, which is slowly coming nearer. People run in from all sides, looking and running here and there to see from which direction it is coming.)

GAMINS

La ritirata!   The tattoo!

BOURGEOIS

La ritirata!   The tattoo!

SEAMSTRESSES, STUDENTS

La ritirata!   The tattoo!

GAMINS

S'avvicinan per di qua?   Are they coming along here?

MUSETTA
(to the waiter)

Il mio conto date a me.   Give me my bill.

SEAMSTRESSES, STUDENTS

No, di là!   No, from there!

GAMINS

S'avvicinan per di là!   They're coming from there!

SEAMSTRESSES, STUDENTS

Vien di qua!   It's coming from here!

GAMINS

No, vien di là!   No, it's coming from there!

MUSETTA
(to the waiter, who hands her the bill)

Bene!   Very well!

BOURGEOIS, VENDORS

Largo! largo!   Make way! Make way!

SOME CHILDREN
(from the windows)

Voglio veder! voglio sentir!   I want to see! I want to hear!

MUSETTA

Presto sommate quello con questo!   Quickly add that one to this one!

CHILDREN

Mamma, voglio veder!   Mamma, I want to see!
Papà, voglio sentir!   Papa, I want to hear!

MAMMAS

Lisetta, vuoi tacer!   Lisetta, will you be quiet?
Tonio, la vuoi finir!   Tonio, will you stop it?

MUSETTA

Papa il signor che stava qui con me! The gentleman who was here with me will pay!

RODOLFO, MARCELLO, SCHAUNARD, COLLINE

Paga il signor!   The gentleman pays!

MAMMAS

Vuoi tacer, vuoi finir?   Will you be quiet? Will you stop it?

SEAMSTRESSES, STUDENTS

S'avvicinano di qua!   They're approaching from here!

THE CROWD

Sì, di qua!	Yes, from here!

GAMINS

Come sarà arrivata	As soon as it's arrived,
la seguiremo al passo!	we'll follow it at its pace!

COLLINE

Paga il signor!	The gentleman pays!

SCHAUNARD

Paga il signor!	The gentleman pays!

MARCELLO

Il signor!	The gentleman!

MUSETTA
(setting the two bills, added together, at Alcindoro's place)

E dove s'è seduto	And where he was seated
ritrovi il mio saluto!	let him find my farewell!

BOURGEOIS

In quel rullìo tu senti	In that drumming you hear
la patria maestà!	the nation's majesty!

RODOLFO, MARCELLO, SCHAUNARD, COLLINE

E dove s'è seduto	And where he was seated
ritrovi il suo saluto!	let him find her farewell!

THE CROWD

Largo, largo, eccoli qua! In fila!	Make way, make way, here they are! Line up!

GAMINS

Ohè! attenti eccoli qua! In fila!	Hey! Watch, here they are! Line up!

MARCELLO

Giunge la ritirata! Che il vecchio non ci veda	The tattoo's coming! Don't let the old man
fuggir con la sua preda!	see us
	flee with his prey!

COLLINE

Che il vecchio non ci veda	Don't let the old man see us
fuggir con la sua preda!	flee with his prey!

RODOLFO

Giunge la ritirata!	The tattoo's coming!

MARCELLO, SCHAUNARD, COLLINE

Quella folla serrata	Let that packed crowd
il nascondiglio appresti!	prepare the hiding place!

(The tattoo crosses the stage.)

The Crowd

Ecco il tambur maggiore!	Here's the drum major!
Più fier d'un antico guerrier!	Haughtier than an ancient warrior!
Il tambur maggior!	The drum major!

Mimi, Musetta, Rodolfo, Marcello, Schaunard, Colline

Lesti, lesti, lesti!	Quickly, quickly, quickly!

The Crowd

I Zappator, I Zappatori olà!	The Pioneers, the Pioneers, hola!
Ecco il tambur maggior!	Here's the drum major!
Pare un general!	He looks like a general!
La ritirata è qua!	The tattoo is here!
Eccolo là! Il bel tambur maggior!	There he is! The handsome drum major!
La canna d'or, tutto splendor!	The gold baton, all splendor!
Che guarda, passa, va!	He looks, passes, and goes on!
Tutto splendor! Di Francia è il più bell'uom!	All Splendor! He's the most handsome man in France!
Il bel tambur maggior! Eccolo là!	The handsome drum major! There he is!
Che guarda, pass, va!	He looks, passes, and goes on!

Rodolfo, Marcello, Schaunard, Colline

Viva Musetta! Cuor birichin!	Long live Musetta! Roguish heart!
Gloria ed onor, onor e gloria	Glory and honor, honor and glory
del quartier latin!	of the Latin Quarter!

(*Musetta, unable to walk because only one foot is shod, is lifted into the arms of Marcello and Colline. The crowd, seeing Musetta borne triumphantly, seizes this excuse to give her noisy ovations. Marcello and Colline with Musetta take up the rear of the tattoo. Rodolfo and Mimi, arm in arm, follow them, and Schaunard with his horn to his lips. Then students and seamstresses, gaily leaping, then boys, bourgeois, women, who fall into the marching step. All this crowd goes off in the background, following the tattoo and singing. Alcindoro, with a well-wrapped pair of shoes, comes back toward the Café Momus, looks for Musetta in vain, and approaches the table. The waiter, who is near it, takes the bills left by Musetta and ceremoniously presents them to Alcindoro, who, seeing the sum and no longer finding anyone, falls on a chair, amazed, aghast.*)

ACT THREE

The Barrière d'Enfer

Beyond the tollgate, the boulevard outside the city, and, in the far background, the Orléans road, which disappears among the tall houses in the February fog. This side, to the left, a tavern and the little square in front of the barrier. At right, the Boulevard d'Enfer; at left, the Boulevard St. Jacques. Also at right the beginning of the Rue d'Enfer, which leads straight to the Latin Quarter. The tavern uses as its sign Marcello's painting "The Crossing of the Red Sea," but below it, instead, in big letters is painted "At the Port of Marseilles." At the sides of the door also are painted frescoes of a Turk and a Zouave with an enormous laurel crown around his fez. In the wall of the tavern that looks toward the tollgate, a ground-floor

*window from which a rosy light comes. The plane trees that flank the square, gray, tall, and
in long rows go from the square, diagonally toward the two boulevards. Between one plane
tree and the next, marble benches. It is February: the snow is everywhere. At the rise of the
curtain in the sky and over the houses there is the uncertain whitening of very early dawn.
Seated before a brazier the customs men are dozing. From the tavern, at intervals, shouts,
clink of glasses, laughter. A customs man comes from the tavern with some wine. The gate
of the barrier is closed. Beyond the closed gate, stamping their feet with the cold and blowing
on their benumbed hands, are some street sweepers.*

SWEEPERS

Ohè, là, le guardie! Aprite! Ohè, là!	Hey there! Guards! Open! Hey there!
Quelli di Gentilly! Siam gli spazzini!	We're the sweepers! Those from Gentilly!

(The customs men remain immobile; the sweepers hammer with their brooms and their shovels on the gate, shouting)

Fiocca la neve . . . Ohè, là!	Snow is falling . . . Hey there!
Qui s'agghiaccia!	We're freezing here!

(The customs men bestir themselves.)

A CUSTOMS MAN
(yawning and stretching his arms, grumbles)

Vengo!	I'm coming!

*(He goes to open. The sweepers come in and go off along the Rue d'Enfer. The customs
man shuts the gate again. From the tavern, gay voices and the clinking of glasses, which
accompany merry singing.)*

VOICES WITHIN

Chi nel ber trovò piacer, nel suo bicchier,	He who in drinking found pleasure, in his glass,
nel suo bicchier, ah!	in his glass, ah!
d'una bocca nell'ardor,	in the ardor of a mouth
trovò l'amor, trovò l'amor!	found love, found love!

MUSETTA
(in the tavern)

Ah! Se nel bicchiere sta il piacer	Ah! if pleasure lies in the glass,
in giovin bocca sta l'amor!	love lies in a young mouth!

VOICES WITHIN

Trallerallè, trallerallè, Eva e Noè!	Trallerallè, trallerallè, Eve and Noah!

*(Sounds of little bells from the Orléans road: these are wagons drawn by mules. Cracking
of whips and cries of carters. Between the wheels they have lighted lanterns covered with
canvas. They go past and go off along the Boulevard d'Enfer.)*

CARTERS

Hopp-là!	Giddap!

MILK WOMEN

Hopp-là!	Giddap!

A CUSTOMS MAN

Son già le lattivendole!	The milk women already!

(From the guardhouse the customs sergeant comes out. He orders the gate to be opened.

The milk women pass the barrier on the backs of little donkeys and go off along different streets.)

CARTERS, MILK WOMEN
Hopp-là! Hopp-là!   Giddap! Giddap!

MILK WOMEN
Buon giorno! Buon giorno! Buon giorno!   Good day! Good day! Good day!

PEASANT WOMEN
(with baskets on their arms)
Burro e cacio! Polli ed ova!   Butter and cheese! Chickens and eggs!
(They pay and the customs men let them pass. When they reach the crossing:)
Voi da che parte andate?   Which way are you going?
A San Michele!   To St. Michel!
Ci troverem più tardi?   Shall we meet later?
A mezzodì!   At midday!
A mezzodì!   At midday!

(They go off along different streets. The customs men take away the benches and the brazier. Mimi comes in from the Rue d'Enfer, looking around carefully, trying to recognize the places, but when she has reached the first plane tree a violent fit of coughing seizes her. When she has recovered and seen the sergeant, she goes over to him.)

MIMI
(to the sergeant)
Sa dirmi, scusi, qual è l'osteria . . .   Can you tell me, forgive me, which is the tav-
                                            ern . . .
(not remembering the name)
. . . dove un pittor lavora?   . ... where a painter is working?

SERGEANT
(pointing to the tavern)
Eccola.   There it is.

MIMI
Grazie.   Thanks.
(A maidservant comes from the tavern. Mimi approaches her.)
O buona donna, mi fate il favore . . .   Oh my good woman, will you do me the fa-
                                            vor . . .
di cercarmi il pittore Marcello?   of looking for the painter Marcello?
Ho da parlargli. Ho tanta fretta.   I have to speak to him. I'm in such a hurry.
Ditegli, piano, che Mimi l'aspetta.   Tell him, softly, that Mimi is waiting for him.

SERGEANT
(to a man passing by)
Ehi, quel paniere!   Hey, that basket!

CUSTOMS MAN
Vuoto!   Empty!

SERGEANT
Passi.   Let him pass.

(From the barrier more people come in, and some one way, some another, all go off. The bells of the Marie Thérèse Hospice ring matins. It is full day, a winter day, sad and misty. Some couples come from the tavern, going home. Marcello comes from the tavern and, with surprise, sees Mimi.)

MARCELLO

Mimì!   Mimi!

MIMI

Speravo di trovarvi qui.   I was hoping to find you here.

MARCELLO

È ver, siam qui da un mese   It's true, we've been here for a month
di quell'oste alle spese.   at the expense of that tavern keeper.
Musetta insegna il canto ai passeggieri   Musetta teaches singing to the travelers,
io pingo quei guerrieri   I'm painting those warriors
sulla facciata.   on the façade.
                              (Mimi coughs.)
È freddo. Entrate.   It's cold. Come in.

MIMI

C'è Rodolfo?   Is Rodolfo there?

MARCELLO

Sì.   Yes.

MIMI

Non posso entrar, no, no!   I can't go in, no, no!

MARCELLO
(surprised)

Perchè?   Why?

MIMI
(bursts into tears)

Oh! buon Marcello, aiuto! aiuto!   Oh, good Marcello! Help! Help!

MARCELLO

Cos'è avvenuto?   What's happened?

MIMI

Rodolfo, Rodolfo, m'ama . . .   Rodolfo, Rodolfo loves me . . .
Rodolfo m'ama e mi fugge,   Rodolfo loves me and flees from me,
il mio Rodolfo si strugge per gelosia.   my Rodolfo is consumed with jealousy.
Un passo, un detto, un vezzo,   A footstep, a word, a compliment,
un fior lo mettono in sospetto . . .   a flower arouse his suspicion . . .
Onde corrucci ed ire.   Whereupon frowns and wrath.
Talor la notte fingo di dormire   At times at night I pretend to sleep
e in me lo sento fiso   and I feel him staring at me,
spiarmi i sogni in viso.   to observe my dreams in my face.
Mi grida ad ogni istante: He shouts at me at every moment:
Non fai per me,   You're not the one for me,

ti prendi un altro amante,
non fai per me!
Ahimè! ahimè!
In lui parla il rovello, lo so,
ma che rispondergli, Marcello?

take another lover for yourself,
you're not the one for me!
Alas! Alas!
Anger is speaking in him, I know,
but what to answer him, Marcello?

MARCELLO

Quando s'è come voi
non si vive in compagnia.

When people are like you two
they don't live together.

MIMI

Dite ben, dite bene.
Lasciarci conviene.
Aiutateci, aiutateci voi;
noi s'è provato più volte, ma invano.

You're right, you're right.
It's best for us to leave each other.
Help us, you help us;
we've tried several times, but in vain.

MARCELLO

Son lieve a Musetta, ell'è lieve a me,
perchè ci amiamo in allegria . . .
Canti e risa, ecco il fior
d'invariabile amor!

I'm easy with Musetta, she's easy with me,
because we love each other gaily . . .
Songs and laughter, there is the flower
of unchanging love!

MIMI

Dite ben, dite ben,
lasciarci convien!
Fate voi per il meglio.

You're right, you're right;
it's best for us to leave each other!
You act for the best.

MARCELLO

Sta ben, sta ben! Ora lo sveglio.

All right, all right! Now I'll wake him.

MIMI

Dorme?

Is he asleep?

MARCELLO

È piombato qui
un'ora avanti l'alba,
s'assopì sopra una panca.
Guardate.

He rushed in here
an hour before dawn;
he dozed off on a bench.
Look.

(Goes to the window and motions to Mimi to look. Mimi coughs.)

Che tosse!

What a cough!

MIMI

Da ieri ho l'ossa rotte.
Fuggì da me stanotte
dicendomi: È finita.
A giorno sono uscita
e me ne venni a questa volta.

Since yesterday I've been exhausted.
He fled from me last night,
saying to me: It's finished.
At daybreak I went out
and I came in this direction.

MARCELLO
(observing Rodolfo inside the tavern)

Si desta . . . s'alza . . . mi cerca . . .
viene . . .

He's waking . . . he's standing up . . . he's
    looking for me . . .
he's coming . . .

MIMI

Ch'ei non mi veda!   Don't let him see me!

MARCELLO

Or rincasate Mimì, per carità!   Go home now, Mimì, please!
Non fate scene qua!   Don't make scenes here!

(*He gently thrusts Mimi towards the corner of the tavern, from which, however, she almost immediately extends her head, curious. Marcello runs to meet Rodolfo.*)

RODOLFO
(*running toward Marcello*)

Marcello. Finalmente!   Marcello. At last!
Qui niun ci sente.   Here no one hears us.
Io voglio separarmi da Mimì.   I want to separate from Mimì.

MARCELLO

Sei volubil così?   Are you fickle like that?

RODOLFO

Già un'altra volta credetti morto   Already another time I believed
il mio cor,   my heart was dead,
ma di quegl'occhi azzurri allo splendor   but at the glow of those blue eyes
esso è risorto.   it revived.
Ora il tedio l'assal . . .   Now boredom assails it . . .

MARCELLO

E gli vuoi rinnovare il funeral?   And you want to repeat its funeral?

(*Mimi, unable to hear the words, seizing the right moment, manages to take refuge behind a plane tree, thus coming closer to the two friends.*)

RODOLFO
(*with grief*)

Per sempre!   Forever!

MARCELLO

Cambia metro.   Change your tune.
Dei pazzi è l'amor tetro   The gloomy love that distills
che lacrime distilla.   tears belongs to madmen.
Se non ride e sfavilla   If it doesn't laugh and sparkle
l'amore è fiacco e roco.   love is weak and hoarse.
Tu sei geloso.   You're jealous.

RODOLFO

Un poco.   A little.

MARCELLO

Collerico, lunatico, imbevuto   Choleric, lunatic, steeped
di pregiudizî, noioso, cocciuto!   in prejudices, boring, stubborn!

MIMI
(*who hears; to herself, uneasy*)

Or lo fa incollerir! Me poveretta!   Now he'll make him angry! Poor me!

RODOLFO

Mimì è una civetta	Mimi is a coquette
che frascheggia con tutti. Un moscardino	who flirts with everyone. A viscount,
di Viscontino	a little dandy,
le fa l'occhio di triglia. Ella sgonnella	makes sheep's eyes at her. She wiggles
e scopre la caviglia	and bares her ankle
con un far promettente e lusinghier . . .	with a promising and flattering manner . . .

MARCELLO

Lo devo dir? Non mi sembri sincer.	Must I say it? You don't seem sincere to me.

RODOLFO

Ebbene, no, non lo son.	Well, no, I'm not.
Invan, invan nascondo	In vain, in vain I hide
la mia vera tortura.	my real torment.
Amo Mimì sovra ogni cosa al mondo,	I love Mimi above everything in the world,
io l'amo, ma ho paura.	I love her, but I'm afraid.
Ma ho paura.	But I'm afraid.

(Mimi, surprised, comes still closer, always hidden behind the trees.)

RODOLFO

Mimì è tanto malata!	Mimi is so ill!
Ogni dì più declina.	Every day she declines further.
La povera piccina è condannata!	The poor little thing is doomed!

MARCELLO

Mimì!?	Mimi!?

MIMI

Che vuol dire?	What does he mean?

RODOLFO

Una terribil tosse	A terrible cough
l'esil petto le scuote	shakes her fragile bosom,
già le smunte gote	already her emaciated cheeks
di sangue ha rosse . . .	are red with blood . . .

MARCELLO

Povera Mimì!	Poor Mimi!

MIMI

Ahimè, morire?!	Alas, to die?!

RODOLFO

La mia stanza è una tana	My room is a squalid den . . .
squallida . . . il fuoco ho spento.	My fire is out.
V'entra e l'aggira il vento	The north wind enters there
di tramontana.	and moves about.
Essa canta e sorride,	She sings and smiles,
e il rimorso m'assale.	and remorse assails me.
Me cagion del fatale	Me, the cause of the fatal
mal che l'uccide.	disease that is killing her.

MARCELLO

Che far dunque?   What to do then?

MIMI
(in anguish)

O mia vita!   Oh, my life!

RODOLFO

Mimì di serra è fiore.   Mimi's a hothouse flower.
Povertà l'ha sfiorita,   Poverty has blighted her;
per richiamarla in vita   to call her back to life
non basta amor, non basta amor!   love's not enough, love's not enough!

MARCELLO

Oh qual pietà! Poveretta!   Oh, what a pity! Poor thing!
Povera Mimì! Povera Mimì!   Poor Mimi! Poor Mimi!

MIMI

Ahimè! Ahimè! È finita!   Alas! Alas! It's finished!
O mia vita . . . ! È finita!   Oh, my life . . . ! It's finished!
Ahimè morir, ahimè morir!   Alas, to die, alas, to die!
(Her cough and her violent sobs reveal Mimi's presence.)

RODOLFO
(seeing her and running to her)

Chè? Mimì! Tu qui?   What? Mimi! You here?
M'hai sentito?   Did you hear me?

MARCELLO

Ella dunque ascoltava?   She was listening, then?

RODOLFO

Facile alla paura   Easily frightened,
per nulla m'arrovello.   I grow angry over nothing.
Vien là nel tepor!   Come in there, in the warmth!
(wants to make her go into the tavern)

MIMI

No, quel tanfo mi soffoca.   No, that moldy smell stifles me.

RODOLFO

Ah, Mimì!   Ah, Mimi!
*(Rodolfo lovingly clasps Mimi in his arms. From the tavern Musetta is heard, laughing
shamelessly. Marcello runs to the window of the tavern.)*

MARCELLO

È Musetta che ride.   It's Musetta who's laughing.
Con chi ride? Ah la civetta!   With whom is she laughing? Ah, the flirt!
Imparerai.   You'll learn.

MIMI
(freeing herself from Rodolfo)

Addio.   Goodbye.

RODOLFO
(surprised, sorrowfully)

Che! Vai?   What! You're going?

MIMI

Donde lieta uscì	To the place she left happily
al tuo grido d'amore,	at your call of love
torna sola Mimì	Mimi is returning alone,
al solitario nido.	to the lonely nest.
Ritorna un'altra volta	She's going back once again
a intesser finti fior!	to weave false flowers!
Addio, senza rancor.	Goodbye, without bitterness.
Ascolta, ascolta.	Listen, listen.
Le poche robe aduna che lasciai	Gather up the few things that I left
sparse. Nel mio cassetto	scattered. In my drawer
stan chiusi quel cerchietto	are shut that little gold
d'or, e il libro di preghiere.	ring, and the prayer book.
Involgi tutto quanto in un grembiale	Wrap everything in an apron
e manderò il portiere . . .	and I'll send the concierge . . .
Bada, sotto il guanciale	Mind you, under the pillow
c'è la cuffietta rosa.	there's the pink bonnet.
Se vuoi . . . se vuoi . . .	If you want . . . if you want . . .
Se vuoi serbarla a ricordo d'amor . . .	If you want to keep it in memory of our love . . .
Addio, addio senza rancor!	Goodbye, goodbye without bitterness!

RODOLFO

Dunque è proprio finita!	Then it's really finished!
Te ne vai, te ne vai, la mia piccina?	You're going away, you're going away, my little one?
Addio sogni d'amor!	Goodbye, dreams of love!

MIMI

Addio dolce svegliare alla mattina!   Goodbye, sweet wakening in the morning!

RODOLFO

Addio sognante vita . . .   Goodbye, dreaming life . . .

MIMI
(smiling)

Addio rabbuffi e gelosie!   Goodbye, rebukes and jealousies!

RODOLFO

. . . che un tuo sorriso acqueta.   . . . that a smile of yours calms.

MIMI

Addio sospetti . . .   Goodbye, suspicions . . .

RODOLFO

Baci . . .   Kisses . . .

MIMI

. . . pungenti amarezze!   . . . poignant bitternesses!

RODOLFO

. . . ch'io da vero poeta   . . . that I, like a true poet,
rimavo con: carezze!   would rhyme with: caresses!

MIMI, RODOLFO

Soli l'inverno è cosa da morire!   Being alone in winter is a thing to die of!

MIMI

Soli!   Alone!

MIMI, RODOLFO

Mentre a primavera c'è compagno il sol!   Whereas in the spring there is the sun as companion!

MIMI

C'è compagno il sol!   There is the sun as companion!
  (*From the tavern a racket of broken plates and glasses. The excited voices of Musetta and Marcello are heard.*)

MARCELLO

Che facevi? Che dicevi . . . ?   What were you doing? What were you saying . . . ?

MUSETTA

Che vuoi dir?   What do you mean?

MARCELLO

. . . presso al fuoco a quel signore? . . . near the fire to that gentleman?

MUSETTA

Che vuoi dir?   What do you mean?

MIMI

Niuno è solo l'april . . .   Nobody's alone in April . . .
  (*Musetta comes out angrily. Marcello follows her, stopping in the doorway.*)

MARCELLO

Al mio venire hai mutato di colore. When I came in you changed color.

MUSSETA

Quel signore mi diceva: That gentleman said to me:
Ama il ballo signorina?   Do you like dancing, miss?

MARCELLO

Vana, frivola, civetta!   Vain, frivolous, flirt!

RODOLFO

Si parla coi gigli e le rose . . .   You speak with lilies and roses . . .

MIMI

Esce dai nidi un cinguettio gentile.   From the nests comes a sweet twittering.

MUSETTA

Arrossendo rispondeva: Blushing, I answered:
ballerei sera e mattina . . .   I would dance evening and morning . . .
ballerei sera e mattina . . .   I would dance evening and morning . . .

MARCELLO

Quel discorso asconde mire disoneste . . . That talk conceals dishonest intentions . . .

MUSETTA

Voglio piena libertà!   I want complete freedom!

MARCELLO
(almost hurling himself against Musetta)
Io t'acconcio per le feste . . .   I'll fix you . . .

MUSETTA

Chè mi canti?   What's this tune of yours?

MARCELLO

. . . se ti colgo a incivettire!   . . . if I catch you flirting!

MIMI, RODOLFO

Al fiorir di primavera c'è compagno il sol! At spring's blossoming there's the sun as
                                            companion!

MUSETTA

Chè mi gridi? Chè mi canti?   What are you shouting at me? What's this
All'altar non siamo uniti.   tune?
                                            We're not united at the altar.

MARCELLO

Bada, sotto il mio cappello   Mind you, under my hat
non ci stan certi ornamenti . . .   certain ornaments don't go . . .

MUSETTA

Io detesto quegli amanti   I hate those lovers
che la fanno da ah! ah! ah! mariti!   who behave like ha! ha! ha! husbands!

MIMI, RODOLFO

Chiacchieran le fontane.   The fountains chatter.
La brezza della sera   The evening's breeze
balsami stende sulle doglie umane.   spreads balms over human sufferings.

MARCELLO

Io non faccio da zimbello   I'm not a laughingstock
ai novizi intraprendenti.   for enterprising novices.

MUSETTA

Fo all'amor con chi mi piace!	I'll make love with whom I please!
Non ti garba?	Don't you like that?
Fo all'amor con chi mi piace!	I'll make love with whom I please!

MARCELLO

Vana, frivola, civetta!	Vain, frivolous, flirt!
Ve n'andate? Vi ringrazio:	Are you going away? I thank you:
or son ricco divenuto.	now I've become rich.

MUSETTA

| Musetta se ne va, sì, se ne va! | Musetta's going away, yes, going away! |

MUSETTA, MARCELLO

| Vi saluto! | I bid you goodbye! |

MIMI, RODOLFO

| Vuoi che aspettiam la primavera ancor? | Do you want us to wait until spring again? |

MUSETTA

| Signor, addio vi dico con piacer! | Sir, I say goodbye to you with pleasure! |

MARCELLO

| Son servo e me ne vo! | I'm your servant, and I'm going away! |

MUSETTA
(goes off furiously, but then, all of a sudden, she stops and shouts at him again,
venomously)

| Pittore da bottega! | Hack painter! |

MARCELLO

| Vipera! | Viper! |

MUSETTA

| Rospo! | Toad! |

MARCELLO

| Strega! | Witch! |

MIMI

| Sempre tua per la vita! | Always yours . . . for life! |

MIMI, RODOLFO

| Ci lascieremo alla stagion dei fior! | We'll leave each other at the season of flowers! |

(They start off. Marcello goes back into the tavern.)

MIMI

| Vorrei che eterno durasse l'inverno! | I would like winter to last eternally! |

MIMI, RODOLFO

| Ci lascierem alla stagion dei fior! | We'll leave each other at the season of flowers! |

ACT FOUR

In the Garret

As in Act One. Marcello is again before his easel, as Rodolfo is seated at his table. Each would like to convince the other that he is working unremittingly, whereas instead they do nothing but chat.

MARCELLO
(*continuing the conversation*)

In un coupé?   In a coupé?

RODOLFO

Con pariglia e livree.   With a pair and livery.
Mi salutò ridendo.   She greeted me, laughing.
Tò, Musetta! Le dissi: Why, Musetta! I said to her:
e il cuor? "Non batte o non lo sento   and your heart? "It isn't beating or I can't hear
grazie al velluto che il copre."   it
                                                thanks to the velvet that covers it."

MARCELLO

Ci ho gusto davver, ci ho gusto davver!   I'm really delighted; I'm really delighted!

RODOLFO
(*aside*)

(Loiola va. Ti rodi e ridi.)   (Hypocrite, go on! You're consumed and you
                                                    laugh.)

MARCELLO
(*ruminating*)

Non batte? Bene! — Io pur vidi . . .   It's not beating? Good! — I also saw . . .

RODOLFO

Musetta?   Musetta?

MARCELLO

Mimì.   Mimì.

RODOLFO
(*starts*)

L'hai vista?   You saw her?
                                                (*recovers himself*)
Oh guarda!   Just think of that!

MARCELLO

Era in carrozza   She was in a carriage
vestita come una regina.   dressed like a queen.

RODOLFO

Evviva. Ne son contento.   Hurrah. I'm pleased.

MARCELLO
(aside)

(Bugiardo, si strugge d'amor.)   (Liar, he's consumed with love.)

RODOLFO

Lavoriam.   Let's work.

MARCELLO

Lavoriam.   Let's work.
                                        (They set to work.)

RODOLFO
(throws down his pen)

Che penna infame!   What a terrible pen!

MARCELLO
(throws down his brush)

Che infame pennello!   What a terrible brush!

RODOLFO

(O Mimì, tu più non torni.   (Oh, Mimi, you return no more.
O giorni belli,   Oh, beautiful days,
piccole mani, odorosi cappelli . . .   little hands, perfumed hair . . .
collo di neve!   snowy neck!
Ah, Mimì, mia breve gioventù!)   Ah, Mimi, my brief youth!)

MARCELLO

(Io non so come sia   (I don't know how it is
che il mio pennello lavori   that my brush works
e impasta colori   and mixes colors
contro voglia mia.   against my will.
Se pingere mi piace o cieli o terre   If I want to paint heavens or lands
o inverni o primavere,   or winters or springs,
egli mi traccia due pupille nere   it draws for me two black eyes
e una bocca procace,   and a saucy mouth,
e n'esce di Musetta il viso ancor . . . and from it comes Musetta's face again . . .
e n'esce di Musetta il viso   and from it comes Musetta's face
tutto vezzi e tutto frode.   all charms and all deceit.
Musetta intanto gode   Musetta meanwhile enjoys herself
e il mio cuor vile la chiama,   and my cowardly heart calls her,
la chiama e aspetta il vil mio cuor.)   my cowardly heart calls her and waits for her.)

RODOLFO

(E tu, cuffietta lieve,   (And you, light bonnet,
che sotto il guancial partendo   which she hid under the pollow
ascose, tutta sai la nostra felicità   on leaving, you know all our happiness:
vien sul mio cuor morto, ah vien!   come upon my dead heart, ah, come!
ah vien sul mio cuor; poichè è morto amor.) Ah, come upon my heart, since love is dead.)

RODOLFO

Che ora sia?   What time can it be?

Giacomo Puccini
(Courtesy of Dorle Soria)

Puccini, left, with the two librettists of *La Bohème*,
Giuseppe Giacosa, center, and Luigi Illica, right

(BOTH *Courtesy of Dorle Soria*)

Puccini's study at Torre del Lago

Drawing of Henri Murger, author of *Scènes de la vie de bohème*,
the novel on which Puccini based his opera

(BOTH *Courtesy of Dorle Soria*)

Giulio Ricordi, Puccini's publisher and close friend

Program of the first performance of *La Bohème* at the Metropolitan Opera

(BOTH *Courtesy of the Metropolitan Opera Archives*)

Act I stage set, original production of *La Bohème* at the Metropolitan Opera

Albert Saléza,
the first Rodolfo
Metropolitan Opera
*(Courtesy of the
Robert Tuggle Collection)*

Nellie Melba, the first Mimi
at the Metropolitan Opera
(Courtesy of Opera News)

Giuseppe Campanari, the first Marcello
at the Metropolitan Opera
(Courtesy of the Robert Tuggle Collection)

Marcella Sembrich as Mimi
(Courtesy of the Robert Tuggle Collection)

Enrico Caruso as Rodolfo
(Courtesy of the Robert Tuggle Collection)

The legendary Geraldine Farrar as Mimi
(Courtesy of the Harvard Theatre Collection)

Lucrezia Bori, who appeared in the role of Mimi
at the Metropolitan Opera for over two decades,
from 1912 until 1936
(Courtesy of the Robert Tuggle Collection)

Jussi Bjoerling as Rodolfo,
Metropolitan Opera, 1938
(Courtesy of the Metropolitan Opera Archives)

Licia Albanese, who appeared as Mimi at the
Metropolitan Opera from 1940 through the fifties
(Courtesy of Opera News)

(Courtesy of the Metropolitan Opera Archives)

Act II, *La Bohème,* Metropolitan Opera, 1930, with, from left to right, Ezio Pinza as Colline, Millo Picco as Schaunard, Pompilio Malatesta, standing, as Alcindoro, Nannette Guilford as Musetta, Beniamino Gigli as Rodolfo, Lucrezia Bori as Mimi, and Giuseppe De Luca as Marcello

Ferruccio Tagliavini as Rodolfo and
Bidù Sayão as Mimi, Metropolitan Opera, 1947
(Photo: Louis Mélançon. Courtesy of the Metropolitan Opera Archives)

Victoria de los Angeles as Mimi, Metropolitan Opera, 1951
(Courtesy of the Metropolitan Opera Archives)

Richard Tucker as Rodolfo and Nadine Conner as Mimi, Metropolitan Opera, 1952
(Photo: Sedge Le Blang. Courtesy of the Metropolitan Opera Archives)

Act II, Café Momus. Set and costume design sketch by Rolf Gérard for his
new production of *La Bohème*, Metropolitan Opera, 1952
(Photo: Sedge Le Blang. Courtesy of the Metropolitan Opera Archives)

Mirella Freni as Mimi and Gianni Raimondi as Rodolfo, Metropolitan Opera, 1965
(Photo: Frank Dunand. Courtesy of the Education Department, Metropolitan Opera Guild)

Renata Tebaldi as Mimi, Metropolitan Opera, 1966
(Photo: Louis Mélançon. Courtesy of the Metropolitan Opera Archives)

Dorothy Kirsten as Mimi
and Luciano Pavarotti as Rodolfo
Metropolitan Opera, 1968
*(Courtesy of the
Metropolitan Opera Archives)*

Act II, Rolf Gérard production, the Metropolitan Opera, 1976,
with Montserrat Caballé as Mimi, Luciano Pavarotti as Rodolfo,
Paul Plishka as Colline, and Allan Monk as Schaunard

(BOTH *Photo: James Heffernan, Metropolitan Opera*)

Act IV, current production, Metropolitan Opera, 1981, with
José Carreras as Rodolfo, Teresa Stratas as Mimi, Renata Scotto
as Musetta, and Richard Stilwell as Marcello

Placido Domingo as Rodolfo, Metropolitan Opera, 1982
(Photo: James Heffernan, Metropolitan Opera)

Act II, sketch of set design by Franco Zeffirelli, current production, Metropolitan Opera

Costume sketches by Peter J. Hall, current production, Metropolitan Opera
(Courtesy of Opera News*)*

MARCELLO

L'ora del pranzo . . . di ieri.   Time for dinner . . . yesterday's.

RODOLFO

E Schaunard non torna?   And Schaunard isn't coming back?
(Enter Schaunard and Colline.)

SCHAUNARD

Eccoci.   Here we are.
(sets four loaves on the table)

RODOLFO

Ebben?   Well?

MARCELLO
(with contempt)
Ebben? Del pan?   Well? Bread?

COLLINE
(displaying a herring)
È un piatto degno di Demostene: It's a dish worthy of Demosthenes:
un'aringa . . .   a herring . . .*

SCHAUNARD

. . . salata!   . . . salty!

COLLINE

Il pranzo è in tavola.   Dinner is on the table.
(They sit around the table, pretending to be at a sumptuous dinner.)

MARCELLO

Questa è cuccagna   This is an abundance
da Berlingaccio.   worthy of Shrove Tuesday.

SCHAUNARD
(sets Colline's hat on the table and places a bottle of water inside it)
Or lo sciampagna   Now let's put
mettiamo in ghiaccio.   the champagne on ice.

RODOLFO
(to Marcello)
Scelga, o barone,   Choose, Baron:
trota o salmone?   trout or salmon?

MARCELLO
(to Schaunard)
Duca, una lingua   Duke, a parrot's
di pappagallo?   tongue?

---

* TRANSLATOR'S NOTE: Colline here makes a pun on the Italian words *aringa* (herring) and *arringa* (harangue).

SCHAUNARD

Grazie, m'impingua.   No thanks, it's fattening.
Stassera ho un ballo.   I have a ball tonight.
(Colline has eaten, and he stands up.)

RODOLFO
(to Colline)
Già sazio?   Sated already?

COLLINE
(solemn)
Ho fretta. Il Re m'aspetta.   I'm in a hurry. The king awaits me.

MARCELLO
C'è qualche trama?   Is there some plot?

RODOLFO
Qualche mister?   Some mystery?

SCHAUNARD
Qualche mister?   Some mystery?

MARCELLO
Qualche mister?   Some mystery?

COLLINE
Il Re mi chiama al minister.   The king is calling me to the ministry.

SCHAUNARD
Bene!   Good!

MARCELLO
Bene!   Good!

RODOLFO
Bene!   Good!

COLLINE
(importantly)
Però . . . vedrò . . . vedrò . . . Guizot!   However . . . I'll see . . . I'll see . . . Gui-
                                                 zot!

SCHAUNARD
(to Marcello)
Porgimi il nappo!   Hand me the goblet!

MARCELLO
(gives him the only glass)
Sì! Bevi, io pappo!   Yes! Drink; I'm feeding!

SCHAUNARD
(*solemn*)

Mi sia permesso   If the noble company
al nobile consesso . . .   will allow me . . .

RODOLFO, COLLINE
(*interrupting him*)

Basta!   Enough!

MARCELLO

Fiacco!   Weak!

COLLINE

Che decotto!   What a concoction!

MARCELLO

Leva il tacco!   Get out!

COLLINE

Dammi il gotto!   Give me the mug!

SCHAUNARD
(*inspired*)

M'ispira irresistibile   The genius of song
l'estro della romanza!   is inspiring me irresistibly!

THE OTHERS
(*shouting*)

No! No! No!   No! No! No!

SCHAUNARD
(*docile*)

Azione coreografica allora?   Choreographic action then?

THE OTHERS
(*applauding*)

Sì! sì!   Yes! Yes!

SCHAUNARD

La danza con musica vocale!   Dance, with vocal music!

COLLINE

Si sgombrino le sale!   Let the halls be cleared!
(*They carry the table and the chairs to one side and take their places for dancing.*)

COLLINE

Gavotta.   Gavotte.

MARCELLO

Minuetto.   Minuet.

RODOLFO

Pavanella.   Pavanella.

SCHAUNARD

Fandango.   Fandango.

COLLINE

Propongo la quadriglia.   I suggest the quadrille.

RODOLFO

Mano alle dame!   Give your hand to the ladies!

COLLINE

Io detto.   I'll call.

SCHAUNARD

Lallera, lallera, lallera, là . . .   Lallera, lallera, lallera, là . . .

RODOLFO
(*gallantly, to Marcello*)

Vezzosa damigella . . .   Charming damsel . . .

MARCELLO

Rispetti la modestia.   Respect my modesty.
La prego.   I beg you.

SCHAUNARD

Lallera, ecc.   Lallera, etc.

COLLINE

Balancez!   *Balancez!*

MARCELLO

Lallera, ecc.   Lallera, etc.

SCHAUNARD

Prima c'è il *Rond*.   First there's the *rond*.

COLLINE

No, bestia!   No, you animal!

SCHAUNARD

Che modi da lacchè.   What lackey's manners!

COLLINE

Se non erro lei m'oltraggia!   If I'm not mistaken, you insult me!
Snudi il ferro!   Draw your sword!
                           (*takes the fire tongs*)

SCHAUNARD
(*takes the shovel*)

Pronti.   Ready.

(wields a blow)

Assaggia.   Taste that.
Il tuo sangue io voglio ber.   I want to drink your blood.

COLLINE
(fighting)
Un di noi qui si sbudella.   One of us here will be disemboweled.

SCHAUNARD
Apprestate una barella.   Prepare a litter.

COLLINE
Apprestate un cimiter.   Prepare a cemetery.
(As they fight, Marcello and Rodolfo dance around them, singing.)

RODOLFO, MARCELLO
Mentre incalza la tenzone   As the combat rages,
gira e balza Rigodone . . .   Rigadoon turns and leaps . . .
(The door is flung open and Musetta enters, greatly upset.)

MARCELLO
(struck)
Musetta!   Musetta!
(All are stunned.)

MUSETTA
(gasping)
C'è Mimì . . .   There's Mimi . . .
(With intense anxiety they surround Musetta.)
Cè Mimì che mi segue e che sta male.   There's Mimi, who's following me and who's
                                                     ill.

RODOLFO
(terrified)
Ov'è?   Where is she?

MUSETTA
Nel far le scale più non si resse.   As she climbed the stairs her strength failed.
(Through the open door Mimi is seen, seated on the top step.)

RODOLFO
Ah!   Ah!
(He rushes toward Mimi; Marcello also rushes out.)

SCHAUNARD
(to Colline)
Noi accostiamo quel lettuccio.   We'll move that cot closer.
(Rodolfo, with the help of Marcello, carries Mimi to the bed, on which he extends her.)

RODOLFO
Là.   There.
(softly, to his friends)

Da bere.   Something to drink.
      (*Musetta runs over with the glass of water and gives Mimi a sip.*)

MIMI
(*recovering herself and seeing Rodolfo near her*)
Rodolfo!   Rodolfo!

RODOLFO
Zitta — riposa.   Hush — rest.

MIMI
O mio Rodolfo! Mi vuoi qui con te?   Oh, my Rodolfo! You want me here with you?

RODOLFO
(*lovingly motions to Mimi to be silent, remaining near her*)
Ah! mia Mimì, sempre, sempre!   Ah, my Mimi! Always, always!

MUSETTA
(*softly, to Marcello, Schaunard, and Colline*)
Intesi dire che Mimì fuggita   I heard it said that Mimi, having fled
dal Viscontino era in fin di vita.   from the viscount, was dying.
Dove stia? Cerca, cerca . . .   Where could she be? I searched and
la veggo passar per via . . .   searched . . .
trascinandosi a stento.   I see her passing in the street . . .
Mi dice: "più non reggo . . .   barely dragging herself along.
muoio, lo sento.   She says to me: "I can stand no more . . .
Voglio morir con lui!   I'm dying, I feel it.
Forse m'aspetta . . . !   I want to die with him!
                                             Perhaps he's waiting for me . . . !

MIMI
Mi sento assai meglio . . .   I feel much better . . .

MUSETTA
. . . M'accompagni, Musetta?"   . . . Will you accompany me, Musetta?"

MIMI
Lascia ch'io guardi intorno.   Let me look around.
Ah come si sta bene qui!   Ah, how comfortable one is here!
Si rinasce, si rinasce.   One is reborn, reborn.
Ancor sento la vita qui . . .   I feel life here again . . .
No, tu non mi lasci più!   No, you won't leave me any more!

RODOLFO
Benedetta bocca,   Blessed mouth,
tu ancor mi parli!   You're speaking to me again!

MUSETTA
(*to the three*)
Che ci avete in casa?   What do you have in the house?

MARCELLO

Nulla!   Nothing.

MUSETTA

Non caffè? Non vino?   No coffee? No wine?

MARCELLO

Nulla! Ah! miseria!   Nothing! Ah, poverty!

SCHAUNARD

(sadly to Colline, drawing him to one side)

Fra mezz'ora è morta!   In half an hour she's dead!

MIMI

Ho tanto freddo . . .   I'm so cold . . .
Se avessi un manicotto! Queste mie mani   If I had a muff! Can these hands of mine
riscaldare non si potranno mai?   never be warmed?

(coughs)

RUDOLFO

(takes her hands in his, warming them)

Qui, nelle mie!   Here, in mine!
Taci! Il parlar ti stanca.   Hush! Talking tires you.

MIMI

Ho un po' di tosse!   I have a little cough!
Ci sono avvezza.   I'm used to it.

(Seeing Rodolfo's friends, she calls them by name; concerned, they rush to Mimi's side.)

Buon giorno, Marcello,   Good day, Marcello,
Schaunard, Colline, buon giorno.   Schaunard, Colline, good day.
Tutti qui, tutti qui sorridenti a Mimì.   All here, all here smiling at Mimi.

RODOLFO

Non parlar, non parlar.   Don't speak, don't speak.

MIMI

Parlo pian. Non temere.   I'm speaking softly. Don't fear.
Marcello, date retta: Marcello, pay attention:
è assai buona Musetta.   Musetta is very good.

MARCELLO

Lo so, lo so.   I know, I know.

(holds out his hand to Musetta)

MUSETTA

(removes her earrings and hands them to Marcello)

A te . . . vendi, riporta   Here . . . sell them, bring back
qualche cordial, manda un dottore!   some cordial, send a doctor!

RODOLFO

Riposa.   Rest.

MIMI

Tu non mi lasci?   You aren't leaving me?

RODOLFO

No! No!   No! No!

MUSETTA
(to Marcello, who is hurrying off)

Ascolta!   Listen!
Forse è l'ultima volta   Perhaps this is the last time
che ha espresso un desiderio, poveretta!   that she's expressed a wish, poor thing!
Pel manicotto io vo. Con te verrò.   I'm going for the muff. I'll come with you.

MARCELLO
(moved)

Sei buona, o mia Musetta.   You're good, Oh, my Musetta.
(Musetta and Marcello leave hurriedly.)

COLLINE
(has removed his overcoat while Musetta and Marcello were talking)

Vecchia zimarra, senti,   Old coat, listen,
io resto al pian, tu ascendere   I'm remaining on the plain, you now
il sacro monte or devi.   must climb the sacred mountain.*
Le mie grazie ricevi.   Receive my thanks.
Mai non curvasti il logoro   You never bowed your worn
dorso ai ricchi ed ai potenti.   back to the rich and the mighty.
Passâr nelle tue tasche   In your pockets,
come in antri tranquilli   as in tranquil grottoes,
filosofi e poeti.   passed philosophers and poets.
Ora che i giorni lieti   Now that the happy days
fuggir, ti dico addio   have fled, I bid you good-bye,
fedele amico mio.   my faithful friend.
Addio, addio.   Goodbye, goodbye.
(making a bundle of it, he places it under his arm, but seeing Schaunard, he says to him in a whisper)
Schaunard, ognuno per diversa via   Schaunard, let us, each in a different way,
mettiamo insieme due atti di pietà;   combine two acts of mercy;
io . . . questo!   I . . . this!
(shows him the coat that he holds under his arm)
E tu . . .   And you . . .
(nodding to Rodolfo, bent over the sleeping Mimi)
lasciali soli là!   leave them alone there!

SCHAUNARD
(moved)

Filosofo, ragioni!   Philosopher, you're reasoning!
È ver . . . ! Vo via!   It's true . . . ! I'm going away!
(He looks around and, to justify his leaving, he takes the water bottle and goes down after Colline, carefully shutting the door.)

---

* TRANSLATOR'S NOTE: a reference to the
Monte di Pietà, or state-run Italian pawn shop.

MIMI

Sono andati? Fingevo di dormire
perchè volli con te sola restare.
Ho tante cose che ti voglio dire
o una sola, ma grande come il mare,
come il mare profonda ed infinita . . .
Sei il mio amor e tutta la mia vita,
sei il mio amore e tutta la mia vita.

Have they gone? I was pretending to sleep
because I wanted to remain alone with you.
I have so many things I want to tell you,
or one alone, but big as the sea,
like the sea, profound and infinite . . .
You're my love and all my life,
You're my love and all my life.

RODOLFO

Ah Mimì, mia bella Mimì!

Ah, Mimi, my beautiful Mimi!

MIMI

Son bella ancora?

Am I beautiful still?

RODOLFO

Bella come un'aurora . . .

Beautiful as a dawn . . .

MIMI

Hai sbagliato il raffronto.
Volevi dir: bella come un tramonto.
"Mi chiamano Mimì, mi chiamano Mimì . . .
il perchè non so."

You've mistaken the comparison.
You meant: beautiful as a sunset.
"They call me Mimi, they call me Mimi . . .
I don't know the reason."

RODOLFO
(tender and caressing)

Tornò al nido la rondine e cinguetta.

The swallow returned to the nest and is twittering.

(He takes Mimi's bonnet from where he had placed it, over his heart, and hands it to her.)

MIMI
(radiant)

La mia cuffietta, la mia cuffietta . . .

My bonnet, my bonnet . . .

(holds her head toward Rodolfo, who puts the bonnet on it. Mimi remains with her head leaning against his chest)

Ah . . . ! Te lo rammenti quando sono en-
trata
la prima volta, là?

Ah . . . ! You remember when I came in
the first time, there?

RODOLFO

Se lo rammento!

Do I remember!?

MIMI

Il lume s'era spento . . .

The light had gone out . . .

RODOLFO

Eri tanto turbata!
Poi smarristi la chiave . . .

You were so upset!
Then you lost the key . . .

MIMI

E a cercarla tastoni ti sei messo!

And you started looking for it, groping!

RODOLFO

E cerca . . . cerca . . .   And I looked . . . and looked . . .

MIMI

Mio bel signorino,   My fine young gentleman,
posso ben dirlo adesso,   I can readily say it now:
lei la trovò assai presto.   You found it very quickly.

RODOLFO

Aiutavo il destino.   I was helping fate.

MIMI
(remembering her meeting with Rodolfo on the evening of Christmas Eve)
Era buio, e il mio rossor non si vedeva . . .   It was dark, and my blushing wasn't seen . . .
(murmurs Rodolfo's words)
"Che gelida manina . . . Se la lasci riscal-   "What an icy little hand . . . Let it be
dar!"   warmed!"
Era buio, e la man tu mi prendevi . . .   It was dark, and you took my hand . . .
(Mimi is seized with a choking fit; she lets her head fall back, exhausted.)

RODOLFO
(frightened)
Oh! Dio! Mimì!   Oh, God! Mimì!
(At this moment Schaunard returns. At Rodolfo's cry he runs over to Mimi.)

SCHAUNARD

Che avvien?   What's happening?

MIMI
(opens her eyes and smiles to reassure Rodolfo and Schaunard)
Nulla. Sto bene.   Nothing. I'm well.

RODOLFO

Zitta, per carità.   Hush, please.

MIMI

Sì, sì, perdona.   Yes, yes, forgive me.
Or sarò buona.   Now I'll be good.
(Musetta and Marcello come in. Musetta is carrying a muff and Marcello, a phial.)

MUSETTA
(to Rodolfo)
Dorme?   Is she sleeping?

RODOLFO

Riposa.   She's resting.

MARCELLO

Ho veduto il dottore!   I've seen the doctor!
Verrà; gli ho fatto fretta.   He'll come; I hurried him.
Ecco il cordial.   Here's the cordial.
(He takes a spirit lamp, sets it on the table, and lights it.)

MIMI
Chi parla?   Who's speaking?

MUSETTA
(approaches Mimi and hands her the muff)
Io, Musetta.   I, Musetta.

MIMI
Oh, come è bello e morbido.   Oh, how beautiful and soft it is.
Non più, non più le mani allividite.   No more, no more, pale hands.
Il tepore le abbellirà.   The warmth will beautify them.
(to Rodolfo)
Sei tu che me lo doni?   Is it you who gives it to me?

MUSETTA
(prompt)
Sì.   Yes.

MIMI
Tu! Spensierato!   You! Carefree man!
Grazie. Ma costerà. Piangi? Sto bene . . .   Thanks. But it must cost. You're crying? I'm
                                                      well . . .
Pianger così perchè?   Why cry like this?
(dozing off little by little)
Qui amor . . . sempre con te . . . !   Here, love . . . always with you . . . !
Le mani . . . al caldo . . . e . . . dor-   My hands . . . in the warmth . . . and . . .
  mire . . .   to sleep . . .
(silence)

RODOLFO
(to Marcello)
Che ha detto il medico?   What did the doctor say?

MARCELLO
Verrà.   He'll come.

MUSETTA
(warms the phial at the spirit lamp and, almost unconsciously, murmurs a prayer)
Madonna benedetta,   Blessed Mother,
fate la grazia a questa poveretta   be merciful to this poor girl
che non debba morire.   who mustn't die.
(breaking off, to Marcello)
Qui ci vuole un riparo   We need a screen here
perchè la fiamma sventola.   because the flame is flickering.
(Marcello sets a book upright on the table forming a screen for the lamp.)
Così.   Like that.
(resumes the prayer)
Madonna santa, io sono   Holy Mother, I'm not worthy
indegna di perdono,   of forgiveness,
mentre invece Mimì   but Mimi instead
è un angelo del cielo.   is an angel from heaven.
(As Musetta prays, Rodolfo has come over to her.)

RODOLFO

Io spero ancora. Vi pare che sia grave?   I still hope. Does it seem serious to you?

MUSETTA

Non credo.   I don't believe so.
(Schaunard has gone over to the couch, then without attracting attention, he has run to
                                Marcello.)

SCHAUNARD
(softly, to Marcello)

Marcello, è spirata . . .   Marcello, she's dead . . .

   (Meanwhile Rodolfo has noticed that the sun from the garret window is about to strike
Mimi's face, and he looks around for some way to prevent this. Musetta notices and points
to her shawl. Rodolfo thanks her with a look, takes the shawl, climbs on a chair, and looks
for a way to spread the shawl over the window. Marcello, in turn, goes to the bed and moves
away from it again, frightened. Meanwhile Colline comes in and places some money on the
table near Musetta.)

COLLINE
(to Musetta)

Musetta . . . a voi!   Musetta . . . take this!
(Then seeing that Rodolfo by himself isn't able to arrange the shawl over the window, he
runs to help him, asking him about Mimi.)
Come va?   How is she?

RODOLFO

Vedi? È tranquilla.   You see? She's calm.
   (He turns towards Mimi. At that moment Musetta signals to him that the medicine is
ready. As Rodolfo rushes over to Musetta he notices the strange attitude of Marcello and
Schaunard, who, filled with dismay, look at him with profound pity.)

RODOLFO

Che vuol dire quell'andare e venire . . .   What does that going and coming mean . . .
que guardarmi così . . . ?   that looking at me like this . . . ?
   (Marcello can't restrain himself any more, runs to Rodolfo and, embracing him hard, murmurs in a choked voice:)

MARCELLO

Coraggio!   Courage!

RODOLFO
(runs to the cot)

Mimì . . . ! Mimì . . . ! Mimì . . . !   Mimi . . . ! Mimi . . . ! Mimi . . . !

NOTES
La Bohème
AT THE METROPOLITAN OPERA

[EDITOR'S NOTE: The first performance of *La Bohème* was in Turin, at the Teatro Regio, on February 1, 1896. The role of Mimì was sung by Cesira Ferrani, the role of Rodolfo by Evan Gorga; Arturo Toscanini was the conductor. The first performance of *La Bohème* at the Metropolitan Opera was on December 26, 1900. Except for the outer acts, redesigned by Joseph Novak in 1944, that 1900 production remained in use until 1952. Rolf Gérard designed new settings and costumes for a production staged by Joseph L. Mankiewicz, first seen on December 27, 1952. On February 23, 1977, a production designed by Pier Luigi Pizzi, on loan for two seasons from the Lyric Opera of Chicago, was introduced. The current Met production by Franco Zeffirelli, with sets by Franco Zeffirelli, costumes by Peter J. Hall, and lighting by Gil Wechsler, was first presented on December 14, 1981.

Along with *Aida* and *Carmen*, *La Bohème* is one of the three most frequently performed operas in the Met repertory, amassing a total of 581 performances in 74 seasons, through the spring of 1982. The following selected casts offer a retrospective view of those artists most often associated with *La Bohème* at the Met.]

DECEMBER 26, 1900

RODOLFO	*Albert Saléza*
MIMI	*Nellie Melba*
MARCELLO	*Giuseppe Campanari*
COLLINE	*Marcel Journet*
SCHAUNARD	*Charles Gilibert*
MUSETTA	*Anita Occhiolini*
BENOIT	*Eugène Dufriche*
ALCINDORO	*Eugène Dufriche*
PARPIGNOL	*Aristide Masiero*

CONDUCTOR	*Luigi Mancinelli*
STAGE DIRECTOR FOR FRENCH AND ITALIAN OPERAS	*William Parry*
STAGE MANAGER	*Frank Rigo*
MAÎTRE DE BALLET	*Luigi Albertieri*

DECEMBER 15, 1902

RODOLFO	*Emilio de Marchi*
MIMI	*Marcella Sembrich*
MARCELLO	*Giuseppe Campanari*

COLLINE	*Marcel Journet*
SCHAUNARD	*Charles Gilibert*
MUSETTA	*Fritzi Scheff*
BENOIT	*Eugène Dufriche*
ALCINDORO	*Eugène Dufriche*
PARPIGNOL	*Roberto Vanni*

CONDUCTOR	*Luigi Mancinelli*	
STAGE DIRECTOR	*Fernand Almanz*	

DECEMBER 3, 1903 (MATINEE)

RODOLFO	*Enrico Caruso*
MIMI	*Marcella Sembrich*
MARCELLO	*Giuseppe Campanari*
COLLINE	*Marcel Journet*
SCHAUNARD	*Eugène Dufriche*
MUSETTA	*Estelle Liebling (debut)*
BENOIT	*Archangelo Rossi*
ALCINDORO	*Archangelo Rossi*
PARPIGNOL	*Aristede Masiero*

CONDUCTOR	*Arturo Vigna*
STAGE DIRECTOR	*Karl Schroeder*

DECEMBER 16, 1904

RODOLFO	*Enrico Caruso*
MIMI	*Nellie Melba*
MARCELLO	*Antonio Scotti*
COLLINE	*Marcel Journet*
SCHAUNARD	*Taurino Parvis*
MUSETTA	*Bella Alten*
BENOIT	*Archangelo Rossi*
ALCINDORO	*Archangelo Rossi*
PARPIGNOL	*Giuseppe Tecchi*

CONDUCTOR	*Arturo Vigna*
STAGE DIRECTOR	*Eugène Dufriche*

NOVEMBER 27, 1907

RODOLFO	*Alessandro Bonci*
MIMI	*Marcella Sembrich*
MARCELLO	*Riccardo Stracciari*
COLLINE	*Marcel Journet*
SCHAUNARD	*Bernard Bégué*
MUSETTA	*Felia Dereyne*
BENOIT	*Eugène Dufriche*

ALCINDORO *Aristide Barrachi*
PARPIGNOL *Giuseppe Tecchi*

CONDUCTOR *Rodolfo Ferrari*
STAGE MANAGER *Eugène Dufriche*

NOVEMBER 21, 1910

RODOLFO *Hermann Jadlowker*
MIMI *Geraldine Farrar*
MARCELLO *Antonio Scotti*
COLLINE *Andres de Segurola*
SCHAUNARD *Adamo Didur*
MUSETTA *Bella Alten*
BENOIT *Antonio Pini-Corsi*
ALCINDORO *Antonio Pini-Corsi*
PARPIGNOL *Angelo Bada*
A SERGEANT *Edoardo Missiano*
A CUSTOMS OFFICER *Pietro Audisio*

CONDUCTOR *Arturo Toscanini*
STAGE MANAGER *Jules Speck*

JANUARY 18, 1911

RODOLFO *Dimitri Smirnoff*
MIMI *Alice Nielsen*
MARCELLO *Antonio Scotti*
COLLINE *Andres de Segurola*
SCHAUNARD *Adamo Didur*
MUSETTA *Bella Alten*
BENOIT *Antonio Pini-Corsi*
ALCINDORO *Antonio Pini-Corsi*
PARPIGNOL *Pietro Audisio*
A SERGEANT *Edoardo Missiano*
A CUSTOMS OFFICER *Pietro Audisio*

CONDUCTOR *Vittorio Podesti*
STAGE MANAGER *Jules Speck*

DECEMBER 2, 1911

RODOLFO *Riccardo Martin*
MIMI *Alma Gluck*
MARCELLO *Antonio Scotti*
COLLINE *Giulio Rossi*
SCHAUNARD *Antonio Pini-Corsi*
MUSETTA *Bella Alten*
BENOIT *Paolo Ananian*

ALCINDORO   *Georges Bourgeois*
PARPIGNOL   *Pietro Audisio*
A SERGEANT   *Edoardo Missiano*

CONDUCTOR   *Giuseppe Sturani*
STAGE MANAGER   *Jules Speck*

FEBRUARY 19, 1912

RODOLFO   *Enrico Caruso*
MIMI   *Geraldine Farrar*
MARCELLO   *Pasquale Amato*
COLLINE   *Andres de Segurola*
SCHAUNARD   *Adamo Didur*
MUSETTA   *Bella Alten*
BENOIT   *Antonio Pini-Corsi*
ALCINDORO   *Georges Bourgeois*
PARPIGNOL   *Pietro Audisio*
A SERGEANT   *Vincenzo Reschiglian*

CONDUCTOR   *Giuseppe Sturani*
STAGE MANAGER   *Jules Speck*

NOVEMBER 16, 1917

RODOLFO   *John McCormack*
MIMI   *Frances Alda*
MARCELLO   *Giuseppe De Luca*
COLLINE   *Andres de Segurola*
SCHAUNARD   *Adamo Didur*
MUSETTA   *Ruth Miller (debut)*
BENOIT   *Pompilio Malatesta*
ALCINDORO   *Robert Leonhardt*
PARPIGNOL   *Pietro Audisio*
A SERGEANT   *Vincenzo Reschiglian*

CONDUCTOR   *Gennaro Papi*
STAGE DIRECTOR   *Richard Ordynski*
STAGE MANAGER   *Armando F. Agnini*

NOVEMBER 20, 1919

RODOLFO   *Charles Hackett*
MIMI   *Frances Alda*
MARCELLO   *Pasquale Amato*
COLLINE   *Andres De Segurola*
SCHAUNARD   *Adamo Didur*
MUSETTA   *Margaret Romaine*
BENOIT   *Pompilio Malatesta*

ALCINDORO   *Paolo Ananian*
PARPIGNOL   *Pietro Audisio*
A SERGEANT   *Vincenzo Reschiglian*

CONDUCTOR   *Gennaro Papi*
STAGE DIRECTOR   *Richard Ordynski*
STAGE MANAGER   *Armando Agnini*

JANUARY 28, 1921

RODOLFO   *Beniamino Gigli*
MIMI   *Lucrezia Bori*
MARCELLO   *Antonio Scotti*
COLLINE   *Giovanni Martino*
SCHAUNARD   *Millo Picco*
MUSETTA   *Anne Roselle*
BENOIT   *Pompilio Malatesta*
ALCINDORO   *Paolo Ananian*
PARPIGNOL   *Pietro Audisio*
A SERGEANT   *Vincenzo Reschiglian*

CONDUCTOR   *Gennaro Papi*
STAGE DIRECTOR   *Samuel Theuman*
STAGE MANAGER   *Armando Agnini*

JANUARY 31, 1923

RODOLFO   *Giacomo Lauri-Volpi*
MIMI   *Frances Alda*
MARCELLO   *Antonio Scotti*
COLLINE   *Leon Rothier*
SCHAUNARD   *Millo Picco*
MUSETTA   *Marie Sundelius*
BENOIT   *Pompilio Malatesta*
ALCINDORO   *Paolo Ananian*
PARPIGNOL   *Pietro Audisio*
A SERGEANT   *Vincenzo Reschiglian*

CONDUCTOR   *Gennaro Papi*
STAGE MANAGER   *Armando Agnini*

FEBRUARY 23, 1923 (MATINEE)

RODOLFO   *Orville Harrold*
MIMI   *Amelita Galli-Curci*
MARCELLO   *Giuseppe De Luca*
COLLINE   *José Mardones*
SCHAUNARD   *Louis D'Angelo*
MUSETTA   *Marie Sundelius*

BENOIT	Pompilio Malatesta
ALCINDORO	José Paolo Ananian
PARPIGNOL	Pietro Audisio
A SERGEANT	Vincenzo Reschiglian

CONDUCTOR Gennaro Papi
STAGE MANAGER Armando Agnini

NOVEMBER 4, 1924

RODOLFO	Miguel Fleta
MIMI	Lucrezia Bori
MARCELLO	Giuseppe De Luca
COLLINE	Leon Rothier
SCHAUNARD	Millo Picco
MUSETTA	Louise Hunter
BENOIT	Paolo Ananian
ALCINDORO	Paolo Ananian
PARPIGNOL	Giordano Paltrinieri
A SERGEANT	Vincenzo Reschiglian

CONDUCTOR Giuseppe Bamboschek
STAGE MANAGER Armando Agnini

NOVEMBER 29, 1924

RODOLFO	Giovanni Martinelli
MIMI	Lucrezia Bori
MARCELLO	Antonio Scotti
COLLINE	Leon Rothier
SCHAUNARD	Millo Picco
MUSETTA	Louise Hunter
BENOIT	Pompilio Malatesta
ALCINDORO	Pompilio Malatesta
PARPIGNOL	G. Marinelli
A SERGEANT	Giuseppe Cottino

CONDUCTOR Giuseppe Bamboschek
STAGE MANAGER Armando Agnini

NOVEMBER 3, 1925

RODOLFO	Edward Johnson
MIMI	Frances Alda
MARCELLO	Giuseppe De Luca
COLLINE	Adamo Didur
SCHAUNARD	Millo Picco
MUSETTA	Louise Hunter
BENOIT	Paolo Ananian

ALCINDORO   *Pompilio Malatesta*
PARPIGNOL   *Max Altglass*
A SERGEANT   *Vincenzo Reschiglian*

CONDUCTOR   *Gennaro Papi*
STAGE MANAGER   *Armando Agnini*

NOVEMBER 27, 1926

RODOLFO   *Giacomo Lauri-Volpi*
MIMI   *Elisabeth Rethberg*
MARCELLO   *Antonio Scotti*
COLLINE   *Leon Rothier*
SCHAUNARD   *George Cehanovsky*
MUSETTA   *Louise Hunter*
BENOIT   *Paolo Ananian*
ALCINDORO   *Pompilio Malatesta*
PARPIGNOL   *Alfio Tedesco*
A SERGEANT   *Paolo Ananian*

CONDUCTOR   *Vincenzo Bellezza*
STAGE MANAGER   *Armando Agnini*

FEBRUARY 8, 1929

RODOLFO   *Giovanni Martinelli*
MIMI   *Maria Mueller*
MARCELLO   *Lawrence Tibbett*
COLLINE   *Ezio Pinza*
SCHAUNARD   *Millo Picco*
MUSETTA   *Nanette Guilford*
BENOIT   *Pompilio Malatesta*
ALCINDORO   *Pompilio Malatesta*
PARPIGNOL   *Max Altglass*
A SERGEANT   *Vincenzo Reschiglian*

CONDUCTOR   *Vincenzo Bellezza*
STAGE MANAGER   *Armando Agnini*

JANUARY 20, 1933 (MATINEE)

RODOLFO   *Giovanni Martinelli*
MIMI   *Elisabeth Rethberg*
MARCELLO   *Richard Bonelli*
COLLINE   *Arthur Anderson*
SCHAUNARD   *Claudio Frigerio*
MUSETTA   *Nina Morgana*
BENOIT   *Paolo Ananian*
ALCINDORO   *Pompilio Malatesta*

PARPIGNOL	Max Altglass
A SERGEANT	Carlo Coscia

CONDUCTOR	Vincenzo Bellezza
STAGE MANAGER	Armando Agnini

DECEMBER 31, 1934

RODOLFO	Dino Borgioli (debut)
MIMI	Lucrezia Bori
MARCELLO	Richard Bonelli
COLLINE	Virgilio Lazzari
SCHAUNARD	Millo Picco
MUSETTA	Nina Morgana
BENOIT	Paolo Ananian
ALCINDORO	Pompilio Malatesta
PARPIGNOL	Max Altglass
A SERGEANT	Carlo Coscia

CONDUCTOR	Vincenzo Bellezza
STAGE DIRECTOR	Désiré Defrère

JANUARY 27, 1936

RODOLFO	Charles Kullmann
MIMI	Eide Norena
MARCELLO	Carlo Morelli
COLLINE	Virgilio Lazzari
SCHAUNARD	George Cehanovsky
MUSETTA	Helen Gleason
BENOIT	Pompilio Malatesta
ALCINDORO	Pompilio Malatesta
PARPIGNOL	Max Altglass
A SERGEANT	Carlo Coscia

CONDUCTOR	Gennaro Papi
STAGE DIRECTOR	Désiré Defrère
CHORUS MASTER	Fausto Cleva

NOVEMBER 24, 1938

RODOLFO	Jussi Bjoerling (debut)
MIMI	Mafalda Favero (debut)
MARCELLO	John Brownlee
COLLINE	Norman Cordon
SCHAUNARD	George Cehanovsky
MUSETTA	Marisa Morel (debut)
BENOIT	Louis D'Angelo
ALCINDORO	Louis D'Angelo

PARPIGNOL *Max Altglass*
A SERGEANT *Carlo Coscia*

CONDUCTOR *Gennaro Papi*
STAGE DIRECTOR *Désiré Defrère*
CHORUS MASTER *Fausto Cleva*

JANUARY 5, 1940

RODOLFO *Jussi Bjoerling*
MIMI *Jarmila Novotna (debut)*
MARCELLO *John Brownlee*
COLLINE *Norman Cordon*
SCHAUNARD *George Cehanovsky*
MUSETTA *Muriel Dickson*
BENOIT *Louis D'Angelo*
ALCINDORO *Louis D'Angelo*
PARPIGNOL *Lodovico Oliviero*
A SERGEANT *Carlo Coscia*

CONDUCTOR *Gennaro Papi*
STAGE DIRECTOR *Désiré Defrère*
CHORUS MASTER *Fausto Cleva*

DECEMBER 1, 1944

RODOLFO *Jan Peerce*
MIMI *Grace Moore*
MARCELLO *John Brownlee*
COLLINE *Norman Cordon*
SCHAUNARD *Hugh Thompson (debut)*
MUSETTA *Frances Greer*
BENOIT *Salvatore Baccaloni*
ALCINDORO *Salvatore Baccaloni*
PARPIGNOL *Lodovico Oliviero*
A SERGEANT *John Baker*

CONDUCTOR *Cesare Sodero*
STAGE DIRECTOR *Désiré Defrère*
CHORUS MASTER *Giacomo Spadoni*

JANUARY 1, 1946

RODOLFO *Jussi Bjoerling*
MIMI *Bidù Sayão*
MARCELLO *John Brownlee*
COLLINE *Norman Cordon*
SCHAUNARD *Arthur Kent*
MUSETTA *Frances Greer*

BENOIT		*Salvatore Baccaloni*
ALCINDORO		*Salvatore Baccaloni*
PARPIGNOL		*Lodovico Oliviero*
A SERGEANT		*John Baker*

CONDUCTOR	*Cesare Sodero*
STAGE DIRECTOR	*Désiré Defrère*
CHORUS MASTER	*Kurt Adler*

JANUARY 10, 1947

RODOLFO		*Ferruccio Tagliavini (debut)*
MIMI		*Licia Albanese*
MARCELLO		*Francesco Valentino*
COLLINE		*Giacomo Vaghi*
SCHAUNARD		*George Cehanovsky*
MUSETTA		*Mimi Benzell*
BENOIT		*Gerhard Pechner*
ALCINDORO		*Gerhard Pechner*
PARPIGNOL		*Lodovico Oliviero*
A SERGEANT		*John Baker*

CONDUCTOR	*Cesare Sodero*
STAGE DIRECTOR	*Désiré Defrère*
CHORUS MASTER	*Kurt Adler*

MARCH 8, 1949 (MATINEE)

RODOLFO		*Giuseppe Di Stefano*
MIMI		*Dorothy Kirsten*
MARCELLO		*John Brownlee*
COLLINE		*Nicola Moscona*
SCHAUNARD		*Clifford Harvuot*
MUSETTA		*Frances Greer*
BENOIT		*Melchiorre Luise*
ALCINDORO		*Melchiorre Luise*
PARPIGNOL		*Anthony Marlowe*
A SERGEANT		*John Baker*

CONDUCTOR	*Giuseppe Antonicelli*
STAGE DIRECTOR	*Désiré Defrère*
CHORUS MASTER	*Kurt Adler*

MARCH 30, 1951

RODOLFO		*Giuseppe Di Stefano*
MIMI		*Victoria de los Angeles*
MARCELLO		*Giuseppe Valdengo*

COLLINE   *Nicola Moscona*
SCHAUNARD   *George Cehanovsky*
MUSETTA   *Lois Hunt*
BENOIT   *Salvatore Baccaloni*
ALCINDORO   *Salvatore Baccaloni*
PARPIGNOL   *Paul Franke*
A SERGEANT   *Carlo Tomanelli*

CONDUCTOR   *Fausto Cleva*
STAGE DIRECTOR   *Désiré Defrère*

DECEMBER 15, 1951

RODOLFO   *Richard Tucker*
MIMI   *Eleanor Steber*
MARCELLO   *Giuseppe Valdengo*
COLLINE   *Cesare Siepi*
SCHAUNARD   *Clifford Harvuot*
MUSETTA   *Hilde Gueden*
BENOIT   *Lorenzo Alvary*
ALCINDORO   *Gerhard Pechner*
PARPIGNOL   *Paul Franke*
A SERGEANT   *Carlo Tomanelli*

CONDUCTOR   *Alberto Erede*
STAGE DIRECTOR   *Désiré Defrère*
CHORUS MASTER   *Kurt Adler*

DECEMBER 27, 1952 (MATINEE)

RODOLFO   *Richard Tucker*
MIMI   *Nadine Conner*
MARCELLO   *Robert Merrill*
COLLINE   *Jerome Hines*
SCHAUNARD   *Clifford Harvuot*
MUSETTA   *Patrice Munsel*
BENOIT   *Lawrence Davidson*
ALCINDORO   *Alessio De Paolis*
PARPIGNOL   *Paul Franke*
A SERGEANT   *Algerd Brazis*

CONDUCTOR   *Alberto Erede*
STAGED BY   *Joseph L. Mankiewicz*
CHORUS MASTER   *Kurt Adler*
DECOR AND COSTUMES BY   *Rolf Gerard*

[EDITOR'S NOTE: This performance of *La Bohème* was sung in English. Translator: Howard Dietz.]

NOTES

NOVEMBER 3, 1956

RODOLFO	*Daniele Barioni*
MIMI	*Lucine Amara*
MARCELLO	*Enzo Sordello (debut)*
COLLINE	*Norman Scott*
SCHAUNARD	*Clifford Harvuot*
MUSETTA	*Laurel Hurley*
BENOIT	*Lawrence Davidson*
ALCINDORO	*Gerhard Pechner*
A SERGEANT	*Calvin March*

CONDUCTOR	*Thomas Schippers*
PRODUCTION BY	*Joseph L. Mankiewicz*
STAGE DIRECTOR	*Nathaniel Merrill*
SETS AND COSTUMES BY	*Rolf Gérard*

FEBRUARY 2, 1957

RODOLFO	*Jan Peerce*
MIMI	*Hilde Gueden*
MARCELLO	*Ettore Bastianini*
COLLINE	*Nicola Moscona*
SCHAUNARD	*George Cehanovsky*
MUSETTA	*Laurel Hurley*
BENOIT	*Lawrence Davidson*
ALCINDORO	*Alessio De Paolis*
PARPIGNOL	*James McCracken*
A SERGEANT	*Calvin Marsh*

CONDUCTOR	*Tibor Kozma*
PRODUCTION BY	*Joseph L. Mankiewicz*
STAGE DIRECTOR	*Nathaniel Merrill*
CHORUS MASTER	*Kurt Adler*
SETS AND COSTUMES BY	*Rolf Gérard*

FEBRUARY 8, 1957

RODOLFO	*Richard Tucker*
MIMI	*Renata Tebaldi*
MARCELLO	*Ettore Bastianini*
COLLINE	*Giorgio Tozzi*
SCHAUNARD	*Clifford Harvuot*
MUSETTA	*Heidi Krall*
BENOIT	*Lawrence Davidson*
ALCINDORO	*Alessio De Paolis*
PARPIGNOL	*Charles Anthony*
A SERGEANT	*Calvin Marsh*

CONDUCTOR	*Thomas Schippers*
PRODUCTION BY	*Joseph L. Mankiewicz*

STAGE DIRECTOR   *Nathaniel Merrill*
CHORUS MASTER   *Kurt Adler*
SETS AND COSTUMES BY *Rolf Gérard*

DECEMBER 8, 1957

RODOLFO	*Carlo Bergonzi*
MIMI	*Victoria de los Angeles*
MARCELLO	*Frank Guarrera*
COLLINE	*Giorgio Tozzi*
SCHAUNARD	*George Cehanovsky*
MUSETTA	*Heidi Krall*
BENOIT	*Ezio Flagello*
ALCINDORO	*Lorenzo Alvary*
PARPIGNOL	*Robert Nagy*
A SERGEANT	*Calvin Marsh*
A CUSTOMS OFFICER	*Robert Nagy*

CONDUCTOR   *Thomas Schippers*
PRODUCTION BY   *Joseph L. Mankiewicz*
STAGE DIRECTOR   *Hans Busch*
CHORUS MASTER   *Kurt Adler*
SETS AND COSTUMES BY *Rolf Gérard*

DECEMBER 10, 1960

RODOLFO	*Richard Tucker*
MIMI	*Lisa Della Casa*
MARCELLO	*Lorenzo Testi*
COLLINE	*Bonaldo Giaiotti*
SCHAUNARD	*Roald Reitan*
MUSETTA	*Laurel Hurley*
BENOIT	*Gerhard Pechner*
ALCINDORO	*Norman Kelley*
PARPIGNOL	*Hal Roberts*
A SERGEANT	*Carlo Tomanelli*
A CUSTOMS OFFICER	*Edward Ghazal*

CONDUCTOR   *Thomas Schippers*
PRODUCTION BY   *Joseph L. Mankiewicz*
STAGE DIRECTOR   *Ralph Herbert*
CHORUS MASTER   *Kurt Adler*
SETS AND COSTUMES BY *Rolf Gérard*

FEBRUARY 26, 1962

RODOLFO	*Ferruccio Tagliavini*
MIMI	*Teresa Stratas*
MARCELLO	*Lorenzo Testi*

COLLINE	*Bonaldo Giaiotti*
SCHAUNARD	*Clifford Harvuot*
MUSETTA	*Brenda Lewis*
BENOIT	*Gerhard Pechner*
ALCINDORO	*Alessio De Paolis*
PARPIGNOL	*Hal Roberts*
A SERGEANT	*Lloyd Strang*
A CUSTOMS OFFICER	*Carlo Tomanelli*

CONDUCTOR	*Martin Rich*
PRODUCTION BY	*Joseph L. Mankiewicz*
STAGE DIRECTOR	*James Lucas*
CHORUS MASTER	*Kurt Adler*
SETS AND COSTUMES DESIGNED BY	*Rolf Gérard*

FEBRUARY 29, 1964

RODOLFO	*Franco Corelli*
MIMI	*Gabriella Tucci*
MARCELLO	*Frank Guarrera*
COLLINE	*Bonaldo Giaiotti*
SCHAUNARD	*William Walker*
MUSETTA	*Elisabeth Söderström*
BENOIT	*Fernando Corena*
ALCINDORO	*Alessio De Paolis*
PARPIGNOL	*Emil Filip*
A SERGEANT	*Lloyd Strang*
A CUSTOMS OFFICER	*Edward Ghazal*

CONDUCTOR	*Fausto Cleva*
PRODUCTION BY	*Joseph L. Mankiewicz*
STAGE DIRECTOR	*Hugh Thompson*
CHORUS MASTER	*Kurt Adler*
SETS AND COSTUMES DESIGNED BY	*Rolf Gérard*

SEPTEMBER 29, 1965

RODOLFO	*Gianni Raimondi (debut)*
MIMI	*Mirella Freni (debut)*
MARCELLO	*Calvin Marsh*
COLLINE	*John Macurdy*
SCHAUNARD	*Clifford Harvuot*
MUSETTA	*Heidi Krall*
BENOIT	*Lorenzo Alvary*
ALCINDORO	*Andrea Velis*
PARPIGNOL	*Emil Filip*
A SERGEANT	*Edward Ghazal*
A CUSTOMS OFFICER	*John Trehy*

CONDUCTOR	Fausto Cleva
PRODUCTION BY	Joseph L. Mankiewicz
STAGE DIRECTOR	Patrick Tavernia
CHORUS MASTER	Kurt Adler
SETS AND COSTUMES DESIGNED BY	Rolf Gérard

NOVEMBER 23, 1968 (MATINEE)

RODOLFO	Luciano Pavarotti (debut)
MIMI	Mirella Freni
MARCELLO	Frank Guarrera
COLLINE	Jerome Hines
SCHAUNARD	Russell Christopher
MUSETTA	Colette Boky
BENOIT	Paul Plishka
ALCINDORO	Lorenzo Alvary
PARPIGNOL	Gene Allen
A SERGEANT	Peter Sliker
A CUSTOMS OFFICER	Lloyd Strang

CONDUCTOR	Francesco Molinari-Pradelli
STAGE DIRECTOR	Nikolaus Lehnhoff
CHORUS MASTER	Kurt Adler
SETS AND COSTUMES DESIGNED BY	Rolf Gérard

DECEMBER 30, 1969

RODOLFO	Nicolai Gedda
MIMI	Gabriella Tucci
MARCELLO	Mario Sereni
COLLINE	Giorgio Tozzi
SCHAUNARD	Robert Goodloe
MUSETTA	Clarice Carson
BENOIT	Paul Plishka
ALCINDORO	Fernando Corena
PARPIGNOL	Hal Roberts
A SERGEANT	Peter Sliker
A CUSTOMS OFFICER	Lloyd Strang

CONDUCTOR	Fausto Cleva
STAGE DIRECTOR	Patrick Tavernia
CHORUS MASTER	Kurt Adler
SETS AND COSTUMES DESIGNED BY	Rolf Gérard

JANUARY 16, 1973

RODOLFO	Richard Tucker
MIMI	Pilar Lorengar
MARCELLO	William Walker

COLLINE	*Paul Plishka*
SCHAUNARD	*Robert Goodloe*
MUSETTA	*Colette Boky*
BENOIT	*Andrij Dobriansky*
ALCINDORO	*Nico Castel*
PARPIGNOL	*William Mellow*
A SERGEANT	*Frank Coffey*
A CUSTOMS OFFICER	*Herman Marcus*

CONDUCTOR	*Henry Lewis*
STAGE DIRECTOR	*Patrick Tavernia*
CHORUS MASTER	*Kurt Adler*
SETS AND COSTUMES DESIGNED BY	*Rolf Gérard*

MARCH 9, 1974

RODOLFO	*Luciano Pavarotti*
MIMI	*Teresa Zylis-Gara*
MARCELLO	*Mario Sereni*
COLLINE	*John Macurdy*
SCHAUNARD	*David Holloway*
MUSETTA	*Edda Moser*
BENOIT	*Richard Best*
ALCINDORO	*Paul Franke*
PARPIGNOL	*Arthur Apy*
A SERGEANT	*Frank Coffey*
A CUSTOMS OFFICER	*Nicola Barbusci*

CONDUCTOR	*Leif Segerstam*
STAGE DIRECTOR	*Patrick Tavernia*
CHORUS MASTER	*David Stivender*
SETS AND COSTUMES DESIGNED BY	*Rolf Gérard*

APRIL 11, 1975

RODOLFO	*José Carreras*
MIMI	*Katia Ricciarelli (debut)*
MARCELLO	*William Walker*
COLLINE	*Giorgio Tozzi*
SCHAUNARD	*Russell Christopher*
MUSETTA	*Rita Shane*
BENOIT	*Andrij Dobriansky*
ALCINDORO	*Charles Anthony*
PARPIGNOL	*Arthur Apy*
A SERGEANT	*Edward Ghazal*
A CUSTOMS OFFICER	*Domenico Simeone*

CONDUCTOR	*Leif Segerstam*
STAGE DIRECTOR	*Patrick Tavernia*
CHORUS MASTER	*David Stivender*
SETS AND COSTUMES DESIGNED BY	*Rolf Gérard*

March 27, 1976

Rodolfo	*Luciano Pavarotti*
Mimi	*Montserrat Caballé*
Marcello	*Mario Sereni*
Colline	*Paul Plishka*
Schaunard	*Allan Monk (debut)*
Musetta	*Maralin Niska*
Benoit	*Italo Tajo*
Alcindoro	*Italo Tajo*
Parpignol	*Arthur Apy*
A Sergeant	*Edward Ghazal*
A Customs Officer	*Herman Marcus*

Conductor	*James Levine*
Stage Director	*Patrick Tavernia*
Chorus Master	*David Stivender*
Set and Costume Designer	*Rolf Gérard*

February 23, 1977

Rodolfo	*Luciano Pavarotti*
Mimi	*Renata Scotto*
Marcello	*Ingvar Wixell*
Colline	*Paul Plishka*
Schaunard	*Allan Monk*
Musetta	*Maralin Niska*
Benoit	*Italo Tajo*
Alcindoro	*Andrea Velis*
Parpignol	*Dale Caldwell*
A Sergeant	*Paul De Paola*
A Customs Officer	*Domenico Simeone*

Conductor	*James Levine*
Production	*Fabrizio Melano*
Chorus Master	*David Stivender*
Set and Costume Designer	*Pier Luigi Pizzi (Debut)*
Lighting Designer	*Gil Wechsler*

[Editor's Note: *La Bohème,* with the above cast, launched the *Live from the Met* telecast series in 1977.]

March 23, 1977

Rodolfo	*José Carreras*
Mimi	*Ileana Cotrubas (debut)*
Marcello	*Ingvar Wixell*
Colline	*Justino Díaz*
Schaunard	*Allan Monk*
Musetta	*Renata Scotto*

BENOIT	*Italo Tajo*
ALCINDORO	*Paul Franke*
PARPIGNOL	*Dale Caldwell*
A SERGEANT	*Paul De Paola*
A CUSTOMS OFFICER	*Domenico Simeone*

CONDUCTOR	*James Levine*
PRODUCTION	*Fabrizio Melano*
CHORUS MASTER	*David Stivender*
SET AND COSTUME DESIGNER	*Pier Luigi Pizzi*
LIGHTING DESIGNER	*Gil Wechsler*

OCTOBER 12, 1977

RODOLFO	*Placido Domingo*
MIMI	*Renata Scotto*
MARCELLO	*Mario Sereni*
COLLINE	*José Van Dam*
SCHAUNARD	*Robert Goodloe*
MUSETTA	*Mary Costa*
BENOIT	*Richard Best*
ALCINDORO	*Paul Franke*
PARPIGNOL	*Donald Junod*
A SERGEANT	*Edward Ghazal*
A CUSTOMS OFFICER	*Domenico Simeone*

CONDUCTOR	*James Conlon*
STAGED BY	*Fabrizio Melano*
DESIGNED BY	*Pier Luigi Pizzi*

DECEMBER 14, 1981

RODOLFO	*José Carreras*
MIMI	*Teresa Stratas*
MARCELLO	*Richard Stilwell*
COLLINE	*James Morris*
SCHAUNARD	*Allan Monk*
MUSETTA	*Renata Scotto*
BENOIT	*Italo Tajo*
ALCINDORO	*Italo Tajo*
PARPIGNOL	*Dale Caldwell*
A SERGEANT	*Glen Bater*
A CUSTOMS OFFICER	*James Brewer*

CONDUCTOR	*James Levine*
PRODUCTION	*Franco Zeffirelli*
CHORUS MASTER	*David Stivender*
SET DESIGNER	*Franco Zeffirelli*
COSTUME DESIGNER	*Peter J. Hall*
LIGHTING DESIGNER	*Gil Wechsler*

MUSICAL PREPARATION *Jeffrey Tate and Joan Dornemann*
ASSISTANT STAGE DIRECTORS *David Kneuss, Lesley Koenig, and David Sell*
STAGE BAND CONDUCTOR *Gildo Di Nunzio*
PROMPTER *Joan Dornemann*

[EDITOR'S NOTE: The statistical data on *La Bohème* which follows was compiled from records kept in the Archives of the Metropolitan Opera. Included is a complete listing of the year of the first performance of every artist in a major role, a complete listing of all conductors, and a complete listing of seasons, from the premiere in 1900 through the season of 1981–1982, in which *La Bohème* has been performed at the Met. Thirteen performances of *La Bohème* have been scheduled for the 1982–1983 season.]

MIMI

Nellie Melba (1900); Marcella Sembrich (1902); Bessie Abott (1906); Lina Cavalieri (1907); Geraldine Farrar (1907); Alice Nielsen (1909); Frances Alda (1909); Gina Ciaparelli (1910); Alma Gluck (1911); Lucrezia Bori (1912); Claudia Muzio (1917); May Peterson (1917); Delia Reinhardt (1923); Amelita Galli-Curci (1923); Maria Mueller (1925); Mary Lewis (1926); Elisabeth Rethberg (1926); Grace Moore (1928); Queena Mario (1928); Editha Fleischer (1930); Eide Norena (1933); Franca Somigli (1937); Bidù Sayão (1937); Rosa Tentoni (1937); Hilda Burke (1937); Mafalda Favero (1938); Jarmila Novotna (1940); Licia Albanese (1940); Dorothy Kirsten (1945); Stella Roman (1946); Nadine Conner (1947); Claudia Pinza (1947); Pia Tassinari (1948); Eleanor Steber (1949); Victoria de los Angeles (1951); Hilde Gueden (1953); Lucine Amara (1953); Renata Tebaldi (1955); Patrice Munsel (1958); Marcella Pobbé (1958); Mary Curtis-Verna (1959); Heidi Krall (1959); Emilia Cundari (1959); Laurel Hurley (1959); Lisa Della Casa (1960); Teresa Stratas (1962); Raina Kabaivanska (1963); Nicoletta Panni (1963); Gabriella Tucci (1964); Mary Ellen Pracht (1964); Jean Fenn (1964); Mirella Freni (1965); Milka Stojanovic (1968); Radmila Bakocevic (1969); Adriana Maliponte (1971); Jeanette Pilou (1971); Anna Moffo (1972); Renata Scotto (1972); Pilar Lorengar (1973); Enriqueta Tarrés (1973); Montserrat Caballé (1974); Teresa Zylis-Gara (1974); Clarice Carson (1974); Colette Boky (1974); Atsuko Azuma (1975); Loretta Di Franco (1975); Katia Ricciarelli (1975); Carole Farley (1975); Ileana Cotrubas (1977); Leona Mitchell (1977); Elena Mauti-Nunziata (1977); Linda Zoghby (1982)

RODOLFO

Albert Saléza (1900); Giuseppe Cremonini (1900); Emilio de Marchi (1902); Carlo Dani (1903); Giovanni Agostini (1903); Enrico Caruso (1903); Andreas Dippel (1905); Alessandro Bonci (1907); Ariodante Quarti (1908); Rinaldo Grassi (1909); Riccardo Martin (1910); Hermann Jadlowker (1910); Dimitri Smirnoff (1911); Giovanni Martinelli (1913); Italo Cristalli (1913); Luca Botta (1914); John McCormack (1917); Giulio Crimi (1918); Hipolito Lazaro (1919); Orville Harrold (1919); Beniamino Gigli (1920); Mario Chamlee (1921); Giacomo Lauri-Volpi (1923); Miguel Fleta (1924); Armand Tokatyan (1925); Edward Johnson (1925); Antonin Trantoul (1930); Frederick Jagel (1934); Nino Martini (1934); Dino Borgioli (1934); Charles Kullman (1936); Bruno Landi (1938); Jan Kiepura (1938); Jussi Bjoerling (1938); Jan Peerce (1944); Ferruccio Tagliavini (1947); Richard Tucker (1947); Giuseppe Di Stefano (1949); Giacinto Prandelli (1952); Eugene Conley (1952); Brian Sullivan (1953); Giulio Gari (1954); Giuseppe Campora (1955); Daniele Barioni (1956); Gianni Poggi (1957); Carlo Bergonzi (1957); Flaviano Labo (1957); Eugenio Fernandi (1958); Barry Morell (1959); Charles Anthony (1959); Dino Formichini (1961); George Shirley (1963); John Alexander (1963); Franco Corelli (1964); Sándor Kónya (1964); Franco Ghitti (1964); Gianni Raimondi (1965); Luciano Pavarotti (1968); Nicolai Gedda (1969); Ion Buzea (1970); Enrico Di Giuseppe (1970); Octaviano Naghiu (1970); Leo Goeke (1972); José Carreras (1975); Raymond Gibbs (1977); Giorgio Casellato-Lamberti (1977); Placido Domingo (1977); Vasile Moldoveanu (1977); Neil Shicoff (1977); Giacomo Aragall (1977); Ermanno Mauro (1981); Giuliano Ciannella (1982)

MARCELLO

Giuseppe Campanari (1900); Antonio Scotti (1904); Riccardo Stracciari (1907); Pasquale Amato (1908); Dinh Gilly (1910); Riccardo Tegani (1915); Giuseppe De Luca (1915); Luigi Montesanto (1918); Millo Picco (1922); Giuseppe Danise (1922); Lawrence Tibbett (1929); Mario Basiola (1929); Richard Bonelli (1932); Armando Borgioli (1933); Carlo Morelli (1935); John Brownlee (1937); Carlo Tagliabue (1938); Francesco Valentino (1942); Martial Singher (1945); Giuseppe Valdengo (1949); Enzo Mascherini (1949); Frank Guarrera (1951); Renato Capecchi (1951); Robert Merrill (1952); Paolo Silveri (1952); Frank Valentino (1953); Ettore Bastianini (1955); Enzo Sordello (1956); Mario Sereni (1958); Mario Zanasi (1958); Clifford Harvuot (1959); Lorenzo Testi (1960); Calvin Marsh (1963); Vladimir Ruzdak (1963); Theodor Uppman (1964); William Walker (1964); Dominic Cossa (1970); Russell Christopher (1971); Matteo Manuguerra (1971); Cornell MacNeil (1974); Robert Goodloe (1975); Lenus Carlson (1975); John Reardon (1975); Ingvar Wixell (1977); Vicente Sar-

dinero (1977); Ryan Edwards (1977); Richard Stilwell (1981); Brent Ellis (1982)

MUSETTA

Anita Occhiolini (1900); Fritzi Scheff (1901); Cleopatre Vicini (1903); Estelle Liebling (1903); Camille Seygard (1903); Bella Alten (1904); Felia Dereyne (1907); Lenora Sparkes (1908); Isabelle L'Huillier (1908); Jane Noria (1910); Elisabeth Schumann (1914); Ida Cajatti (1915); Edith Mason (1916); Ruth Miller (1917); Helen Kanders (1918); Margaret Romaine (1918); Marie Sundelius (1919); Anne Roselle (1920); Marie Tiffany (1921); Yvonne D'Arle (1921); Grace Anthony (1922); Nannette Guilford (1924); Louise Hunter (1924); Mary Mellish (1924); Elizabeth Kandt (1926); Thalia Sabanieeva (1927); Editha Fleischer (1928); Augusta Oltrabella (1929); Santa Biondo (1930); Nina Morgana (1932); Helen Gleason (1933); Aida Doninelli (1933); Stella Andreva (1937); Margaret Daum (1937); Lucy Monroe (1937); Muriel Dickson (1937); Natalie Bodanya (1938); Marisa Morel (1938); Annamary Dickey (1940); Frances Greer (1942); Christina Caroll (1943); Marita Farell (1944); Mimi Benzell (1947); Lois Hunt (1949); Anne Bollinger (1951); Patrice Munsel (1951); Hilde Gueden (1951); Ljuba Welitsch (1952); Brenda Lewis (1952); Regina Resnik (1953); Jean Fenn (1953); Virginia MacWatters (1954); Heidi Krall (1954); Laurel Hurley (1956); Gloria Lind (1959); Elizabeth Söderström (1961); Dorothy Coulter (1961); Maria Gray (1963); Janet Pavek (1963); Jolanda Meneguzzer (1963); Anneliese Rothenberger (1963); Joy Clements (1964); Beverly Bower (1965); Marie Collier (1967); Judith De Paul (1968); Colette Boky (1968); Clarice Carson (1968); Maralin Niska (1973); Christine Weidinger (1973); Edda Moser (1974); Betsy Norden (1974); Loretta Di Franco (1974); Rita Shane (1975); Mary Costa (1975); Renata Scotto (1977); Josephine Barstow (1977); Leona Mitchell (1977); Julia Migenes-Johnson (1982); Patricia Craig (1982)

SCHAUNARD

Charles Gilibert (1900); Marcel Journet (1903); Archangelo Rossi (1903); Eugène Dufriche (1903); Taurino Parvis (1904); Jules Simard (1906); Bernard Bégué (1907); Giulio Rossi (1908); Enzo Bozzano (1908); Adamo Didur (1909); Antonio Pini-Corsi (1909); Vincenzo Reschiglian (1913); Riccardo Tegani (1914); Louis D'Angelo (1917); Thomas Chalmers (1918); Millo Picco (1920); George Cehanovsky (1926); Claudio Frigerio (1931); Wilfred Engelman (1937); Hugh Thompson (1944); Arthur Kent (1946); Clifford Harvuot (1949); Calvin Marsh (1959); Roald Reitan (1960); William Walker (1963); Robert Patterson (1964); Russell Christopher (1964); Robert Goodloe (1965); Gene Boucher (1967); Raymond Gibbs (1971); David Holloway (1974); Raymond Michalski (1974); Allan Monk (1976); Mario Sereni (1981)

COLLINE

Marcel Journet (1900); Charles Gilibert (1903); Aristide Barrachi (1908); Adamo Didur (1908); Guilio Rossi (1909); Andres de Segurola (1909); Leon Rothier (1913); José Mardones (1917); Giovanni Martino (1920); Ezio Pinza (1920); Pavel Ludikar (1927); Tancredi Pasero (1929); Arthur Anderson (1932); Virgilio Lazzari (1934); Norman Cordon (1937); Nicola Moscona (1945); Giacomo Vaghi (1946); Italo Tajo (1949); Cesare Siepi (1951); Norman Scott (1952); Jerome Hines (1952); Giorgio Tozzi (1956); Louis Sgarro (1959); William Wildermann (1959); Bonaldo Giaiotti (1960); Anton Diakov (1963); Justino Díaz (1964); John Macurdy (1964); Nicola Ghiuselev (1966); Paul Plishka (1970); Ezio Flagello (1972); Raymond Michalski (1974); Malcolm Smith (1975); James Morris (1975); Philip Booth (1977) José Van Dam (1977); Julien Robbins (1982)

BENOIT

Eugène Dufriche (1900); Archangelo Rossi (1903); Paolo Ananian (1908); Antonio Pini-Corsi (1909); Robert Leonhardt (1914); Pompilio Malatesta (1915); Louis D'Angelo (1935); Salvatore Baccaloni (1941); Gerhard Pechner (1942); Melchiorre Luise (1947); Lorenzo Alvary (1949); Lawrence Davidson (1952); Alessio De Paolis (1956); Ezio Flagello (1957); Fernando Corena (1959); Elfego Esparza (1965); Raymond Michalski (1966); Paul Plishka (1968); Richard Best (1970); Andrij Dobriansky (1971); Andrea Velis (1973); Robert Schmorr (1975); Nico Castel (1975); Italo Tajo (1976); Renato Capecchi (1982)

ALCINDORO

Eugène Dufriche (1900); Archangelo Rossi (1903); Aristide Barrachi (1907); Concetto Paterna (1908); Fernando Gianoli-Galletti (1909); Antonio Pini-Corsi (1910); Georges Bourgeois (1911); Paolo Ananian (1913); Robert Leonhardt (1915); Pompilio Malatesta (1916); Louis D'Angelo (1935); Salvatore Baccaloni (1945); Melchiorre Luise (1949); Gerhard Pechner (1950); Lawrence Davidson (1951); Alessio De Paolis (1951); Lorenzo Alvary (1954); Osie Hawkins (1959); Norman Kelley (1960); Mariano Caruso (1964); Fernando Corena (1969); Robert Schmorr (1972); Nico Castel (1972); Paul Franke (1973); Andrij Dobriansky (1974); Charles Anthony (1975); Italo Tajo (1977); Renato Capecchi (1982)

CONDUCTOR

Luigi Mancinelli (1900); Arturo Vigna (1903); Rodolfo Ferrari (1907); Francesco Spetrino (1908); Vittorio Podesti (1909); Arturo Toscanini (1910); Giuseppe Sturani (1911); Giorgio Polacco (1912); Gaetano Bavagnoli (1915); Gennaro Papi (1916); Giuseppe Bamboschek (1924); Vincenzo Bellezza (1926); Pietro Cimara (1932); Paul Breisach (1942); Cesare Sodero (1942); Giuseppe Antonicelli (1948); Alberto Erede (1951); Fausto Cleva (1951); Tibor Kozma (1956); Thomas Schippers (1956); Kurt Adler (1958); Martin Rich (1959); Ignace Strasfogel (1959); George Schick (1961);

Nino Verchi (1961); Jan Behr (1964); Francesco Molinari-Pradelli (1968); Carlo Franci (1969); Henry Lewis (1972); Leif Segerstam (1973); James Levine (1976); James Conlon (1977); Jeffrey Tate (1982)

PERFORMANCES BY SEASON

1900–01 (5); 02–03 (3); 03–04 (3); 04–05 (3); 05–06 (5); 06–07 (7); 07–08 (7); 08–09 (7); 09–10 (7); 10–11 (6); 11–12 (8); 12–13 (6); 13–14 (8); 14–15 (7); 15–16 (5); 16–17 (5); 17–18 (5); 18–19 (6); 19–20 (4); 20–21 (9); 21–22 (7); 22–23 (7); 23–24 (8); 24–25 (7); 25–26 (8); 26–27 (7); 27–28 (4); 28–29 (6); 29–30 (7); 30–31 (6); 31–32 (4); 32–33 (7); 33–34 (3); 34–35 (6); 35–36 (6); 36–37 (4); 37–38 (5); 38–39 (6); 39–40 (5); 40–41 (3); 41–42 (4); 42–43 (6); 43–44 (7); 44–45 (7); 45–46 (7); 46–47 (5); 47–48 (7); 48–49 (10); 49–50 (8); 50–51 (5); 51–52 (11); 52–53 (11); 53–54 (15); 54–55 (5); 55–56 (6); 56–57 (14); 57–58 (9); 58–59 (17); 60–61 (14); 61–62 (9); 63–64 (19); 65–66 (16); 66–67 (11); 68–69 (17); 69–70 (9); 70–71 (11); 71–72 (3); 72–73 (16); 73–74 (11); 74–75 (9); 75–76 (1); 76–77 (14); 77–78 (15); 81–82 (20) —581 performances in 74 seasons

SELECTED DISCOGRAPHY

[EDITOR's NOTE: * indicates recordings not currently available; (I) indicates recordings available as imports from Europe.]

COMPLETE RECORDINGS

Lorenzo Molajoli, cond.; La Scala Chorus and Orchestra (1929)
Rosetta Pampanini (Mimi), Luba Mirella (Musetta), Luigi Marini (Rodolfo), Gino Vanelli (Marcello), Aristide Baracchi (Schaunard), Tancredi Pasero (Colline), Salvatore Baccaloni (Benoit, Alcindoro)
COLUMBIA OP-5* (78 rpm)
Highlights: EMI/ITALY 3C-063-17802 (mono)

Umberto Berretoni, cond.; La Scala Chorus and Orchestra (1938)
Licia Albanese (Mimi), Tatiana Menotti (Musetta), Beniamino Gigli (Rodolfo), Afro Poli (Marcello), Aristide Baracchi (Schaunard), Duilio Baronti (Colline), Carlo Scattola (Benoit, Alcindoro)
SERAPHIM 6038-IB (mono)

Arturo Toscanini, cond.; chorus and NBC Symphony Orchestra (1946)
Licia Albanese (Mimi), Anne McKnight (Musetta), Jan Peerce (Rodolfo), Francesco Valentino (Marcello), George Cehanovsky (Schaunard), Nicola Moscona (Colline), Salvatore Baccaloni (Benoit, Alcindoro)
RCA VICTROLA VICS-6019 ("electronic stereo")

Giuseppe Antonicelli, cond.; Metropolitan Opera Chorus and Orchestra (1947)
Bidù Sayão (Mimi), Mimi Benzell (Musetta), Richard Tucker (Rodolfo), Francesco Valentino (Marcello), George Cehanovsky (Schaunard), Nicola Moscona (Colline), Salvatore Baccaloni (Benoit, Alcindoro)
CBS/ODYSSEY Y2-32364 (mono)

Alberto Erede, cond.; Chorus and Orchestra of Accademia Santa Cecilia, Rome (1950)
Renata Tebaldi (Mimi), Hilde Gueden (Musetta), Giacinto Prandelli (Rodolfo), Giovanni Inghilleri (Marcello), Fernando Corena (Schaunard), Raffaele Arié (Colline), Melchiorre Luise (Benoit, Alcindoro)
RICHMOND RS-62001* (mono)

Gabriele Santini, cond.; Radio Italiana Chorus and Orchestra (1951)
Rosanna Carteri (Mimi), Elvira Ramella (Musetta), Ferruccio Tagliavini (Rodolfo), Giuseppe Taddei (Marcello), Pier Luigi Latinucci (Schaunard), Cesare Siepi (Colline), Mario Zorgniotti (Benoit, Alcindoro)
CETRA-SORIA LP-1237* (mono)

Alberto Paoletti, cond.; Rome Opera House Chorus and Orchestra (1952)
Frances Schimenti (Mimi), Mafalda Micheluzzi (Musetta), Giacomo Lauri-Volpi (Rodolfo), Giovanni Ciavola (Marcello), Enzo Titta (Schaunard), Victor Tatozzi (Colline), Piero Passerotti (Benoit, Alcindoro)
REMINGTON R-199-99* (mono)

Sir Thomas Beecham, cond.; New York City Opera Chorus, RCA Victor Orchestra (1956)
   Victoria de los Angeles (Mimi), Lucine Amara (Musetta), Jussi Bjoerling (Rodolfo), Robert Merrill (Marcello), John Reardon (Schaunard), Giorgio Tozzi (Colline), Fernando Corena (Benoit, Alcindoro)
   SERAPHIM 6099-IB ("electronic stereo")

Antonino Votto, cond.; La Scala Chorus and Orchestra (1956)
   Maria Callas (Mimi), Anna Moffo (Musetta), Giuseppe Di Stefano (Rodolfo), Rolando Panerai (Marcello), Manuel Spatafora (Schaunard), Nicola Zaccaria (Colline), Carlo Badioli (Benoit, Alcindoro)
   ANGEL 3560-BL (mono)

Francesco Molinari-Pradelli, cond.; San Carlo Opera Chorus and Orchestra, Naples (1957)
   Antonietta Stella (Mimi), Bruna Rizzoli (Musetta), Gianni Poggi (Rodolfo), Renato Capecchi (Marcello), Guido Mazzini (Schaunard), Giuseppe Modesti (Colline), Melchiorre Luise (Benoit), Giorgio Onesti (Alcindoro)
   COLUMBIA M2L-401*; PHILLIPS 6720-008 (I)

Tullio Serafin, cond.; Chorus and Orchestra of Accademia Santa Cecilia, Rome (1958)
   Renata Tebaldi (Mimi), Gianna d'Angelo (Musetta), Carlo Bergonzi (Rodolfo), Ettore Bastianini (Marcello), Renato Cesari (Schaunard), Cesare Siepi (Colline), Fernando Corena (Benoit, Alcindoro)
   LONDON/JUBILEE JL-42002

Antonino Votto, cond.; Chorus and Orchestra of Maggio Musicale Fiorentino (1961)
   Renata Scotto (Mimi), Jolanda Meneguzzer (Musetta), Gianni Poggi (Rodolfo), Tito Gobbi (Marcello), Giorgio Giorgetti (Schaunard), Giuseppe Modesti (Colline), Virgilio Carbonari (Benoit, Alcindoro)
   DEUTSCHE GRAMMOPHON 2726-086

Erich Leinsdorf, cond.; Rome Opera House Chorus and Orchestra (1961)
   Anna Moffo (Mimi), Mary Costa (Musetta), Richard Tucker (Rodolfo), Robert Merrill (Marcello), Philip Maero (Schaunard), Giorgio Tozzi (Colline), Fernando Corena (Benoit), Giorgio Onesti (Alcindoro)
   RCA GOLD SEAL AGL2-3969
   Highlights: RCA RED SEAL LSC-2655

Thomas Schippers, cond.; Rome Opera House Chorus and Orchestra (1963)
   Mirella Freni (Mimi), Mariella Adani (Musetta), Nicolai Gedda (Rodolfo), Mario Sereni (Marcello), Mario Basiola Jr. (Schaunard), Ferruccio Mazzoli (Colline), Carlo Badioli (Benoit), Paolo Montarsolo (Alcindoro)
   ANGEL 3643-BL
   Highlights: ANGEL 36199

Herbert von Karajan, cond.; German Opera Chorus and Berlin Philharmonic Orchestra (1973)
   Mirella Freni (Mimi), Elizabeth Harwood (Musetta), Luciano Pavarotti (Ro-

dolfo), Rolando Panerai (Marcello), Gianni Maffeo (Schaunard), Nicolai
Ghiaurov (Colline), Michel Sénéchal (Benoit, Alcindoro)
LONDON OSA-1299
Highlights: LONDON OS-26399

Sir Georg Solti, cond.; John Alldis Choir, London Philharmonic Orchestra (1973)
Montserrat Caballé (Mimi), Judith Blegen (Musetta), Placido Domingo (Ro-
dolfo), Sherrill Milnes (Marcello), Vicente Sardinero (Schaunard), Ruggero
Raimondi (Colline), Noel Mangin (Benoit), Nico Castel (Alcindoro)
RCA RED SEAL ARL2-0371

Colin Davis, cond.; Covent Garden Royal Opera House Chorus and Orchestra
(1979)
Katia Ricciarelli (Mimi), Ashley Putnam (Musetta), José Carreras (Rodolfo),
Ingvar Wixell (Marcello), Håkan Hagegård (Schaunard), Robert Lloyd (Col-
line), Giovanni de Angelis (Benoit), William Elvin (Alcindoro)
PHILIPS 6769-031

James Levine, cond.; Ambrosian Opera Chorus, National Philharmonic Orches-
tra (1979)
Renata Scotto (Mimi), Carol Neblett (Musetta), Alfredo Kraus (Rodolfo),
Sherrill Milnes (Marcello), Matteo Manuguerra (Schaunard), Paul Plishka
(Colline), Italo Tajo (Benoit), Renato Capecchi (Alcindoro)
ANGEL 3900-ZBX

HIGHLIGHTS

(*Excerpts from Acts III, IV*) Vincenzo Bellezza, cond.; Covent Garden Royal
Opera House Orchestra (performance, June 8, 1926)
Dame Nellie Melba (Mimi), Aurora Rettore (Musetta), Browning Mummery
(Rodolfo), John Brownlee (Marcello), Frederic Collier (Schaunard), Edouard
Cotreuil (Colline)
EMI/HMV RLS-719* (mono) (I)

(*Act IV complete*) Sir Thomas Beecham, cond.; London Philharmonic Orchestra
(1935)
Lisa Perli (Mimi), Stella Andreva (Musetta), Heddle Nash (Rodolfo), John
Brownlee (Marcello), Robert Alva (Schaunard), Robert Easton (Colline)
EMI/HMV HQM-1234* (mono) (I)

(*Che gelida manina; Mi chiamano Mimì; O soave fanciulla; Musetta's Waltz;
Addio di Mimì; Quartet; O Mimì, tu più non torni; Sono andati? . . . Finale*)
Renato Cellini and Victor Trucco, cond.; RCA Victor Orchestra (1952?)
Licia Albanese (Mimi), Patrice Munsel (Musetta), Giuseppe Di Stefano (Ro-
dolfo), Leonard Warren (Marcello), George Cehanovsky (Schaunard), Nicola
Moscona (Colline)
RCA VICTOR LM-1709* (mono)

(*Che gelida manina; Mi chiamano Mimì; O soave fanciulla; Musetta's Waltz;
Addio di Mimì*) Fausto Cleva, cond.; Metropolitan Opera Orchestra (1952/53)

Dorothy Kirsten (Mimi, Musetta), Richard Tucker (Rodolfo)
COLUMBIA ML-4981* (mono)

(*Abridged*) Fausto Cleva, cond.; Metropolitan Opera Chorus and Orchestra
(195–?)
   Lucina Amara (Mimi), Heidi Krall (Musetta), Daniele Barioni (Rodolfo),
   Frank Valentino (Marcello), Clifford Harvuot (Schaunard), Nicola Moscona
   (Colline), Alessio de Paolis (Alcindoro)
   METROPOLITAN OPERA RECORD CLUB MO-610* (mono)

INDIVIDUAL EXCERPTS

ACT I: Rodolfo's Narrative (Che gelida manina)

Giacomo Aragall (197–?)	London OS-26499*
Jussi Bjoerling (1936)	Metropolitan Opera Guild MET-110
Jussi Bjoerling (1951)	RCA Victor LM-1841*
Alessandro Bonci (1905)	Rubini RDA-002 (I)
Alessandro Bonci (1908)	Court Opera Classics CO-343 (I)
Enrico Caruso (1906)	RCA Red Seal ARM1-2766, CRM1-1749
Giulio Crimi (1920)	Rubini GV-521 (I)
Miguel Fleta (1927)	Lebendige Vergangenheit LV-96 (I)
Beniamino Gigli (1931)	EMI/Italy 3C-153-03480/6 (I)
Charles Hackett (1924)	EMI/HMV RLS-743 (I)
Charles Hackett (1926)	OASI-515
Jan Kiepura (1937)	EMI/Electrola 1C-147-29135/6 (I)
Giacomo Lauri-Volpi (1926)	Lebendige Vergangenheit LV-36 (I)
Giovanni Martinelli (1913)	Lebendige Vergangenheit LV-271 (I)
Giovanni Martinelli (1926)	Lebendige Vergangenheit LV-1301 (I)
Galliano Masini (1935)	OASI-542
John McCormack (1908)	Arabesque 8105-2
John McCormack (1910)	Pearl GEMM-155/160 (I)
Luciano Pavarotti (1981)	London LDR-72009
Aureliano Pertile (1930)	Lebendige Vergangenheit LV-279 (I)
Tito Schipa (1913)	Rubini GV-29 (I)
Ferruccio Tagliavini (194–?)	Cetra LPC-50143*
Richard Tucker (1959)	Columbia MS-6604, M-30118, D3M-33448
Giovanni Zenatello (1908)	Court Opera Classics CO-414

ACT I: Mimi's Narrative (Mi chiamano Mimi)

Licia Albanese (195–?)	RCA Victrola AVM1-0715*
Frances Alda (1915)	Court Opera Classics CO-383 (I)
Gemma Bellincioni (1904/05)	Rubini GV-568 (I)

Lucrezia Bori (1910)	CBS/Odyssey 32-16-0207
Lucrezia Bori (1914)	RCA Victor LCT-1006*, LM-1909*
Lucrezia Bori (1926)	Lebendige Vergangenheit LV-298 (I)
Montserrat Caballé (1970)	Angel 36711
Maria Callas (1954)	Angel 35195
Ileana Cotrubas (1976)	Columbia M-34519
Victoria de los Angeles (1955)	Seraphim 60326
Geraldine Farrar (1912)	Court Opera Classics CO-368 (I)
Cesira Ferrani (1903)	EMI/HMV RLS-724* (I)
Dorothy Kirsten (1947)	RCA Victrola VIC-1552*
Pilar Lorengar (1966)	London OS-26381*
Nellie Melba (1906)	EMI/HMV RLS-719* (I)
Nellie Melba (1907 & 1910)	RCA/Australia VRL5-0365 (I)
Leona Mitchell (1979)	London OS-26591
Anna Moffo (1960)	RCA Victor LSC-2504*
Grace Moore (1940)	RCA Victor LCT-7004*
Claudia Muzio (1911)	OASI-526
Claudia Muzio (1917/18)	OASI-568
Claudia Muzio (1921)	Odyssey Y-33793*
Claudia Muzio (1935)	Seraphim 60111
Magda Olivero (1940)	Cetra LPO-2041 (I)
Rosetta Pampanini (1928)	Lebendige Vergangenheit LV-221 (I)
Rosa Ponselle (1923)	Scala 803; OASI-621
Leontyne Price (1971)	RCA Red Seal LSC-3337
Elisabeth Rethberg (1925)	Lebendige Vergangenheit LV-170 (I)
Bidù Sayão (1941)	Odyssey Y-31151
Elisabeth Schwarzkopf (1959)	Angel 36434*
Margherita Sheridan (1926)	Lebendige Vergangenheit LV-201 (I)
Antonietta Stella (1957)	EMI/Italy 3C-053-01736 (I)
Pia Tassinari (1930)	OASI-638
Renata Tebaldi (1949)	Cetra LPO-2043 (I)

ACT I: Love Duet (O soave fanciulla)

Anna-Lisa Bjoerling, Jussi Bjoerling (949)	EMI/HMV RLS-715 (I)
Frances Alda, Giovanni Martinelli (1918)	Court Opera Classics CO-383 (I)
Lucrezia Bori, John McCormack (1914)	Court Opera Classics CO-382 (I)
Maria Caniglia, Beniamino Gigli (1937)	EMI/HMV RLS-729 (I)
Geraldine Farrar, Enrico Caruso (1912)	Court Opera Classics CO-368 (I)
Nellie Melba, Enrico Caruso (1907)	RCA Red Seal ARM1-2766
Hjoerdis Schymberg, Jussi Bjoerling (1941)	Capitol G-7248*
Pia Tassinari, Piero Pauli (1933)	OASI-638
Maria Zamboni, Beniamino Gigli (1919)	EMI/HMV RLS-729 (I)

ACT II: Musetta's Waltz Song (Quando m'en vo' soletta per la via)
Licia Albanese (195–?)   RCA Victrola AVM1-0715 *
Lucrezia Bori (1927)   Lebendige Vergangenheit LV-298
                                  (I)

Alma Gluck (1916)   Rococo 6215 *
Claudia Muzio (1917/18)   OASI-564
Leontyne Price (1971)   RCA Red Seal LSC-3337
Bidù Sayão (1947)   Odyssey Y-31151
Renata Scotto (1974)   Columbia M-33435
Ljuba Welitsch (1948)   Seraphim 60202 *

ACT III: Mimi-Marcello duet (Mimi? Speravo di trovarvi qui)
Geraldine Farrar, Antonio Scotti (1909)   Court Opera Classics CO-368

ACT III: Mimi's Farewell (Donde lieta uscì)
Licia Albanese (195–?)   RCA Victrola AVM1-0715
Frances Alda (1918)   Club 99 CL-99-45
Lucrezia Bori (1925)   Lebendige Vergangenheit LV-298
                                  (I)

Montserrat Caballé (1970)   Angel 36711
Maria Callas (1954)   Angel 35195
Victoria de los Angeles (1954)   Seraphim 60326
Florence Easton (192–?)   IRCC L-7022 *
Geraldine Farrar (1912)   Court Opera Classics CO-368 (I)
Dorothy Kirsten (1947)   RCA Victrola VIC-1552 *
Nellie Melba (March and   EMI/HMV RLS-719 * (I)
  October, 1904; in French,
  1908)
Zinka Milanov (1958)   RCA Victrola VICS-1198 *
Claudia Muzio (1935)   Seraphim 60111
Magda Olivero (195–?)   Cetra LPO-2008 (I)
Leontyne Price (1971)   RCA Red Seal LSC-3337
Bidù Sayão (1945)   CBS/Odyssey Y-31151
Elisabeth Schwarzkopf (1950)   Angel 3915-ZDX
Pia Tassinari (194–?)   Cetra LPO-2036 (I)
Renata Tebaldi (194–?)   Cetra LPO-2043 (I)
Renata Tebaldi (1951)   Metropolitan Opera Guild MET-
                                  109

ACT III: Quartet (Mimi, Musetta, Rodolfo, Marcello: Addio, dolce svegliare)
Geraldine Farrar, Gina Viafora,   RCA Red Seal ARM1-2767
  Enrico Caruso, Antonio Scotti
  (1908)
Pia Tassinari, Maria Huder,   Cetra LPO-2036 (I)
  Ferruccio Tagliavini, Enzo
  Mascherini (194–?)

ACT IV: Rodolfo-Marcello duet (O Mimi, tu più non torni)
Jussi Bjoerling, Robert Merrill (1951)   RCA Victor LM-2736
Enrico Caruso, Antonio Scotti (1907)   RCA Red Seal ARM1-2766
Placido Domingo, Sherrill Milnes   RCA Red Seal LSC-3182
  (1970)

Beniamino Gigli, Titta Ruffo (1926)   Seraphim 60314
Beniamino Gigli, Giuseppe de Luca   Pearl GEMM-146 (I)
   (1927)
John McCormack, Mario Sammarco   Court Opera Classics CO-382 (I),
   (1910)   Pearl GEMM-155/60 (I)

ACT IV: Colline's Coat Song (Vecchia zimarra)
   Enrico Caruso (1916)   RCA Red Seal ARM4-0302 *
   Feodor Chaliapin (1924)   Harvest H-1002 *
   Tancredi Pasero (1927)   Lebendige Vergangenheit LV-34
                      (I)
   Ezio Pinza (1927)   Metropolitan Opera Guild MET-
                       105
   Ezio Pinza (1946)   Odyssey Y-31148
   Italo Tajo (194–?)   OASI-632
   Vanni-Marcoux (1927)   Rubini GV-19 (I)

ACT IV: Mimi-Rodolfo duet (Sono andati?)
   Lucrezia Bori, Tito Schipa (1925)   Lebendige Vergangenheit LV-185
   Pia Tassinari, Arturo Ferrara (193–?)   OASI-638

Selected Bibliography

Ashbrook, William. *The Operas of Puccini.* New York: Oxford University Press, 1968.

Carner, Mosco. *Puccini.* London: Duckworth, 1958.

Greenfeld, Howard. *Puccini.* New York: G. P. Putnam's Sons, 1980.

Marek, George R. *Puccini.* New York: Simon & Schuster, 1951.

Murger, Henri. *Bohemian Life.* tr. George B. Ives. Philadelphia, The Rittenhouse Press, 1899.

Seligman, Vincent. *Puccini Among Friends.* New York: Macmillan, 1938.

Weaver, William. *Puccini.* New York: Dutton, 1977.

NOTES ON THE CONTRIBUTORS

V. S. PRITCHETT was born in England in 1900. He has published a number of volumes of short stories, including *The Sailor and the Saint, Blind Love, The Camberwell Beauty,* and in 1982, his *Collected Stories.* His memoirs, *A Cab at the Door* and *Midnight Oil,* were published in 1968 and 1972 respectively. He has also written biographies of Balzac and Turgenev, and two of his volumes of critical essays are *The Myth Makers* and *The Tale Bearers.* His novels include *Mr. Beluncle, Dead Man Leading,* and *The Key to My Heart.* Mr. Pritchett is a foreign honorary member of the American Academy of Arts and Letters and of the Academy of Arts and Sciences. In 1975 he received a knighthood. He lives in London with his wife.

WILLIAM MANN was principal music critic of *The Times* in London for more than two decades. He is a member of the editorial board of *Opera* and has contributed to *Grove's Dictionary, Chambers's Encyclopaedia,* and the *Oxford Junior Encyclopaedia.* He is also author of *An Introduction to the Music of J. S. Bach, Richard Strauss: A Critical Study of the Operas,* and in 1977, of *The Operas of Mozart.*

WILLIAM WEAVER, who was born in America and graduated from Princeton University, has lived most of his life in Italy. He is the Arts correspondent for the *Financial Times* in London and a regular contributor to numerous magazines. He has published *Seven Verdi Librettos, Verdi: A Documentary Study, Puccini, The Golden Century of Opera,* and in 1981, *Seven Puccini Librettos.* His translations have won the National Book Award on two occasions. Since 1965 he has lived on his farm in Tuscany.